Global Crises and the Challenges of the 21st Century

GLOBAL CRISES AND THE CHALLENGES OF THE 21ST CENTURY

ANTISYSTEMIC MOVEMENTS AND THE TRANSFORMATION OF THE WORLD-SYSTEM

edited by
Tom Reifer

Political Economy of the World-System Annuals, Volume XXXII
Immanuel Wallerstein, Series Editor

Paradigm Publishers
Boulder • London

Copyright © 2014 Paradigm Publishers

Published in the United States by Paradigm Publishers, 5589 Arapahoe Avenue, Boulder, CO 80303 USA.

Paradigm Publishers is the trade name of Birkenkamp & Company, LLC, Dean Birkenkamp, President and Publisher.

Library of Congress Cataloging-in-Publication Data

Global crises and the challenges of the 21st century : antisystemic movements and the transformation of the world-system / edited by Tom Reifer.
  p. cm.
 ISBN 978-1-59451-919-2 (hardcover : alk. paper)
 ISBN 978-1-59451-920-8 (paperback : alk. paper)
 1. Global Financial Crisis, 2008–2009. 2. Globalization—Economic aspects.
I. Reifer, Tom.
 HB37172008 G556 2012
 330.9001'12—dc23

                                                                    2012007392

Printed and bound in the United States of America on acid-free paper that meets the standards of the American National Standard for Permanence of Paper for Printed Library Materials.

Designed and Typeset by Straight Creek Bookmakers

18 17 16 15 14 1 2 3 4 5

For Giovanni Arrighi

CONTENTS

PREFACE AND ACKNOWLEDGMENTS

All the chapters of this book except one were originally presented at the Political Economy of the World-Systems Conference held at the University of San Diego, April 23–25, 2009. Many people, departments, and organizations helped in making this event a great success. First off, I would like to thank USD Provost, Dr. Julie Sullivan, for generous financial support committed early on, without which the conference would have never taken place. Thanks also to the Ethnic Studies Department, Student Affairs, Carl Jubran, the International Center, and Dr. Dean Boyd, Chair of the College of Arts and Sciences. Most especially, I want to thank all of my colleagues in the Sociology Department who helped make me aware that I was part of a larger team, team USD. Thanks also to Ramon Grosfoguel and Immanuel Wallerstein for their usual sage advice about the organization of the conference. Thanks also to countless others at USD for their help, especially Denise Ward. Thanks also for invaluable editorial assistance to my lifelong friend Tom Dobrzeniecki.

The volume brings together state-of-the-art scholarship on today's global crises, antisystemic movements, and the challenges of the twenty-first century, from the varieties of contemporary globalization to social movements and regional efforts aiming to transform the system in more democratic, peaceful, and egalitarian directions. Topics explored include: comparative forms of white settler colonialism and decolonization; indigenous and racial, ethnical, class, national, and transnational struggles for peace and justice; and explorations from indigenous Native American perspectives of the role of violence and the sacred in the global system. Related civilizational themes that challenge the Eurocentric imaginary are also explored, from food, the sacred, and religion in the struggle of Latin farmworkers in the chapter "The Tortilla Priest & the People of Corn," which focuses on struggles in the Southwest United States and religious battles over old and new world foods (wheat versus corn), to current battles over the role of the veil in the modern world-system. Since the conference from which this volume has come was originally held, the polarization of wealth and power in the world-system has given rise to the most sustained resurgence of antisystemic movements across the globe since 1968, whose continuation it represents as Immanuel Wallerstein has noted, first with the revolutionary wave that toppled one dictator after another in the Arab Spring, and then the development and global spread of the Occupy Wall Street movement, adding additional voices to those Europeans protesting massive waves of austerity throughout their Continent (see Reifer, 2009–10; 2/23/11; 2011).

The current movements remind one of Nobel Prize–winning economist Amartya Sen's insights expressed in *Development as Freedom* (1999), where he explains that thousands of years ago Aristotle, in his *Nicomachean Ethics,* noted: "wealth is evidently not the good we seek, for it is merely useful ... for the sake of something else." This line resonated strongly with a similar discussion between a husband and wife recounted in the *Brihadaranyaka Upanishads* around roughly the same time. Much of the rest of Sen's book is devoted to noting the potential role of wealth and public investments in increasing human capability, going on to redefine poverty as "capability deprivation."

Today's Occupy Wall Street protests continue this ancient discussion about the purposes of wealth, with its slogan—we are the 99%—echoing too Aristotle's famous distinction in his *Politics* about the conflict between oligarchy (rule of the rich) and democracy (the rule of the demos/the people), most of whom are without property, or poor. As Simon Johnson, former chief economist of the IMF, noted recently, "the U.S. is unique ... just as we have the world's most advanced economy, military and technology, we also have its most advanced oligarchy." The great moral philosopher and economist Adam Smith long ago critiqued what he called "prodigals and prospectors," defined by the 1616 *Shorter Oxford English Dictionary* as "a promoter of bubble companies; a speculator; a cheat," echoing today's anger at promoters of subprime mortgages and credit default swaps, the latter having grown from $631.5 billion of over $62 trillion in notional value between 2001 and 2007, expressed too in 2008 Republic Presidential candidate John McCain's critique of the "greed of Wall Street."

The statistics are compelling. In 2007, for example, the Congressional Budget Office (CBO) revealed that the increase in the incomes of the richest 1% of the US population from 2003–2005 came to $524.8 billion, a change of 42.6%, greater than the total combined income of the poorest 20% of Americans. Today, the top 1% of the income bracket in the United States has greater wealth than at any time since 1929, the eve of the Wall Street crash. The Great Depression was the end result of the speculative mania that characterized the roaring twenties, a decade eerily similar to the speculative housing bubble of the 2000s that culminated in the 2008 global financial crisis and the Great Recession. Moreover, a newly released CBO report reveals that average inflation-adjusted after-tax income of the top 1% of the US income bracket between 1979–2007 increased by 275 percent. At the same time, recently released figures reveal that US student loan debt has topped the $1 trillion mark. This is not surprising, given skyrocketing tuition costs combined with savage cuts to public education and programs supporting these struggling students.

Today, we are told by the 1% and their political representatives that we can no longer afford money for public education, even as trillions go to Wall Street. One is reminded of the words of the famous educator, philosopher, and sociologist John Dewey, who noted that "Nothing in the history of education is more touching than to hear some successful leaders denounce as undemocratic attempts to give all the children at public expense the fuller education that their own children enjoy as a matter of course." Dewey said: "the price that democratic societies will have to pay for their continuing health is the elimination of an oligarchy—the most exclusive and dangerous of all—that attempts to monopolize the benefit of intelligence and of the best methods for the profit of a few privileged ones, while practical labor, requiring less spiritual effort and less initiative remains the lot of the great majority." Already, the Occupy Wall Street Movement, with many students in the forefront, is achieving success. Recently, for example, President Obama bypassed the Republican Congress by signing a new executive order to provide some relief to students overburdened by the crushing weight of student loan debt.

Along with this concentration of income at the top 1%, the Great Recession has seen astonishing declines in incomes for the vast majority, but most especially for racial and ethnic minorities in the United States, with wealth gaps between whites, blacks, and Latinos hitting historic highs. Between 2005–2009, the median wealth of Latinos, blacks, and Asians in the United States fell by 66, 53, and 54 percent, respectively. And despite massive pain and suffering for ordinary people, as the *Wall Street Journal* and *New York Times* recently reported, corporations are holding greater shares of cash than at any time in nearly half a century, with banks in particular being awash with cash. The global distribution of wealth is even more skewed. As detailed in the UN's study, The World Distribution of Household Wealth, the richest 1% of the world's population owned 40% of global assets in 2000, with the richest 10% accounting for 85% of total world wealth, in contrast to the world's bottom half, which owned "barely 1% of global wealth."

These facts and figures, coming in the context of the recent global financial, economic, and related social crises, are not coincidental. For it is these very wealth inequalities, as in the 1920s, that provide the most fertile ground for financial bubbles and their bursting and concomitant crises, as the rich awash in cash seek to make money off financial speculation, while the majority of the population tries to stay afloat by taking on increasing levels of debt. For a time, the speculative boom, like in the roaring twenties, was kept afloat by new forms of financing via household indebtedness, but with the bursting of that superbubble in 2008, ordinary working people, the poor and middle income families, have increasingly run out of options.

For a time, protest over the trillions of dollars going to bail out the super-rich on Wall Street was stymied by President Obama's electoral victory and the hope of many Americans that he would take steps to address the financial and larger economic crisis. Instead, for the most part, the Obama administration turned to the very Wall Street figures that were responsible for the deregulation of finance that produced the financial crisis in the first place, such as Larry Summers. Feeling like they had exhausted the formal channels of the political system, people have now turned to mass protest. This too has resonance in American history. People often forget that FDR, following what was then called the Wall Street–Treasury view, was cutting the federal budget as late as 1937, triggering the so-called Roosevelt recession. The Roosevelt recession, in turn, provided the final death knell for the Wall Street–Treasury view and led to the overthrowing of the Money Trust that had dominated US politics since the late nineteenth century. So it should come as no surprise, then, that initial reactions to the crisis by the political elite have been to enact massive cuts to health, education, and social welfare, with devastating consequences to communities in both the United States and across the globe. Today's global protests represent the rebellion of reasonable minds, with the overall message that the economies should serve all the people, not just the super-rich top 1%. In his landmark "Beyond Vietnam: A Time to Break the Silence" speech on April 4, 1967, exactly a year before he was assassinated, the Reverend Martin Luther King, Jr., put it this way: "we as a nation must undergo a radical revolution of values. We must rapidly begin the shift from a thing-oriented society to a person-oriented society. When machines and computers, profit motives and property rights, are considered more important than people, the giant triplets of racism, extreme materialism, and militarism are incapable of being conquered." At the time, King was talking about integration as "shared power and radical redistribution." Unfortunately, since King's death there has been a radical redistribution of wealth and power, but in the opposite direction, towards the top 1%. But King's critique here of the entwined evils of militarism and materialism and the related need for a revolution of values, have been echoed recently, most notably by Cornell West, in the context of the new monument to King and the civil rights movement on the National Mall in Washington, DC.

King's words also echo those of other religiously inspired activists, before and after. For example, Peter Maurin, one of the founders of Dorothy Day's Catholic Worker movement, in his "A Case for Utopia," noted: "The world would be better off if people tried to become better, and people would become better if they stopped trying to become better off. For when everyone tries to become better off nobody is better off. But when everyone tries to become better everybody is better off. Everyone would be rich if nobody tried to become richer, and nobody would be poor if everybody tried to be the poorest. And everybody would be what he ought to be if everybody tried to be what he wants the other fellow to be."

Father Ignacio Ellacuria, then rector of the University of Central America in El Salvador, put it this way in Europe, speaking to the West, just a few days before he was assassinated by US-trained government forces in San Salvador in November of 1989: "[You] have organized your lives around inhuman values ... inhuman because they cannot be universalized. The system rests on a few using the majority of the resources, while the majority can't even cover their basic necessities. It is crucial to define a system of values and a norm of living that takes into account every human being." Perhaps today the world is finally heeding these eloquent messages about the purposes of wealth and the need to subordinate the economy to the needs of society—as Karl Polanyi argued in his *Great Transformation*—most especially the vast majority, and above all the global poor, with its echoes too in liberation theology. That is the great hope and clarion call of this new global movement.

On Friday, October 18, 2011, police arrested some 50 protesters in San Diego, California, and they have been moving steadily to arrest resisters all across the United States. But as the saying goes, you can jail the resisters, but not the resistance, with the latest count of Occupy Wall Street protests reaching 1,039 occupation events in 87 countries. As one sign in the Occupy Wall Street movement put it, The Beginning is Near. The global protest movement is out for nothing less than remaking the world on a more just, democratic, and egalitarian basis. There are not enough jails in the world to jail all those who will stand in solidarity with that message.

Not surprisingly, it turns out that the editor of *The Occupied Wall Street Journal* told commentators that he was inspired by one of world-systems analysis guiding lights, Giovanni Arrighi, whose *The Long Twentieth Century: Money, Power and the Origins of Our Times* (2nd edition, 2010), and his related *Adam Smith in Beijing* (2007) are still the best analysis of today's global crisis, and the most helpful in understanding the origins and prospects of the Occupy Wall Street Movement and the shift of the center of the global political economy from the declining West to the rising East. Sadly, cancer took Giovanni before he was able to see these latest revolutionary waves, which surely would have lifted his spirits in final struggle. But Giovanni's lives on among scholars and activists. Thus, appropriately, this book is dedicated to the memory of Giovanni Arrighi, 1937–2009, a pioneering scholar-activist whose legacy will live on in the countless numbers of students, colleagues, friends, scholars, and activists that he inspired over many years. *A luta continua.*

References

Reifer, Tom. 2009–2010. "Lawyers, Guns & Money: Wall Street Lawyers, Investment Bankers and Global Financial Crises, Late 19th to 21st Century." *Nexus: Chapman University Journal of Law & Public Policy*, special issue on "The 80th

Anniversary of the Great Crash of 1929: Law, Markets & the Role of the State." 15, 119–133. http://www.tni.org/paper/lawyers-guns-and-money-wall-street-lawyers -investment-bankers-and-global-financial-crises.

————. 2011. "The 'Arab 1848': Reflections on US Policy & the Power of Non-violence." *Transnational Institute* (February 23, 2011) http://www.tni.org/article/ %E2%80%9Carab-1848%E2%80%9D-reflections-us-policy-power-nonviolence.

————. 2011. "Global Inequalities, Alternative Regionalisms & the Future of Social-ism." *Austrian Journal of Development Studies, Special Issue on Giovanni Arrighi: A Global Perspective.* Guest editors, Amy Holmes and Stefan Schmalz, XXVII (1: Summer), 72–94. http://www.tni.org/paper/global-inequalities-alternative -regionalism-and-future-socialism.

1

"CRISIS, WHAT CRISIS?"

Immanuel Wallerstein

In 1982, I published a book, jointly with three colleagues, entitled *Dynamics of Global Crisis*. This was not its original title. We had proposed the title, *Crisis, What Crisis?* The United States publisher did not like that title, but we used it in the French translation. The book consisted of a joint introduction and conclusion and a separate essay by each of us on the topic.

We opened the book with our observation that "throughout the 1970s, 'crisis' became an increasingly familiar theme: first in obscure discussions among intellectuals, then in the popular press, and finally in political debates in many countries." We noted that there were many different definitions of the so-called crisis as well as different explanations of its origin.

By the 1980s, the term "crisis" seemed to disappear from world discourse, to be replaced by another buzzword, one with a much more optimistic gloss—"globalization." It is only beginning in 2008 that the tone has turned dour again, and the word "crisis" has resurfaced, this time more sharply than in the 1970s, but just as loosely. So the question, "crisis, what crisis?" seems again very relevant.

*   *   *

1

Something did indeed happen to the world-system in the late 1960s and early 1970s. This moment marked the beginning of the downturn in two absolutely normal cycles in the operation of the modern world-system. It was the moment when both the hegemonic cycle and the overall economic cycle each began its downturn. The period 1945 to circa 1970 had been the moment of the height of United States hegemony in the world-system and also the moment of the most expansive Kondratieff A-upturn that the capitalist world-economy had ever known in its history. The French refer to that period as "les trente glorieuses" (the Thirty Glorious Years), a most apt expression.

I call these downturns absolutely normal. To understand why, one must bear in mind two things. All systems have cyclical rhythms. It is the way they live, the way they deal with the inevitable fluctuations of their operations. The second thing to bear in mind has to do with how capitalism as a world-system functions. There are two key issues: how producers make profit; and how states guarantee the world order within which producers may make profit. Let us take each in turn.

Capitalism is a system in which the endless accumulation of capital is the *raison d'être*. To accumulate capital, producers must obtain profits from their operations. However, truly significant profits are possible only if the producer can sell the product for considerably more than the cost of production. In a situation of perfect competition, it is absolutely impossible to make significant profit. If there is perfect competition (that is, a multitude of sellers, a multitude of buyers, and universally available information about prices), any intelligent buyer will go from seller to seller until he finds one who will sell at a penny above the cost of production, if not indeed below the cost of production.

Obtaining significant profit requires a monopoly, or at least a quasi-monopoly of world-economic power. If there is a monopoly, the seller can demand any price, as long as he does not go beyond what the elasticity of demand permits. Any time the world-economy is expanding significantly, one will find that there are some "leading" products, which are relatively monopolized. It is from these products that great profits are made and large amounts of capital can be accumulated. The forward and backward linkages of these leading products are the basis of an overall expansion of the world-economy. We call this the A-phase of a Kondratieff cycle.

The problem for capitalists is that all monopolies are self-liquidating. This is because there exists a world market into which new producers can enter, however well politically defended is a given monopoly. Of course, entry takes time. But sooner or later, others are able to enter the market, and the degree of competition increases. And when competition increases, prices go down, as the heralds of capitalism have always told us. However, at the same time, profits go down. When profits for the leading products go down sufficiently, the world-economy ceases to expand, and it enters into a period of stagnation. We call this the B-phase of a Kondratieff cycle. Empirically, the A- and B-phases together have tended to be 50–60 years in length, but the exact lengths have varied. Of course, after a certain time in a B-phase, new monopolies can be created and a new A-phase can begin. How this has been done is not our topic here.

* * *

The second condition for capitalist profit is that there exists some kind of relative world order. While world wars offer the possibilities for some entrepreneurs to do very well, they also occasion enormous destruction of fixed capital and considerable interference with world trade. The overall world-economic balance sheet of world wars is not positive, a point Schumpeter repeatedly made. A relatively stable situation is necessary for a positive overall balance sheet. Ensuring this relatively stable situation is the task of a hegemonic power, that is, a power strong enough to impose such relative stability on the world-system as a whole. Hegemonic cycles have been much longer than Kondratieff cycles. It is not so easy, in a world of multiple so-called sovereign states, for one state to establish itself as the hegemonic power. It has in fact been done only three times in several hundred years: first by the United Provinces in the mid-seventeenth century, then by the United Kingdom in the mid-nineteenth century, and finally by the United States in the mid-twentieth century.

* * *

The rise of a hegemonic power is the result of a long struggle with other potential hegemonic powers. It has been won each time up to now by that state which, for various reasons and by various methods, has been able to put together the most efficient productive machinery, and then to win a "thirty years' war" with its principal rival. Again, how this is done is not our topic here. The key point is that once a given state finally achieves hegemony, it is able to set the rules by which the interstate system operates, seeking simultaneously to assure its smooth functioning and to maximize the flow of accumulated capital to its citizens and productive enterprises. One could call this a quasi-monopoly of geopolitical power.

The problem for the hegemonic power is the same as the problem for a leading industry. The monopoly is self-liquidating. This is so for two reasons. On the one hand, to maintain the order it imposes, the hegemonic power has to make use on occasion of its military power. But potential military strength is always more intimidating than actually used military strength. Using military strength is costly in money and lives. It has a negative impact on the citizens of the hegemonic power, whose initial pride in victory tends to turn to distress as they pay the increasing costs of military action, and they begin to lose enthusiasm. Furthermore, big military operations tend almost always to be less efficacious than both supporters and opponents of the hegemonic power had expected, and this strengthens the future resistance of others who wish to defy the hegemonic power.

There is a second reason. Even if the hegemonic power's economic efficiency does not immediately falter, that of other countries begins to rise. And as the others rise, they are less ready to accept the dictates of the hegemonic power. The hegemonic power enters into a process of slow decline relative to the rising powers. The decline may be slow but it is nonetheless essentially irreversible.

*   *   *

The conjoining, circa 1965–1970, of the two kinds of decline—that marking the end of the historically most-expansive Kondratieff-A phase and that marking the beginning of decline of the historically most-powerful hegemonic power—is what made that turning point so remarkable. It is no accident that the world revolution of 1968 (actually 1966–1970) took place at that turning point, as an expression of the turning point.

The world revolution of 1968 marked a third downturn, one, however, that has occurred only once in the history of the modern world-system: the decline of the traditional antisystemic movements of the world-system, the so-called Old Left. The Old Left—essentially the two varieties of world social movements, the Communists and the Social Democrats; plus the national liberation movements—arose slowly and laboriously across the world-system, primarily throughout the last third of the nineteenth century and the first half of the twentieth century. The Old Left movements ascended from a position of political marginality and weakness as of say 1870 to one of political centrality and considerable strength as of say 1950.

*   *   *

These movements reached the summit of their mobilizing power in the period from 1945 to 1968—exactly the moment of both the extraordinary Kondratieff A-phase expansion and the height of US hegemony. I do not think this was fortuitous, although it might seem counter-intuitive. The incredible world economic expansion led to a strong preference on the part of entrepreneurs not to suffer interruptions of their production processes because of conflict with the workers. It followed that they tended to believe that concessions to the material demands of their workers cost them less than such interruptions. Of course, over time, this meant rising costs of production, one of the factors that led to the end of the quasi-monopolies of leading industries. But most entrepreneurs make decisions that maximize short-term profits—let us say, profits over the succeeding three years—and leave the future to the gods.

Parallel considerations influenced the policies of the hegemonic power. Maintaining relative stability in the world-system was an essential objective. The United States had to weigh the cost of repressive activity on the world scene against the cost of concessions to the demands of national liberation movements. Reluctantly at first, but later more deliberately, the United States began to favor a controlled "decolonization" and this had the effect of bringing such movements to power.

Hence, by the middle of the 1960s, one could say that the Old Left movements had achieved their historic goal of state power almost everywhere—at least on paper. Communist parties ruled one-third of the world—the so-called socialist bloc. Social-democratic parties were in power, at least alternating power, in most of another third of the world—the pan-European world. One also has to bear in mind that, at this time, the principal policy of the social-democratic parties—the welfare state—was accepted and practiced as well by their conservative alternating parties. And of course, the national liberation movements had come to power in most of the former colonial world (as well as various versions of populist movements in Latin America).

* * *

To be sure, I have said "at least on paper." Most analysts and militants tend today to be very critical of the performance of all these movements, and doubt that their coming to power made much difference. But this is a retrospective view and is historically anachronistic. The critics forget the sense of worldwide triumphalism that pervaded the Old Left movements and their supporters at precisely that time, a triumphalism based precisely on their achievement of state power. The critics forget as well the sense of deep fear that pervaded the world's wealthier and more conservative strata about what looked to them like a juggernaut of destructive egalitarianism.

The world revolution of 1968 changed all that. Three themes pervaded the analyses and the rhetoric of those who engaged in the multiple uprisings. All three themes bespoke a revised triumphalism. The first theme was that the US hegemonic power had overstretched and was vulnerable. The Vietnam War was the model example, albeit not the only one. The Tet offensive was taken to be the death knell of the US military operation. As part of the new atmosphere, the revolutionaries attacked the role of the Soviet Union, which they saw as a collusive participant in US hegemony, a feeling that had been growing everywhere, since at least 1956.

The second theme was that the Old Left movements—of all three varieties—had failed to deliver their historic promises. All three varieties had built their strategy on the so-called two-step strategy—first take state power, then change the world. The militants said, in effect: "You have taken state power but have not at all changed the world. If we wish to change the world, we must replace you with new movements and new strategies. And we shall do this." The Chinese cultural revolution was taken by many as the model example of this possibility.

* * *

The third theme was that the Old Left movements had ignored the forgotten peoples—those downtrodden because of their race, their gender, their ethnicity, their sexuality. The militants insisted that the demands for equal treatment by all of these groups could no longer be deferred to some putative future time after the main Old Left parties had achieved their historic objectives. These demands, they said, constituted part of the urgent present, not the deferred future. In many ways, the Black Power movement in the United States was the model example.

The world revolution of 1968 was an enormous political success. The world revolution of 1968 was an enormous political failure. It rose like a phoenix, burned very bright indeed across the globe, and then by the mid-1970s seemed to be extinguished almost everywhere. What had been accomplished by this wild brushfire? Actually, quite a bit. Centrist liberalism had been dethroned as the governing ideology of the world-system. It was reduced to being simply one alternative among others. And the Old Left movements were destroyed as mobilizers of any kind of fundamental change. But the immediate triumphalism of the revolutionaries of 1968, liberated from any subordination to centrist liberalism, proved shallow and unsustainable.

*   *   *

The world right was equally liberated from any attachment to centrist liberalism. It took advantage of the world economic stagnation and the collapse of the Old Left movements (and their governments) to launch a counter-offensive, which we call neoliberal (actually quite conservative) globalization. The prime objectives were to reverse all the gains of the lower strata during the Kondratieff A-period. The world right sought to reduce all the major costs of production, to destroy the welfare state in all its versions, and to slow down the decline of US power in the world-system. The onward march of the world right seemed to culminate in 1989. The ending of Soviet control over its East-Central European satellite states and the dismantling of the Soviet Union itself led to a sudden new triumphalism of the world right. One more illusion!

The offensive of the world right was a great success. The offensive of the world right was a great failure. What was sustaining the accumulation of capital since the 1970s was the turning from seeking profits via productive efficiency to seeking profits via financial manipulations, more correctly called speculation. The key mechanism of speculation is encouraging consumption via indebtedness. This was of course what has happened in every Kondratieff B-period.

The difference this time has been the scale of the speculation and the indebtedness. After the biggest A-period expansion in the history of the capitalist world-economy, there has followed the biggest speculative mania. The bubbles moved through the whole world-system; from the national debts of the Third World countries and the socialist bloc in the 1970s, to the junk bonds of large corporations in the 1980s, to the consumer indebtedness of the 1990s, to the US government indebtedness of the Bush era, the system has gone from bubble to bubble. The world is currently trying one last bubble—the bailouts of the banks and the printing of dollars.

*   *   *

The depression into which the world has fallen will continue now for quite a while and will go quite deep. It will destroy the last small pillar of relative economic stability, the role of the US dollar as a reserve currency of safeguarding wealth. As this happens, the main concern of every government in the world—from the United States to China, from France to Russia to Brazil, not to speak of all the weaker governments on the world scene—will be to avert the uprising of the unemployed workers and the middle strata whose savings and pensions disappear. The governments are turning to protectionism and printing money as their first line of defense, as ways of dealing with popular anger.

Such measures may postpone the dangers the governments fear, and may assuage momentarily the pain of ordinary people. But they will eventually probably make the situation even worse. We are entering a gridlock of the system, from which the world will find it extremely difficult to extract itself. The gridlock will express itself in the form of a constant set of ever-wilder fluctuations, which will make short-term predictions—both economic and political—virtually guesswork. And this in turn will aggravate popular fears and alienation.

*   *   *

Some are claiming that the greatly improved relative economic position of the Asian nations—especially first Japan, then South Korea and Taiwan, then China and to a lesser extent India—is allowing or will allow a resurgence of capitalist enterprise, with a simple geographical shift of location. One more illusion! The relative rise of Asia is a reality, but precisely one that undermines further the capitalist system. It does so by overloading the numbers of persons to whom surplus-value is distributed. The top end of the capitalist system can never be too large, for this reduces (not increases) the overall accumulation of capital. China's economic expansion accelerates the structural profit squeeze of the capitalist world-economy.

Where do we go from here? It is at this point that we must put into the discussion the other element, the secular trends of the world-system, as opposed to its cyclical rhythms. All kinds of systems function in the same formal fashion. The cyclical rhythms are how they operate on a continuing basis, how they breathe if you will. There are innumerable ups and downs, some more fundamental than others. But the B-phases never end at the same point as where the preceding A-phases began. There is always a systemic price to pay for renewing the upward phase of the cycles. The system has always to move just a little further from equilibrium, even its moving equilibrium.

We may think of each upturn as a contribution to slow-moving upward curves, each heading towards its asymptote. In the capitalist world-economy, it is not all that difficult to discern which curves matter most. Since capitalism is a system in which the endless accumulation of capital is paramount, and since one accumulates capital by making profits in the market, the key issue for all capitalists is how to produce products for prices that are lower, preferably far lower, than the prices for which they can be sold.

*   *   *

We therefore have to discern what goes into the costs of production and what determines the prices. Logically, there are three different kinds of costs of production: the costs of personnel (all personnel); the costs of inputs (all kinds of inputs); and the costs of taxation (all kinds of taxation). I think it is not too hard to demonstrate that all three costs have been going up over time as a percentage of the actual prices for which products are sold. And this is so despite the repeated efforts of capitalists to push them down, and despite the repeated technological and organizational improvements that have increased the so-called efficiency of production. I shall state briefly why this is so, and then state briefly why there are limits to the elasticity of demand.

The costs of personnel may be divided into three categories: the relatively unskilled workforce, the intermediate cadres, and the top managers. The costs of the unskilled tend to go up in A-periods as a result of some kind of syndical action. When these costs go too high for given entrepreneurs and particularly for those in the leading industries, relocation to historically lower-wage areas in the B-period is the main remedy. When there is later on similar syndical action in the new location, a new move occurs. The moves are costly but effective. But worldwide there is a ratchet effect. The reductions never eliminate totally the increases. Over 500 years, this repeated process has exhausted the loci into which to move. This can be measured by the deruralization of the world-system.

*   *   *

The increase in the costs of cadres is the result of two different considerations. One, the increased scale of productive units requires more intermediate personnel, whose salaries augment the personnel bill. And two, the political dangers that result from the repeated syndical organization of the relatively low-skilled personnel is countered by the creation of a larger intermediate stratum who can be both political allies for the ruling stratum and models of a possible upward mobility for the unskilled majority, thereby blunting its political mobilization.

The increase in the costs of top managers is the direct result of the increased complexity of entrepreneurial structures—the famous separation of ownership and control. This makes it possible for these top managers to appropriate ever larger portions of the firm's receipts as rent, thereby reducing what goes to the "owners" as profit or to reinvestment by the firm. This last increase was spectacular in size during the last few decades.

The costs of inputs have been going up for analogous reasons. The basic effort of capitalists is to externalize costs, that is, to not pay the full bill for the inputs they use. There are three main costs one may externalize: handling toxic waste, renewing raw materials, and building infrastructure. For a very long time, from the origins of the capitalist world-economy in the sixteenth century to the 1960s, such externalization of costs has been taken as absolutely normal. It was basically unquestioned by political authorities.

* * *

In the twenty-first century, when climate change is widely debated, and "green" and "organic" have become universal buzzwords, it is hard to remember that, for five centuries, toxic waste was normally and almost always simply dumped in the public domain. What happened is that the world has been running out of such vacant public domains—the equivalent of deruralization of the world's work force. Suddenly, the health consequences and costs have become so high and so close to home that a major political response has occurred, in the form of demands for environmental clean-up and control.

The second externalization, that of renewing resources, has also only recently become a major concern, the consequence of the sharp increase in world population. Suddenly, there is a wide concern about shortages—of energy sources, of water, of forestation, of products of the soil, of fish and meat. Suddenly, we are worried about who uses what, for what purposes, and who pays the bill.

The third externalization has been that of infrastructure. Products produced for sale on the world market need transport and communication, the costs of which have gone up as they have become more efficient and faster. Entrepreneurs have historically only paid a small part of the real bill for infrastructure. The costs for entrepreneurs thus go down, while the government's cost of providing the infrastructure goes up.

The consequence of all of this has been a political thrust for governments to assume directly some of the necessary costs of detoxification, resource renewal, and further infrastructure expansion. To do this, governments must increase taxes. And, unless they wish to go bankrupt, governments have to insist on more internalization of costs by entrepreneurs, which of course cuts sharply into margins of profit of enterprises.

* * *

Finally, taxation has been going up. There are multiple political levels of taxation. There is also the private taxation of corruption and organized mafias. For the entrepreneur, it does not really matter to whom the taxes go. They are a cost.

The size of private taxation has risen as the extensiveness of world economic activity has gone up and the structuration of state bureaucracies has expanded. However, the major impetus for increased taxation has been the impact of the world's antisystemic movements on political culture—what might be called the democratization of world politics.

Popular movements have pushed for three basic state guarantees: education, health, and lifelong revenue flows. Each of these has expanded in two ways over the past 200 years: in the levels of services demanded; and the geographical locales in which the demands have been made. The welfare state is good shorthand for such demands. And there is no government today exempt from the pressure to maintain a welfare state, even if the levels vary, primarily according to the collective wealth of the country.

*   *   *

All three costs of production have risen steadily as a percentage of the real sales prices of products, albeit in the form of an A-B ratchet, over 500 years. The most dramatic increases have been in the post-1945 period. Cannot the prices for which products are sold simply be raised, in order to maintain the margins of real profit? That is precisely what has been tried in the post-1970 period. This has taken the form of price increases, sustained by expanded consumption, in turn sustained by indebtedness. The economic collapse in the midst of which we find ourselves is nothing but the expression of the limits of elasticity of demand. When everyone lives far beyond their real incomes, there comes a point where someone has to stop, and fairly quickly everyone feels they have to stop.

The coming together of the three elements—the magnitude of the "normal" crash, the real rise in costs of production, and the extra pressure on the system of Chinese (and Asian) growth—means that Humpty Dumpty has fallen off the wall, and the pieces can no longer be put together again. The system is very, very far from equilibrium, and the fluctuations are enormous. As a consequence, the short-term predictions have become impossible to make, and this tends to freeze consumption decisions. This is what one calls structural crisis.

From here on in, we are living amidst the bifurcation of the systemic process. The question is no longer, how will the capitalist system mend itself, and renew its forward thrust? The question is: what will replace this system? What order will be chosen out of this chaos?

Of course, not everyone is aware of this as yet. Most people continue to operate as though somehow the system were continuing, using its old rules. They are not really wrong. The system does continue to operate, using its old rules. But now, using the old rules only exacerbates the structural crisis. However, some actors are quite aware that we are in a bifurcation. And they know, perhaps only tacitly, that at some point in a bifurcation, the collectivity of all actors leans definitively in one direction or another. One can say that a decision has been made, even if the use of the word "decision" sounds anthropomorphic.

* * *

We may think of this period of systemic crisis as the arena of a struggle for the successor system. The outcome may be inherently unpredictable but the nature of the struggle is very clear. We are before alternative choices. They cannot be spelled out in institutional detail, but they can be suggested in broad outline.

We can "choose" collectively a new stable system that essentially resembles the present system in some basic characteristics—a system that is hierarchical, exploitative, and polarizing. There are no doubt many forms this could take, and some of these forms could be harsher than the capitalist world-system in which we have been living. Alternatively, we can "choose" collectively a radically different form of system, one that has never previously existed—a system that is relatively democratic and relatively egalitarian.

I have been calling the two alternatives "the spirit of Davos" and "the spirit of Porto Alegre." But the names are unimportant. What is important is to see the possible organizational strategies on each side in this definitive struggle—a struggle that has been going on in some form since the world revolution of 1968 and may not be resolved before circa 2050.

* * *

Before, however, one looks at strategies, one must note two crucial characteristics of a structural crisis. Because the fluctuations are so wild, there is little pressure to return to equilibrium. During the long, "normal" lifetime of the system, these pressures were the means by which extensive social mobilizations (so-called revolutions) had always been limited in their effects. But when the system is far from equilibrium, exactly the opposite happens. Small social mobilizations have very great effects.

This is what complexity science refers to as the "butterfly" effect. We might also, in ancient philosophic discourse, call it the moment when free will prevails over determinism. Prigogine calls this way of understanding complex systems the "narrow path between two conceptions that both lead to alienation: a world ruled by deterministic laws, which leaves no place for novelty, and a world ruled by a dice-playing God, where everything is absurd, acausal, and incomprehensible."[1]

* * *

The second crucial characteristic of a structural crisis is that neither of the two camps has, or can have, a vertical structure with a small group at the top calling all the shots. There is neither a functioning executive committee of the ruling class nor a politburo of the oppressed masses, nor can there be. Even among those aware of and committed to the struggle for a successor system, there are multiple players, pushing different emphases, coordinating poorly with each other. These two groups of aware militants on both sides also find it difficult to persuade the larger groups that form the potential base of their strength of the utility and possibility of organizing the transition. In short, the chaos of the structural crisis is reflected as well in the relatively chaotic structures of the two camps struggling over the successor system.

What we can do, while in the very middle of this structural crisis, is to try to analyze the emerging strategies that each camp is developing, the better to orient our own political choices in the light of our own moral preferences. We can start with the strategy of the camp of the "spirit of Davos." They are deeply divided. There are those who wish to institute a highly repressive system that openly propagates a worldview glorifying the role of skilled, secretive, highly privileged rulers and submissive subjects. They not only propagate this worldview but also propose to organize the network of armed enforcers needed to crush opposition.

There is a second group who believe that the road to control and privilege is via a highly meritocratic system that would co-opt the large number of cadres necessary to maintain the system with a minimum of force and a maximum of persuasion. This group speaks a language of fundamental change, utilizing all the slogans that have emerged from the antisystemic movements—including a green universe, a multicultural utopia, and meritocratic opportunities for all—all this, while maintaining a polarized and unequal system.

*   *   *

On the side of the camp of the "spirit of Porto Alegre," there is a parallel split. There are those who envisage a highly decentralized world, one which privileges rational long-term allocations over economic growth, one which makes possible innovation without creating cocoons of expertise unanswerable to the larger society. This group envisages a system in which a universal universalism will be built out of the never-ending piecing together of the multiple wisdoms that humans have created and will continue to create in their different cultural flowerings.

There is a second group who have been, and continue to be, more oriented to transformation from above, by cadres and specialists who believe they see more clearly than the rest. Far from being decentralizing, they envisage an ever more coordinated and integrated world-system, a formal egalitarianism without real innovation and without the patience to construct a truly universal but multifaceted universalism.

So, far from a simple twofold battle for the successor system, I envisage a fourfold battle—one between the two great camps and a second one within each of the great camps. This is a confusing situation—confusing intellectually, morally, and politically. All the more reason to insist that the outcome is fundamentally unpredictable and uncertain.

*   *   *

What, then, can we say of the practical steps any of us, as individuals and as groups of diverse kinds and strengths, can and should take to further this process? There is no formulaic agenda of action. There are only lines of emphasis. I would put at the head of the list actions that we can take, in the short run, to minimize the pain—the pain that arises from the breakdown of the existing system, the pain that arises from the confusions of the transition. Personally, I would not sneer at winning an election, at obtaining more benefits within the states for those who have the least materially. I would not sneer at some protection of judicial and political rights. I would not sneer at combating some further erosion of our planetary wealth and conditions for collective survival. I would not sneer at any of these, even though I do not consider any of these achievements more than momentary palliatives for immediate pain. They are not in themselves in any way steps towards creating the new successor system that we want.

The second thing that we can do is engage in endless serious intellectual debate about the parameters of the kind of world-system we want, and the strategy of transition. We not only need to do this ceaselessly, but we need to do it with a willingness to hear, as part of the debate, persons we deem of good will if not of our immediate viewpoint. A constant open debate may bring more insight, will surely build greater camaraderie, and will keep us perhaps from falling into the sectarianism that has always defeated antisystemic movements.

The third thing we can do is construct, here and there and everywhere, on small and large scales, alternative decommodified modes of production. We can learn from doing this the limits of many particular methods. We can demonstrate by doing this that there are modes of ensuring sensible and sustainable production other than reliance on the profit motive as the basis of our reward system.

The fourth thing we can do is engage in moral debate, to sharpen our sense of the moral negatives of any and all particular modes of action, to realize that balances must be made between the realization of alternative good outcomes. One of the reasons there are so many different progressive organizations is the differing emphases on priorities.

And through all of this, we must put at the forefront of our consciousness and our action the struggle against the three fundamental inequalities of the world—gender, class, and race/ethnicity/religion. This is the hardest task of all, since there are none of us guiltless and none of us pure. And the entire world culture that we have all inherited militates against this.

Finally, we must run like the plague from any sense that history is on our side, that the good society is certain to come, if only x or y. History is on no one's side. A century from now, our descendants may regret all that we have done. We have at best a 50-50 chance of creating a better world-system than the one in which we now live. But 50-50 is a lot. We must try to seize Fortuna, even if it escapes us. What more useful thing can any of us do?

Note

1. Ilya Prigogine, *The End of Certainty* (New York: The Free Press, 1996), 187–188.

2

LONG-TERM WORLD-SYSTEMIC CRISES

"AN SICH" OR "VON SICH"?

W. L. Goldfrank

Commentators and analysts from the far right to the far left have lately been in astonishing agreement that the world economy is now undergoing a severe and at least temporarily crippling crisis, however much they disagree about its causes, its multiple aspects, and its possible outcomes. A large majority of these observers are drawn toward an analogy with the Great Depression of the 1930s and offer policy prescriptions to the G-8, the US government, or the IMF focused on stimulus packages, regulatory reforms, and/or monetary fixes. However useful or not these prescriptions may prove in the short term, the analogy is seriously misleading in one major respect: despite all the current disturbances in the "arc of instability," world politics are far more stable during the current crisis than during the 1930s, when aggressive German and Japanese military expansionisms were gathering steam, British hegemony was a distant memory, and the definitive ascendance of the United States had yet to be forged in the crucible of the Second World War. Transnational institutions are now vastly thicker than seventy-five years ago—corporations, IGOs, NGOs—as especially core countries have forged constructed instruments of cooperation that dwarf the organizational reach of the League of Nations and others from that earlier era. Hence in the short term, it seems likely that sooner or later something will pull the world economy out of its doldrums and into a new phase of growth, something like a makeshift turn from fossil fuel-based, Washington Consensus neoliberalism to quasi-green global Keynesianism. But what of durations that typically receive far less attention except among world-system scholars and a handful of others, viz, the medium term and especially the long term?

In discussing alternative visions of the future, a loose rhetorical analogy to Marx's famous distinction between a social class in itself, "an sich," and a social class for itself, "für sich," may prove useful. A class "an sich" is objectively identifiable, while a class "für sich" is subjectively disposed to political action, even potentially transformative political action. Turn now to the world-system and its history of hegemonic crises, tracing them back in time, from British to US dominance via the world wars of the first half of the twentieth century, from Dutch to British sway via the Napoleonic Wars, and possibly that from the Hapsburgs to the Dutch via the Thirty Years' War. However much they disagree about the details, most world-system scholars understand these crises as crises "an sich," crises in the system, crises within the system's logic. With the benefit of hindsight, to be sure, we can see that these crises were phases in an ongoing process of expanded reproduction (Wallerstein's emphasis) and organizational evolution (Arrighi's emphasis). One could perhaps argue that exceptionally visionary politicians (William Pitt? George Kennan?) understood them as such as the crises were occurring.

What then can we say about the current crisis? In so far as it entails the decline—the eclipse, even—of US hegemony, it appears to be another "an sich" crisis in the system, and those who understand it this way have at one time or another cast Japan, or China, or a United States (military) plus East Asia (finance) combination as the hegemonic successor. But one must also point to anomalies in the current crisis that suggest a simultaneous and overlapping possibility. In addition to this recurrent crisis "an sich," the world-system may well have entered a crisis "von sich," a crisis of itself, a crisis from which there is no exit via war, geographic expansion, increased proletarianization and commodification, or technological advances. Five salient anomalies imply that the current crisis differs significantly from past instances.

In his "Postscript to the 2010 Second Edition of *The Long Twentieth Century,*" Arrighi points out one such anomaly. Each of the two last hegemonic successors was territorially larger and militarily more powerful than its predecessor, as well as being more successful economically. In contrast, the United States has retained overwhelming military superiority even as it has lost ground in production, commerce, and finance, shifting from a position as the world's leading creditor to that of the world's leading debtor. This is without historical precedent, as Great Britain and its primary competitor France clearly overshadowed the Dutch Republic in the eighteenth century, and the United States and its primary competitor Germany outmuscled the British by the time of World War I. No currently constituted national state looms militarily as even a challenger to the United States. A second anomaly is that the B-phase of the current Kondratieff long wave is lasting much longer than the typical 20–30 years, having started around 1970 and showing few signs of ending, belying Wallerstein's (and others') expectations that a new A-phase would have started by the turn of the millennium, or at any rate well before now (see, e.g., "Peace, Stability, and Legitimacy, 1990–2025/2050," chapter 2 in Immanuel Wallerstein's book *After Liberalism* [New York: New Press, 1995], 28–29).

Before attempting further to parse this "an sich"/"von sich" distinction, three additional anomalies deserve mention: one in the sphere of culture and ideology; one in the sphere of ecology; and one in the sphere of warfare. During prior hegemonic transitions and cyclical economic shifts, most self-conscious participants in world politics believed in liberal notions of progress, including the conservatives who wanted to slow it down so as to diminish its disruptive consequences and also the radicals who wanted to speed it up so as to hasten the realization of its egalitarian promises. The present crisis, however, has let loose an ideological cacophony that dwarfs previous dissent from the consensus about progress. Fundamentalist and quietist religious formations, "small is beautiful" anti-materialism, and post-modern rejections of grand narratives are all instances of defection from the long-dominant sway of liberal ideology. Meanwhile, ecologically, whereas previous crises and transitions entailed an intensification of fossil fuel-based technologies such as the substitution of coal for wood or petroleum for coal, the current crisis includes the increasingly evident threat of severe climate change unless quite radical innovations in sustainable energy production are undertaken—not to mention possible impending global shortages of both water and arable land. Finally, whereas all previous hegemonic transitions were accomplished in part via major wars among the great powers of their day, in the current crisis two factors make global war highly unlikely: one is the aforementioned absence of one or more challengers to the United States, and the other is the virtual impossibility of winning a nuclear war, since even if one's enemies are destroyed, one's own territory will most probably be rendered uninhabitable as well.

Logically, then, there are two ways to approach the current crisis, and they are not mutually exclusive nor contradictory, but neither are they cleanly separable. And their referents are most probably interactive. The "an sich" approach looks toward the emergence of a variant version of the long-term structure of the capitalist world-economy. As Arrighi once envisioned, this variant might entail a return to the bifurcated hegemony first instanced in the sixteenth century by the combination of Genoese finance and Hapsburg military might, only now in the guise of East Asian money and US armed forces. Or, as hypothesized by Leslie Sklair and by William Robinson, this variant might entail the consolidation of a global capitalist class that uses the US military as its primary instrument of coercion. Neither of these variants would greatly disturb the existing hierarchies of wealth and power, although movement within those hierarchies would almost surely include the continued rise of some—China, India, Brazil—and the stagnation or decline of others, most likely in Eastern Europe, Central Asia, Africa, and possibly Latin America. Yet both of these variants also entail the kinds of changes in enterprise organization, geographical scale, and class relations Arrighi identified as crucial elements of previous transitions from one "systemic cycle of accumulation" to the next.

The "von sich" approach both tends to use a longer time frame—say fifty to seventy-five years instead of twenty to thirty years—and typically envisions a future with considerably more radical alternatives. These alternatives are by no means necessarily positive: the planet could be rendered uninhabitable in short order by a nonregional nuclear conflict. Or it could be rendered uninhabitable over the long haul by environmental degradation, climate change, or ozone depletion. Several analysts have conjured a third dystopian alternative: a global world-empire enforcing a Social Darwinist order, justified perhaps by an alleged need to prevent irruptive terrorism or to manage epidemiological threats. Its *raison d'être* would be to preserve ("Western") civilization. Call it barbarism, call it global fascism, it cannot be ruled out so long as military might remains concentrated so intensively in a very small number of hands. And for all the alleged democratizing potentialities of the Internet, it may well be that computer-based technologies are increasing the administrative and surveillance capabilities of powerful states even faster. Repeated insurgencies from the global South could provoke countermovement in this authoritarian direction. (My own initial projection of this possibility may be found in "Socialism or Barbarism: The Long Run Fate of the Capitalist World-Economy," in T. Boswell and A. Bergesen, eds., *America's Changing Role in the World-System*, [New York: Praeger, 1987].)

On the other hand, the "von sich" angle depicts two possible progressive long-run transformations of the world-system, both of them implied in Wallerstein's original 1973 announcement of the world-system perspective "The Rise and Demise of the Capitalist World-Economy," when he foresaw a "socialist world government" as a fourth conceivable type of socioeconomic totality, in addition to the historically known mini-systems, world-empires, and world-economies. One version of a socialist world government would be a global social-democratic welfare state; the other a global socialist commonwealth. How these two differ is perhaps less important than how they are similar, as both would entail large-scale redistributions in class, race, gender, and geographical (core/periphery) terms—not merely redistributions of wealth and power but also of headquarters functions. Both are compatible with the more progressive future Arrighi imagines, that of a "non-capitalist" world market of civilizational equals. Achieving either would almost certainly require the leadership of the large semiperipheral states like China, India, and Brazil allied with progressive forces in the core. Creating and sustaining global social democracy would almost surely make more likely the gradual evolutionary achievement of full-blown socialism with democratically accountable and ecologically viable investment planning. And this evolutionary route is more plausible than one via a stage-skipping world revolution. (For a fuller elaboration of these alternatives, see my "Beyond Cycles of Hegemony: Economic, Social, and Military Factors," pp. 66–76 in V. Bornschier and C. Chase-Dunn, *The Future of Global Conflict* [Beverly Hills: Sage, 1999].)

To resume the story so far: the present situation simultaneously presents: (1) aspects of a typical "an sich" transition; and (2) anomalies indicating the onset of a "von sich" transformation into one of the alternative systems just sketched. To advance both of these angles and conclude this *tour d'horizon*, let us briefly review the major limits to the ceaseless accumulation of capital in a world-economy now in its sixth century of continuous—and discontinuously expanding—existence. To put it another way, let us look at the extent to which the most significant previous "an sich" crisis-relieving mechanisms remain available. Take geographical expansion, which in the past enabled capitalists to incorporate new markets, new laborers, and new and/or cheaper raw materials. At present, the world-economy is encroaching upon the last redoubts of indigenous peoples and of wilderness, with tragic consequences for humans and other species alike. No wonder then that advances in education and communication have enabled increasing indigenous resistance, most recently, for example, in the Amazonian Ecuador and around the Freeport-McMoran gold mine in West Papua (Indonesia), but also in international forums. No wonder, as well, that local and global environmental movements figure so prominently on the current political landscape. Geographical expansion cannot proceed much further; undersea mining and space exploration are more fantasy than plausible economic lifelines—the world has run out of space.

Take proletarianization, another reliable crisis-relieving mechanism of the past. It is in no way accidental that the most dramatic recent advances in capitalist expansion have been occurring in China and India, the two most abundant sources of peasant and semi-proletarian households. These two streams of new proletarians, plus rural sources in sub-Saharan Africa and elsewhere in the global South, project a picture quite different from the geographical one: there are probably between two and three billion peasants to proletarianize before this limit is reached. Other past mechanisms are likely to sustain the capitalist world-economy into and perhaps through the middle run as well. Income redistribution downward to the working and middle classes in some semiperipheral countries—again China and India most prominently, but not exclusively—could well fuel another A-phase, as will marketing products from a range of new technological breakthroughs in fields such as renewable energy, molecular biology, and robotics. Although theoretically limitless, further mechanization implies a different sort of limit to capitalism in its capacity to set free from drudgery people who might then make political waves. And income redistribution downward would almost surely further empower strata and states in the global South who have a continuing interest in furthering the cause of global equalization and eventually eliminating the core/periphery division of labor itself.

These considerations, finally, lead us back to the observed anomaly that while each prior hegemonic transition gave rise to a new dominant power larger in size, population, and global reach than its predecessor, the current transition shows no signs whatever of yielding a single successor to the United States. And it shows many signs of alterations in the international system of competing national states: regional formations such as the EU, NAFTA, the ASEAN bloc; a thickening of intergovernmental and non-governmental organizations; tentative moves in the direction of a world state, such as the proposed dethroning of the dollar as the world's sole reserve currency. Chaos, anarchy, a *sauve-qui-peut* mentality: yes, this too is a possible future. But this seems to me considerably less likely than first a middle-run "an sich" transition to a viable, if comparatively unstable, structure of renewed accumulation, followed by a long-run "von sich" transformation towards barbarism or socialism, those hoary alternatives that refuse to die.

3

BELATED DECOLONIZATION

SOUTH AFRICA, NORTHERN IRELAND, AND ISRAEL/ PALESTINE COMPARED

Gershon Shafir

Introduction

The coincidence in peacemaking in South Africa, in Israel/Palestine, and in Northern Ireland in the early 1990s—the unbanning of the ANC on February 11, 1990, and the first democratic elections in the history of South Africa from April 26 to 29, 1994; the signing of the Oslo DOP on September 13, 1993; the December 15, 1993, Downing Street Declaration and subsequent cease fire declaration by the Provisional IRA on August 31, 1994—have been noted by many an observer but usually seen as fortuitous. I wish to argue that these peacemaking attempts and the simultaneity of timing point to significant similarities between the three societies, while their partial differences account for their greatly varied measure of success.

The thesis of this chapter is that all three countries are sites of colonial settlement in which the consolidation of the homogenous post-settlement societies remained incomplete and self-contradictory, leading to twisted, partial, and belated decolonization. The peace processes in South Africa, Israel, and Northern Ireland, as I will demonstrate in Section One, are in fact decolonization processes, and their agonies are closely related to that very fact. I will then highlight the combined local-global dynamic behind these decolonization drives. The stage, as shown in Section Two, was set by the modernization of South African, Israeli, and Irish economies which have shattered the ethnic, racial, or religious solidarity of their post-settler populations and, as laid out in Section Three, freed their business elites to experiment with new social models made attractive by economic globalization in the mid-1980s. Section Four will focus on the differences in outcomes. I will highlight the effectiveness of the late twentieth century international model of conflict-resolution through leveling citizenship in South Africa, where it was applied in a single society; its utter failure in the Israel and Palestine, where two societies exist side-by-side; and limited but expanding effectiveness in Northern Ireland, where it was used to integrate conflicting groups within a single political framework but slowed down by the desire to unify it with a foreign political entity—the Republic of Ireland. These differences led to the peaceful but tense coexistence in South Africa and heavily escalated confrontation between Israelis and Palestinians, which place these two at the opposite end of the continuum, and a delayed and incomplete restructuring, which locates Northern Ireland in between the other two.

One: Intractable Conflicts and Decolonization

The earliest colonial experience was Ireland, where Tudor, Stuart, Cromwellian, and Williamite state-building conquests and settlements established patterns of ethnic and religious differentiation which have persisted to the present day. Understanding their consequence is indispensable for understanding Northern Ireland (O'Leary and McGarry 1993, 56). The plantation of Protestant settlers made Ireland different from Wales and Scotland; though once a site for the attempted diffusion of the dominant culture of the British Isles, English-speaking Anglicanism, the Ulster colony became a major obstacle to the successful incorporation of Ireland into the emerging British nation (O'Leary and McGarry 1993, 62). Dutch and then British colonization of southern Africa began in the Cape of Good Hope, from which it spread inland. This involved an ongoing struggle between the Boers and the British, especially after the discovery of diamonds and gold, and led to the creation of the Union of South Africa. Unlike the Eastern European romantic nationalist movements it resembled, the Zionist movement was based, after 1882, on immigration to and colonization of Palestine. Israel, as the product of a settlement movement, is therefore not so different from some of the other European overseas societies that were shaped in the process of settlement and sustained conflict with already existing societies they were displacing (Shafir 1989).

*   *   *

In studying colonization—the founding of "new societies"—I have followed George Fredrickson's cogent argument that colonization was not made of one cloth. Fredrickson distinguishes between *occupation, mixed, plantation,* and *pure settlement* colonies. The first evolved to ensure military control of strategic locations without, however, undertaking to transform their economic order. Examples of this model abound in South East Asia and coastal Africa. The other three were settler colonies with sizeable European populations but differed in the labor force employed to cultivate appropriated native land. The alternative labor forces consisted of native, "imported," and white workers respectively. Mixed colonies used coercive methods to elicit labor from the native population, but potential antagonism between the two groups was dampened through miscegenation. The mountainous regions of Latin America supply us with obvious examples of mixed colonies. In the plantation colony, lacking "a docile indigenous labor force," the settlers acquired land directly and imported an indentured or unfree labor force to work their monocultural plantations. Examples of this method of settlement are the South in the United States and the Caribbean sugar islands. Finally, the pure settlement colony established "an economy based on white labor" which, together with the forcible removal or the destruction of the native population, allowed the settlers "to regain the sense of cultural and ethnic homogeneity that is identified with a European concept of nationality." Among colonial societies, the pure, or homogenous, settlement colonies had the largest post-settler population, members of which sought to become the majority in their chosen land. These colonies have also reproduced consequently, in varying degrees, the complex economies and social structures of metropolitan societies. Australia and the North in the United States exemplify this type (Fredrickson 1981; 1988, 218–221).

*   *   *

Anti-colonial struggles have their own particular forms of resolutions, and I believe that the rhythm and reason of colonialism and decolonization mirror each other, such that the diversity of colonial projects is recapitulated in a corresponding pattern of decolonizations. Consequently, I suggest that we can extend the reach of Fredrickson's typology by constructing a systematic framework to account for decolonization as well.

Waves of colonial expansion, as Albert Bergesen has argued, resulted from rivalries between great powers wanting to enhance their strategic and economic positions and, I will suggest, conversely, decolonization corresponds to the assumption of international hegemony by a single power (Bergesen and

Schoenberg 1980) which, instead of employing expensive political tools of domination, supports rapid economic expansion and simultaneously cajoles and exerts control to establish its own, much vaunted, version of Pax Britannica, or Americana. The cycles of colonial expansion correspond to protectionism, while decolonization goes hand-in-hand with trade and financial expansion, namely what we have come to label economic globalization.

The first wave of decolonization was of *mixed* and *plantation colonies* and took place in the heyday of international British hegemony. A new wave of international instability began in the 1870s, when British hegemony was challenged by other European great powers. Colonial control, consequently, was expanded into Africa and Asia while a neo-mercantilist protectionism reshaped trade relations. In the post–Second World War era, the second massive wave of decolonization of *occupation colonies* in Asia and Africa—a period that wrongly monopolized the designation of "the era of decolonization"—took place with great rapidity. This second wave of decolonization coincided with the rise of the United States and of multinational corporations. And in the 1990s, the fall of the USSR and the disintegration of its imperial borderlands occurred simultaneously with the rise of the United States to the position of sole superpower. Under US hegemony, a process of globalization led to the integration of financial markets, the building of regional trading blocks, and the expansion of international trade opportunities. This is also leading to a belated, third, decolonization drive in which South African, Israeli, and Northern Irish elites show willingness to jettison the overt practices even if not all the vestiges of their colonial past and near-present.

Among the ripples of the end of the Cold War we can count, therefore, not only the disintegration of the "socialist bloc," but also the following additional ripples: the disintegration of multi-ethnic empires; the decline of one-party regimes; military coups and dictatorships; as well as the last wave of decolonization. Peacemaking in South Africa, Israel, and Northern Ireland signals decolonization in instances of partially successfully established *pure settlement colonies*.

*   *   *

Whereas settler-immigrants and their descendants on Europe's other "frontiers of settlement" mixed, to differing extents, with the native populations, marginalized and destroyed them, or were expelled, the colonial standoffs in South Africa, Israel, and Northern Ireland continued. Africans and other non-whites, Palestinians, and Irish Catholics continued to pose a basic challenge to the resolve and the identity of post-colonial or post-settlement whites in South Africa, Jews in Israel, and Ulster Protestants in Northern Ireland, respectively. Two shared characteristics account for this challenge.

(a) The first is the post-settler populations' relatively small size, *vis-à-vis* their respective black African, Palestinian Arab, and Irish Catholic neighbors, animated the latter's continuous struggle and justified their hopes. Demography, however, is not destiny; a group's populations can be counted and compared in different ways since they rarely overlap with cultural identities and invariably possess a more salient political dimension. At the same time, a distinct characteristic of settler colony dynamics is their demographic rivalry and polarization. A significant part of colonial conflict takes place in maternity wards and generates the fear of demographic threats or the *revanche des berceaux* (revenge of the cradles) as part of the post-settlers' general siege culture.

The biggest demographic ratio gap of the three cases is in South Africa, where in the late 1980s the black African population represented 75.2 percent, white 13.6 percent, Colored 8.6 percent, and Indian 2.6 percent, of the 43 million inhabitants. Until the 1990s the size of the white population was artificially inflated by undercounting the rest of the population The share of the Catholic population of Northern Ireland, at 33.5 percent of the population, has remained static for many decades, in part because during the Stormont years they composed approximately 60 percent of the emigrants and thus contributed to the continued demographic preponderance of Protestants (O'Leary and McGarry 1993, 131). But it began inching up, and in 1991, out of a population of 1,577,836, the share of Catholics jumped to 38.4 percent, while Protestants fell to 50.6 percent (Table 22.1 in Doherty 1996, 201). Catholics are also 45.4 percent of the 0–4 age groups, while Protestants are 40.7 percent. These numbers seem to predict a Catholic majority within twenty years or so (Mulholland 2002, 182–183).

Palestinians are conceived by many Israelis not only as political antagonists but as a "demographic threat" on three levels. In the domestic sphere, the Israeli population in 2012 stood at 7,836,000, of which 1.6 million are Palestinian Arab. The 2.6 percent annual growth among Israeli Palestinian citizens is one of the highest in the world (as compared with 2.8 percent in Jordan and Syria and 2.1 percent in Egypt), though lower than in the Palestinian Authority. Combining the number of citizens in Palestine and those in the West Bank and Gaza, which is estimated at between 2.7 and 3.9 million, the former mandate of Palestine will have a Palestinian majority within less than a generation. Finally, the opposition to the Palestinian refugees' right of return, which would threaten the Jewish character of the otherwise mostly secular Israeli state, is an ironclad principle of all Israeli Jewish political parties and rules out all resolutions of the conflict based on universal human rights ("*Population, by Population Group,*" Monthly Bulletin of Statistics, *Israel Central Bureau of Statistics,* 2012. http://www.cbs.gov.il/www/yarhon/b1_e.htm.).

The minority status of whites in South Africa, and the tenuous majority of Protestants in Northern Ireland and of Israeli Jews everywhere except within the green line of 1948 weighed heavily on post-settler politics. At the same time, the demographic threat should not be exaggerated. Demographic interests are only part of larger socioeconomic dynamics, as demonstrated by the fact that the most peaceful accommodation took place in South Africa, where this threat should have been the gravest.

*   *   *

(b) The *second reason* for the delay in and the checkered character of these decolonizations is that in these three cases no single predominant colonial model was able to prevail. In Fredrickson's words: "the modern South African situation has evolved out of the interaction among [pure] settlement, plantation, and occupational tendencies, but none has been carried to a logical conclusion." The Afrikaner *Herrenvolk* approach emerged from the struggle against Great Britain and viewed South Africa as a quintessentially white society in which Africans were temporary alien sojourners. White liberals, mostly associated with or hailing from the corporate elite, worked with the model of a plantation colony and expressed a willingness to partially absorb the African agricultural or mining proletariat, but until recently were unwilling to go as far as agreeing to a "one man, one vote" system. Finally, the European minority only reluctantly has, and in many cases has not yet, overcome the view of being an outpost of Europe in Africa, thus retaining the mentality typical to an occupation colony, and indeed within the African nationalist movement, the Pan-Africanist perspective held that white minority rule was an alien occupation (Frederickson 1995).

Similarly, in Northern Ireland, loyalist Protestants viewed ties with Britain as decisive for their status and prominence, hence members of this group still retain the type of association typical to occupation colonies. In their relationship with the Catholic population, their preference has been for a plantation colony in which the populations are segregated into hierarchically organized economic niches. On occasion, small groups have raised the possibility of a separate Ulster nationalism. Finally, there is a long historical tradition of nonsectarian Irish nationalism, which emerged during the French Revolution and has found periodic expression.

*   *   *

In the case of Israel, the victory of the pure settlement colony model during the *Second Aliya,* which led to a willingness to accept territorial partition in 1936 and in 1947, was challenged after the 1967 War by three waves of settlement in the West Bank, Gaza, and the Golan Heights. The ethnic settlement colony in the West Bank challenged the purity of Jewish settlement within the 1948 boundaries, and the subsequent inability to draw a line of separation along the Green Line and within Jerusalem made problematic Peace Now's desire to return to a homogenous Jewish state. Continued colonization even subsequent to the Oslo Accord further undermined the older Labor Zionist project of Israel as a pure settlement colony. As an aside, I will mention that in the United States there was also a contention of two models, but the Civil War afforded the Northern model decisive victory, in turn leading to subsequent stability.

The continued colonial dimension of these three societies accounted for the anachronistic dimension in South African, Israeli, and Irish histories. Frederik Van Zyl Slabbert, the leader of the Progressive Democratic Party and the founder of Institute for Democratic Alternatives in South Africa (IDASA), explains the anomalous position of South Africa in the world following the Second World War as the result of the refusal of its whites to undergo a process of decolonization when the rest of Africa already had done so. The setting up of the apartheid regime itself, starting in 1948, was the direct continuation of the white minority rule which was the hallmark of the continuous colonial character of South Africa (Slabbert 1986, 3).

Walid Khalidi, the doyen of Palestinian scholars and the founder of the *Journal of Palestine Studies,* finds the parallels to the Palestinian experience in the comparative historical context of the European colonization of North America, Australia, and New Zealand. Khalidi (like Van Zyl Slabbert in regard to South Africa) is left puzzled by the anachronistic character of Zionism: its encroachment on Palestine came late, at the post-heyday of the last wave of European imperialism and, therefore, the War of Independence already coincided with the demise of Europe's old colonies (Khalidi 1992).

The violent struggle against the Catholic civil rights movement throughout the 1970s and 1980s, when civil rights and multicultural advocates were winning their battles for integration in other post-colonial societies, is another indication of an anachronistic streak in Ulster's history. Even more dramatically, the abolition of the Stormont regime, the assumption of direct British rule, and the return of the British troops to Northern Ireland in 1972, have reinstated a particularly blatant colonial dimension absent since 1919. Against this background, Britain's assertion that it has no selfish strategic or economic interest in Northern Ireland (Aughey and Morrow 1996, 215) can be seen as an official end to this colonial dimension.

Two: The Breakup of the Post-Settler Solidarity

In each of these societies, ethnic, religious, or racial unity, or paternalistic solidarity, played an important role in protecting privilege. These settler societies reduced potential class conflict by keeping access open to all, especially unskilled working class or agricultural workers, of the post-settler group. The struggle for a "civilized" or "European way of life" or for "Hebrew labor" served as important rallying cries for this unity. Such alliances always remained costly and problematic, and led to the creation of large, unwieldy, and frequently wasteful, state sectors. When the interests of the post-settler elites were better served by alternative economic arrangements or the European standard seemed secured, the constraints imposed by the alliance began wearing off. Central to the willingness of the elites of these post-settler societies to embark on belated and partial decolonization-cum-peacemaking in these cases was the economic modernization which had undermined and sometimes shattered the alliances between the dominant middle and working classes. The transformation of their class structures accounts, in large part, for the new-found openness to peacemaking.

The clearest demonstration of the formation of such alliances in South Africa is the formation of the "Pact Government" in 1924. In the 1920s, poor whites, who fled to the towns to escape the turmoil in the agrarian sector, encountered the competition of lower-paid blacks and colored people who threatened their "civilized wages" and, therefore, way of life. Dan O'Meara's brilliant *Volkskapitalisme* (2009) demonstrated how the formation of the Afrikaner identity and the exclusivist Afrikaner economic institutions were bound together and led to the formation of Afrikaner political power. A series of legislative acts were enacted to protect white workers by means of massive and entrenched non-market mechanisms and featherbedding of government employment. Starting in 1924, the South African Pact Government adopted a series of legislative acts enacted to protect white workers by means of non-market mechanisms. The adoption of the apartheid regime in 1948 was a further entrenchment of this alliance. It prevented African workers from staying in the cities where they would compete with white workers and would be better equipped to organize in opposition to apartheid itself. At the same time, Afrikaners became an upper caste of skilled workers delineated from the lower caste, which was exclusively occupied by black Africans by a rigid "color bar."

*   *   *

As apartheid redistributed wealth and employment to large cross-sections of the Afrikaner community the old system of privilege began losing its appeal and the new Afrikaner professional and middle class forged a new alliance with its English speaking counterpart. The gap between the FCI (Federated Chamber of Industries), ASSOCOM, and the AHI (Afrikaanse Handelsinstituut—the organization of small-scale Afrikaner manufacturing and commerce), gradually disappeared and the representatives of white-owned business spoke with one voice regardless of the language in which they spoke (Greenberg 1985). As the gap between the English and Afrikaner business class eroded, the Afrikaner working class was absorbed into the middle class. The 1991 census reports that there were 920,976 black, 131,813 Colored, and only 7,072 white laborers in South Africa (*SA Labour Bulletin*, March/April 1993, Vol 17, No. 2, pp. 53–55). In short, apartheid made unskilled whites disappear. Both classes in the Afrikaner "nation" had been "emancipated" from the racial conflict through the brutal exploitation of the African population. Afrikaners were able to lock in their privileges though educational and occupational credentials and experiences. The changing socioeconomic character of the National Party's Afrikaner constituency also subverted many of the arguments in favor of apartheid. With the social mobility of un- and semi-skilled working class Afrikaners their fear of loss of privilege declined, and the trading of political power for the preservation of privilege through the end of apartheid became an acceptable outcome. Of our three cases, the South African has been the most peaceful, in large part, because privilege was not destroyed (Adam and Moodley 1993; Adler and Webster 1995; Consultative Business Movement 1993; du Preez et al. 1989).

Jewish employers in Palestine, like elsewhere, preferred to employ cheaper workers, in this case Palestinians (Shafir 1989; Shapira 1977). As a consequence, in the Israeli society-in-the-making, the ashkenazi (Jews of European descent) agricultural workers launched a struggle not for a color bar but for exclusionary "Hebrew Labor." Their goal was to create a "closed shop" of Jewish workers, and in order to prevent undercutting by Palestinian workers, they elected to underrate all levels of labor, from skilled to unskilled. The two institutional pillars of Zionist colonization, the World Zionist Organization's Jewish National Fund and the agricultural workers' Histadrut (labor federation), allied to monopolize a section of the land and labor markets and, in this fashion, create a large, horizontally and vertically integrated, separate co-operative Jewish sector of the economy. After 1948, the ashkenazi labor force has found even stronger protection from uneven competition when a caste based labor market was institutionalized and the Palestinian Arab population placed under military government (until 1965). With the absorption of a large share of the ashkenazi labor force into the new government bureaucracy and the Histadrut's own economic sector, the lower rungs of the economy came to be filled with mizrachi (Jews of North African and Middle Eastern provenance) workers. In Palestine, the settlers and the indigenous population formed two mutually exclusive societies, while in South Africa the indigenous groups were incorporated into the settler society, though without, obviously, attaining legal and social equality. South African society was based on supremacist principles (but practices of incorporation); Israeli society on separatist designs.

* * *

It was only in the mid-1980s that a relatively autonomous Israeli business class began to emerge. With the collapse of the Histadrut, the role played by the trade unions in the shaping of economic policy was also radically reduced. The business community became one of the main champions of the peace process, for example by putting behind-the-scene pressure on the Shamir government to negotiate with the Palestinians (Rossant 1989, 58; Kochan 1992). "Israeli businessmen know that without peace with the Arabs," one journalist found, "there is little chance of the country building a stable civilian economy." It is against this conviction, at a time when the economy had already been restructured into "Israel Inc." much to the delight of business and is slated for a take-off, that "many Israeli businessmen are joining the Bush Administration in leaning on Prime Minister Yitzhak Shamir to become more flexible in his approach to negotiations." Eli Hurvitz, the Director of Teva Pharmaceuticals and Israel's largest drug company and past president of the Israeli Manufacturers Association (IMA), expressed this consensus by stating that from this economic perspective "the future is problematic without peace" (Rossant 1989, 54) and the same role was played by Dov Lautman, his successor, throughout the Oslo process and later. In this case, therefore, the support for peacemaking was more half-hearted, being an ashkenazi elite project which suffered from lower-class mizrachi misgivings.

*   *   *

The earliest form of the class alliance among Protestant landlords, gentry, and peasants in Northern Ireland was formed to protect the control of land in the late nineteenth century. The bond became even stronger during the violent struggle to prevent Home Rule and the independence of all of Ireland. The adoption of this solidarity to industry presumed the attachment of the Ulster economy to the British imperial market and was dominated by production of capital goods such as shipbuilding, heavy engineering, and linen (McGovern and Shirlow 1997, 183). But the main industries in Ulster were in continuous decline, as was the empire, leaving the region with the highest rate of unemployment in the UK, and therefore their provision of "Protestant" employment became ever more crucial (see, for example, Mulholland 2002, 49–50).

The dramatic extension of the British welfare state under Labor governments after the Second World War undercut the Ulster control system (Collins 1999; Coulter 1999; Elliott 2000; Ruane and Todd 1996). "The British government made their new welfare programs extremely attractive by offering to make up whatever shortfall would exist if the Northern Ireland government provided services at UK standards while imposing tax rates similar to Britain." Catholics in Northern Ireland began to interact with state institutions and expect more from them, thus becoming more British (O'Leary and McGarry 1993, 157). So now in addition to the decline of industries that employed Protestant workers, the expansion of public employment by growing British subvention created more equitable opportunities for Catholics (O'Leary and McGarry 1993, 189). "The result is a tendency to consolidate non-sectarian middle-class solidarity while at the same time alienating sections of both Catholic and Protestant working-class" (McGovern and Shirlow 1997, 190). These changes turned the tide against internal Protestant solidarity.

"As the cross-class alliance between the Protestant bourgeoisie and the working class began to dissolve, some Protestant workers looked to politicians and community leaders who spoke the language of suppression and draconian state action against the Catholic minority. In the vacuum which now existed between the State and the Protestant working class the UVF was re-launched and began to engage in a sectarian campaign of murder and intimidation of Catholics" (McGovern and Shirlow 1997, 187). Though Protestant workers

suffered from downward mobility, the worst deprivation continued to be experienced by Catholic workers, who provided the bulk of the supporters of the
Provisional IRA and other Catholic paramilitaries. In fact, "most of those who
have played a direct role in the conflict have been drawn from the working class
communities. The security forces have in the main recruited from the respect-
able elements of the Protestant working class. The agents of unofficial forms
of violence have also come overwhelmingly from working class backgrounds"
(Coulter 1999, 71; see also, O'Brien 1993; Nelson 1984).

The disappearance or breakup of the coalitions that protected the privileges of post-settlers and thus overrode their class divisions eased the peace
process South Africa. This allowed the business and professional elites to embark
on decolonization in both Northern Ireland and Israel but also produced many
of its opponents from among the now "abandoned" lower-class post-settlers.

Three: Global Opportunities

These three economies, especially their subsidized oversized state sectors, found
themselves in the 1980s between particularly acute crises and the attractions of
rapid economic growth promised to those integrated into the global economy.

South African economists repeatedly told the story of the wasted 1980s.
The growth of the South African economy declined from 5.5 percent annual
rate in the 1960s to 2.9 percent in the 1970s, and "in the decade 1981–1990,
economic growth collapsed to 0.6 percent per annum." The real output of
manufacturing, mining, and construction contracted in the 1981–1991 years
with negative annual growth rates between 0.8 and 2.3 percent. Fixed investments declined by 30 percent. A talk presented by businessman Christo Nel
to IDASA in April 1988 summed up the ailments of South Africa from the
perspective of all its racial groups as "declining productivity, increased cost of
living, declining standards of living, large-scale poverty, unemployment, and
widespread social unrest and conflict" (Nel 1988). A confidential report of the
President's Economic Advisory Council from August 1986 stated that the past
"course cannot be pursued much longer" and called for "certain fundamental
adjustments" in the economy and its environment (Economic Advisory Council
1990, 1). The business community, now thoroughly politicized through its
Consultative Business Movement, played a key role in securing the transition
of power from the Nationalist party to the ANC.

The Israeli policy of accelerated economic growth through inflows of
unilateral capital transfers and immigration worked remarkably well, with
some interruptions, from the 1920s until the Yom Kippur War and energy
crisis year of 1973. As economists report, that "fateful year marked a watershed
in economic performance" (Rivlin 1992, 10) and "the period which started
with the Yom Kippur War and lasted until the … wave of immigration [from

the ex-Soviet Union] which began in 1990 is known as the 'lost years'" (Razin and Sadka 1993, 16). A factor analysis, run by Aryeh Shahar and Maya Chosen on national indicators from the World Bank's *World Development Report* with the intention of measuring the change in Israel's relative position in the global context between 1965 and 1989, demonstrated that Israel had been and remained lodged in the interstice between the upper layer of the developing and the bottom layer of developed countries. Not only has it failed to make it into the ranks of the developed countries of the world but "the disparities between Israel and the countries of the developed world are growing, while the disparities with the upper section of the developing countries are decreasing." The prolonged continuation of this trend was likely, therefore, to move Israel from its "intermediate position ... into the large group of developing countries" (Shahar and Chosen 1993, 324). Consequently, it was argued that "if Israel resembles many East Asian states prior to the 1970s, since then it favors the Latin American states" (Barnett 1996, 134; see also Silver 1990).

*   *   *

In Northern Ireland, the Troubles radically altered the economy of Northern Ireland, above all making it dependent on the UK. The two largest branches of the private sector, manufacturing and tourism, declined, while the share of public sector production doubled between 1970 and 1984 from 15 to 30 percent (Considine and O'Leary 1999, 113: Table 7.3). British subventions financed the dramatic expansion of the public sector, from 27 percent of the total labor force in the early 1970s to 42 by the mid-1970s, creating what some have called a workhouse economy with a large non-tradable sector (Bew et al. 1997, 91–93). Consequently, the economy of Northern Ireland, more than that of any other state in Western Europe, is characterized by abnormal public-sector dominance (McGovern and Shirlow 1997, 191). There was no assurance of such large continued subvention.

In addition to these profound structural crises, both the Israeli and South African economies suffered from economic boycotts, which blocked their way to international markets and the growing benefits of globalization. Already in the 1940s, the Arab League imposed a primary boycott on Israel, prohibiting Arab countries from trading with her directly, as well as a secondary boycott, which forbade Arab countries and companies to do business with foreign companies that maintained business relations with Israel. In November 1992, President of the Israeli Manufacturer's Association Dov Lautman added the Arab boycott to his list of conditions that hurt Israel, and in this context argued that the business community made a mistake in the past decade by not placing at the top of the list of its priorities the creation of a close linkage between peace and growth (*Ha'aretz*, November 17, 1992). He was seconded by Danny Gilerman, the President of the Israeli Chambers of Commerce, who, relying on a study of his organization, alleged that Israel lost $44 billion as a result of the Arab boycott. Gilerman called on Rabin to view the abolition of the boycott as a top priority (*Ha'aretz,* August 7, 1992).

South Africa was subjected to an international arms embargo and economic sanctions, starting with OPEC's oil embargo in 1973, growing throughout the 1980s, and leading to a host of restrictive regulations and laws by foreign countries and bodies, such as the US's Comprehensive Anti-Apartheid Act (CAAA), which resulted in 350 foreign corporations disposing of their South African investments. The most damaging sanction was the decision of a number of international banks in 1985 not to renew short-term credits to South Africa, leading to a severe debt crisis and to massive capital flight. These sanctions threatened South Africa with the absence of technological renewal. This forbidding prospect weighed heavily on the South African business community.

*   *   *

But already the ongoing modernization of the South African and Israeli economies began pointing in new directions that would be rewarded by greater access to international markets. As Robert Price among many others argued, the eclipse of mining and agriculture by manufacturing in the 1970s exposed the limits placed by apartheid on South Africa's economic development. Manufacturing requires a stable, literate, technically skilled, and relatively permanent urban labor force, but by the late 1960s there was a shortage of skilled whites and the large black population began filling the jobs created by the maturing industrial sector (Price 1991). Furthermore, the erosion of black labor control and the failure of the "homelands" to arrest or slow down black urbanization removed the *raison d'être* of apartheid. In Israel, in response to a French-imposed weapons embargo after the 1967 War, the government developed an Israeli military-industrial complex. The military industries became the engine of growth and the focus of knowledge dissemination for advanced high technology industries, as well as the primary influence in the modernization of industry and large segments of the economy. The new industries trained and recruited technological and managerial manpower, part of which, subsequently, moved to private and/or civilian industry as employees and entrepreneurs. Military production led to spinoffs of civilian uses and, at the end of the 1970s, high-tech civilian companies began to expand rapidly, while the complex of military industries also became the main source of growth for exports. Not only did military production produce relatively high added value, but it also helped pry open doors for Israeli civilian products. With the crisis of the military industrial production since the mid-1980s, civilian production and exports continued to grow on their own. In Northern Ireland, the path was less direct. The economy of the Republic of Ireland during the same period was named a "Celtic tiger," and served as an example of what Northern Ireland was missing out on. The highly skilled labor force contributed to the growth of knowledge intensive industries in electronics, computers, and pharmaceuticals. Foreign investment also played an important role in expanding employment and the share of exports in the GDP rose considerably (Considine and O'Leary 1999, 120–122). South African manufacturing and Israeli and Irish high-tech production provided tangible alternatives to the older economic models by being modern and export-oriented and less dependent on state regulation or subsidies.

The impact of global economic forces on South African, Irish, and Israeli economies made less viable the unique extra-market features that are the result of their establishment and reproduction as post-colonial societies. These were the massive, but inefficient and costly, extra-market mechanisms and institutions that provided mostly Afrikaans-speaking, Protestant, and Jewish post-settler-immigrants with conditions favorable for settlement and prosperity.

Four: Conflict Resolution Regimes

Though there are many differences between the colonial and post-colonial regimes established in Northern Ireland, South Africa, and Israel, the impact of only one can be explored in the space available here on their respective de-colonizations. That difference concerns internal versus external decolonization, the latter being an obstacle to peacemaking.

In the Republic of South Africa, the legacy of a single labor market created a single political arena in which decolonization was played out. The ANC's historical demand was always for equal citizenship, but even when apartheid was slowly dismantled, and even after the unbanning of the ANC, the idea of "one man, one vote" gained currency among whites only slowly. Compromise solutions failed: in 1984, the apartheid regime disenfranchised nonwhites and when it undertook to integrate Indians and Colored in a subsidiary position in 1984 into separate assemblies, while leaving black Africans without the vote, massive opposition broke out. The granting of the ANC's central demand effectively transferred parliamentary and political power to the black majority and lead to a relatively peaceful transition.

The IRA's goal of unification of the six counties of Northern Ireland with the three which compose the Republic of Ireland, in order to overturn the 1920 division of the island into two separate political entities, added a clear external dimension to its desire to end British presence in Northern Ireland. The adoption of a reformist strategy of equal citizenship in the 1960s in place of the denial of the legitimacy of the Ulster state was a radical shift and served as the most serious challenge to unionist domination (Patterson 1996, 43). Under the combined influence of the civil rights movement in the United States and the new British welfare state, Catholic students and members of the middle class engaged in a civil rights movement of their own, the People's Democracy, in the late 1960s and early 1970s. Though using the generic language of civil rights, frequently the goal was the attainment of a full complement of British citizenship rights.

The combination of goals for internal and external decolonization held back and repeatedly threatened the Northern Irish peace process. Internal decolonization, here as in South Africa, proved within reach. In many of its major documents, for example the Anglo-Irish Agreement of November 15, 1985, the integrationist goal of accommodating the rights and identities of both Protestants and Catholics by protecting human rights and preventing discrimination became central (O'Leary and McGarry 1993, 222), while the Good Friday agreement of April 10, 1998, created power-sharing agreements with broad veto powers for each community (Mulholland 2002, 178; Ruane and Todd, 2007). At the same time, the "re-unification" of Ireland was not accomplished and, though consultative north-south ministerial councils on transport, agriculture, education, tourism were established (Mulholland 2002, 177–178), the loyalist Protestants won multiple guarantees against forced unification. Great Britain, on its part, agreed to abide by a referendum which wishes to make Ulster part of a united island (Cradden and Collins 1999; Crotty 1998). Peacemaking in Northern Ireland, therefore, is an interim case, between the other two.

The Israeli path of state-building through the bifurcation of the economy of Palestine into two sectors contributed to the maintenance of two distinct societies and, especially after the Israeli conquests of all of Palestine the 1967 War, has a closer fit with a model of external decolonization through territorial partition (known as the land-for-peace formula). The Oslo Agreement recognized the principle of withdrawal and territorial partition even if it remained vague in regard to its dimensions. Subsequent plans, such as the Road Map of 2002, proposed by the United States, the EU, Russia, and the UN made the two state solution explicit. One of greatest obstacles to such external decolonization is the continued colonization by the Israeli government, which has by 2009 settled over 300,000 Jewish settlers in the West Bank (not including East Jerusalem), and the subsequent high levels of violence.

Conclusion

The three peace processes of the last decade of the 20th century examined here, I argue, were in fact belated processes of partial decolonization in partially successful, and by now anachronistic, pure settlement colonies. Notwithstanding disparate institutional contexts and different rates of development, due to their post-colonial similarities the three economies displayed marked structural similarities in the 1980s. Economic modernization began to challenge the heavily interventionist economies in South Africa, Northern Ireland, and Israel, while economic globalization provided their business and professional sectors with appealing alternatives. The crumbling of the post-settler groups class alliances was a key factor in the willingness of their middle and entrepreneurial classes to seek peaceful accommodations. The practical disappearance of the Afrikaner working class greatly facilitated the peaceful transition, whereas in Israel, members of the working class were opposed to, and in Northern Ireland engaged in, violence to thwart the transition. The relative success of peacemaking in South Africa reflects the existence of a single political framework. The decolonization of the West Bank and Gaza, on its part, is the result of the failure so far of external decolonization when territorial colonization is still ongoing. Northern Ireland falls somewhere in the middle of the continuum between these two cases with its relatively effective internal decolonization and postponement of external decolonization through the unification of Ireland.

References

Adam, Heribert, and Kogila Moodley. 1993. *The Opening of the Apartheid Mind.* Berkeley, CA: University of California Press.

Adler, Glen, and Eddie Webster. 1995. "Challenging Transition Theory: The Labor Movement, Radical Reform, and Transition to Democracy in South Africa." *Politics and Society* 23(1:March): 75–106.

Anderson, James, and James Goodman. 1994. "Northern Ireland: Dependency, Class and Cross-Border Integration in the European Union." Unpublished paper.

Aughey, Arthur, and Duncan Morrow, eds. 1996. *Northern Ireland Politics,* London: Longman.

Barnett, Michael. 1996. "Israel in the World Economy: Israel as an East Asian State?" In his *Israel in Comparative Perspective,* 107–140. New York: SUNY Press.

Beilin, Yossi. 1992. *Israel: A Concise Political History.* New York: St. Martin's.

Bergesen, Albert, and Ronald Schoenberg. 1980. "Long Waves of Colonial Expansion in the World-System." in *Studies of the Modern World-System,* edited by A. Bergesen. New York: Academic Press.

Bew, Paul, et al. 1997. *Between War and Peace: The Political Future of Northern Ireland.* London: Lawrence and Wishart.

Chug Mashov in the Labor Party. 1991. *Mashov's Fifth Congress: Proposed Resolutions,* Efal, (4 May). In Hebrew.

Collins, Neil. 1999. *Political Issues in Ireland Today* (Second ed.). Manchester: Manchester University Press.

Considine, John, and Eoin O'Leary. 1999. "The Growth Performance of Northern Ireland and the Republic of Ireland: 1960 to 1995." In *Political Issues in Ireland Today,* edited by Neil Collins, 106–125.

Consultative Business Movement. 1993. *Managing Change: A Guide to the Role of Business in Transition.* Johannesburg: Ravan Press.

Coulter, Colin. 1999. *Contemporary Northern Irish Society.* London: Pluto.

Cradden, Terry, and Neil Collins. 1999. "The Northern Ireland Peace Agreement." In *Political Issues in Ireland Today,* edited by Neil Collins, 190–205.

Crotty, William, and David E. Schmitt (eds.). 1998. *Ireland and the Politics of Change.* London: Longman.

Doherty, Paul. 1996. "The Numbers Game: The Demographic Context of Politics." In

Northern Ireland Politics, edited by Arthur Aughey and Duncan Morrow, 199–209. London: Longman.

Dotan, Shmuel, 1981. *The Struggle for Eretz-Yisrael.* Tel Aviv, Ministry of Defense: 114–118 (in Hebrew).

du Preez, Max et al. (eds.). 1989. *The Broederstroom Encounter.* Johannesburg: CBM.

Economic Advisory Council of the State President. 1990. "Proposed Long-Term Economic Strategy." September 7, 1990.

Elliott, Marianne. 2000. *The Catholics of Ulster: A History.* London: Allen Lane.

Federated Chamber of Industries (FCI). 1986. *Charter of Economic, Social and Political Rights.*

Fredrickson, George M. 1981. *White Supremacy: A Comparative Study in American and South African History.* New York: Oxford University Press.

———. 1988. *The Arrogance of Race: Historical Perspectives on Slavery, Racism, and Social Inequality.* Middletown, CT: Wesleyan University Press.

———. 1995. *Black Liberation: A Comparative History of Black Ideologies in the United States and South Africa.* New York: Oxford University Press.

Greenberg, Stanley B. 1985. *Race and State in Capitalist Development.* New Haven, CT: Yale University Press.

Keren, Michael. 1994. "Israeli Professionals and the Peace Process." *Israel Affairs* 1(1:Autumn): 149–163.

Khalidi, Walid. 1992. *All That Remains: The Palestinian Villages Occupied and Depopulated by Israel in 1948.* Washington: Institute for Palestine Studies.

Kleiman, Ephraim. 1967. "The Place of Manufacturing in the Growth of the Israeli Economy." *Journal of Development Studies* 3(April): 226–248.

Kochan, Nicholas. 1992 "Israel: Bidding to Be the Next 'Economic Dragon.'" *Multinational Business* (Spring).

Levi-Faur, David. 1996. "Nationalism and the Power of Business: The Manufacturers' Association of Israel." *Environment and Planning C: Government and Policy* 14: 193–209.

Magliolo, Jacques. 1995. "Liebenberg Eases Tax for Foreign Investors." *Business Mail* (March 17–23).

McGovern, Mark, and Peter Shirlow. 1997. "Counter-Insurgency, Deindustrialization and the Political Economy of Union Loyalism." In *Who are "the People"? Unionism, Protestantism and Loyalism in Northern Ireland,* edited by Shirlow and McGovern, 176–198. London: Pluto Press.

McGrath, Mike, and Merle Holden. 1992. "Economic Outlook 1981–1992." *Indicator SA,* 9(4:Spring).

McGregor, Robin, and Anne McGregor. 1995. *McGregor's Who Owns Whom,* (15th Edition). Rustenburg: Purdey Publishing.

McKittrick, David, and David McVea. 2000. *Making Sense of the Troubles.* Belfast: Blackstaff.

Meretz, Platform for the 1992 Elections (in Hebrew).

Mulholland, Marc. 2002. *The Longest War: Northern Ireland's Troubled History.* Oxford: Oxford University Press.

Nel, Christo. 1988. "The Viability of a Mixed Economy in Post-Apartheid South Africa." Paper presented to the IDASA seminar: "A View of the Economy Beyond Apartheid," April 22, 1988.

Nelson, Sarah. 1984. *Ulster's Uncertain Defenders: Protestant Political, Paramilitary and Community Groups and the Northen Ireland Conflict.* Belfast: Appletree.

O'Brien, Brendan. 1993. *The Long War: The IRA and Sinn Féin, 1985 to Today.* Syracuse, NY: Syracuse University Press.

O'Leary, Brendan, and John McGarry, 1993. *The Politics of Antagonism: Understanding Northern Ireland.* London: Athelone.

O'Meara, Dan. 2009. *Volkscapitalisme.* Cambridge: Cambridge University Press.

Patterson, Henry. 1996. "Nationalism" In *Northern Ireland Politics,* edited by Arthur Aughey and Duncan Morrow, 39–47. London: Longman.

Price, Robert M. 1991. *The Apartheid State in Crisis.* New York: Oxford University Press.

Quigley, George. 1992. "Ireland—An Island Economy." Speech delivered to the Confederation of Irish Industry, Dublin, February.

Razin, Assaf, and Efraim Sadka. 1993. *The Economy of Israel: Malaise and Promise.* Chicago: University of Chicago Press.

Rivlin, Paul. 1992. *The Israeli Economy.* Boulder, CO: Westview.

Rosholt, A. M. 1985. "Reform for Our Sake." *Financial Mail: Supplement on Investment in 1986* (November 29): 74–78.

Rossant, John. 1989. "Israel Has Everything It Needs—Except Peace." *Business Week* (December 9, 1989).

Ruane, Joseph, and Jennifer Todd. 1996. *The Dynamics of Conflict in Northern Ireland: Power, Conflict, and Emancipation.* Cambridge: Cambridge University Press.

———. 2007. "Path Dependence in Settlement Processes: Explaining Settlement in Northern Ireland." *Political Studies,* 1–17.

Shafir, Gershon. 1989. *Land, Labor, and the Origins of the Israeli-Palestinian Conflict, 1882–1914.* Cambridge: Cambridge University Press.

Shahar, Aryeh, and Maya Chosen. 1993. "Israel Among the Nations: A Comparative Study of the Israel's Place Between the Developed World and the Developing World." *Mechkarim Begeographia shel Eretz-Yisrael* [Studies in the Geography of Palestine] 14: 312–324 (in Hebrew).

Shapira, Anita. 1977. *Futile Struggle: The Jewish Labor Controversy, 1929–1939.* Tel Aviv: Hakibbutz Hameuchad (in Hebrew).

Shirlow, Peter, and Mark McGovern (eds.). 1997. *Who are "the People"? Unionism, Protestantism and Loyalism in Northern Ireland.* London: Pluto Press.

Silver, Beverly. 1990. "The Contradictions of Semiperipheral 'Success:' The Case of Israel." In William G. Martin ed., *Semiperipheral States in the World-Economy* edited by William G. Martin, 161–181. New York: Greenwood.

Slabbert, Frederik Van Zyl. 1986. "Sanctions Against South Africa." Press release by FCI on August 7, 1986.

Welsh, David. 1988. "Politics and Business in South Africa." *Optima* 36(3: September): 161–168.

———. 1994. "Liberals and the Future of the New Democracy in South Africa." *Optima* 40(2: November): 39–44.

———. 1995. "Maintaining Peace in South Africa: An Analysis of the Transition." Paper Delivered at the Conference on "The Resolution of Intractable Conflicts: The Israeli-Palestinian and the South African Experience," The Tami Steinmetz Center for Peace Research, Tel Aviv, 19–21 March 1995.

4

DEMOCRATIZING GLOBAL GOVERNANCE

STRATEGY AND TACTICS IN EVOLUTIONARY PERSPECTIVE

Christopher Chase-Dunn and Bruce Lerro

Over the last four centuries global governance has evolved in a more democratic direction, as indicated by the emergence of parliamentary democracy in the core, its diffusion to the non-core, the abolition of slavery and formal colonialism and the establishment of a global human rights regime, though the latter is only partially institutionalized and enforced. The political ideal of democracy, despite continuing contestation about its meaning, has become increasingly adopted by the world's peoples, and the existing institutions of global governance fair badly by comparison to even the most tepid definitions of democracy. The majority of the peoples of the Earth have little knowledge about, or say over, the existing institutions of global governance. Democracy within nation-states, though a laudable goal and in many cases a valuable achievement, does not add up to global democracy, because it says little about the nature of relations among nation-states or about governance at the global level. Existing global governance institutions mainly reflect the outcome of World War II and the might-makes-right rules of global governance by hegemony.

Contested Definitions of Global Democracy

Democracy is a contested concept in both theory and practice even at the national level (Robinson 1996). And the idea of global democracy is even more contested. Most political theorists do not apply the idea at the global level, and when one does it immediately brings up the issue of European cultural hegemony and the relevance of the idea of democracy to non-European civilizations. For many, global democracy is simply the addition of more and more national democracies—parliamentary governments in which fair elections decide the political leadership of the national state. This is the subject of most of the democratization literature in the social sciences and is the guiding approach that forms the basis of most of the discourse in global politics, as states seek to justify their actions by appealing to the idea of democracy. But a growing number of transnational activists contend that global democracy should mean much more than this. The peoples of the world live in a single social system, and decisions about what will happen in that system are the relevant foci for understanding the meaning of global democracy. In a global democracy the majority of the people of the Earth would have say over the decisions that affect their lives. The simple addition of national democracies does not necessarily add up to global democracy, because national states have unequal power, and the question of global democracy turns importantly on the nature of relations among the national states. When the problems are global, the democracy should be global, meaning that the majority of the people of the Earth should be able to have meaningful influence over the institutions of global governance. These institutions have evolved over the past several centuries, and an analysis of the prospects for global democracy needs to begin with an understanding of the historical evolution of global governance.

Our approach questions the idea that parliamentary democracy in single states, even when most of the states in the system have this kind of political system, adds up to global democracy. Some states are much more powerful than others, and their policies affect people all over the Earth. We call this the problem of *global vs. single-state democracy.*

The second focus of our essay is on the issue of the contested nature of the idea of democracy. Here we will note that the definitions of democracy have themselves been issues of political struggle, both within the discourse of the European Enlightenment and in the discourse about Eurocentrism. Our goal is to move toward the formulation of a global consensus about the meaning of the idea of popular democracy. This requires knowledge of this history of political struggles all over the Earth and an understanding of the historical evolution of human societies over the last fifty thousand years (Chase-Dunn 2007).

The democratization literature mainly has studied how and why some societies have been able to institutionalize parliamentary systems for the peaceful transition of power by means of popular elections. This is a very important literature and much has been learned about the conditions that are favorable for stable parliamentary regimes. Charles Tilly's (2007) summary and conclusions, based on decades of studying the political history of national societies, provide a useful roadmap to the conditions under which a national state responds to the will of its average citizens. Tilly's analysis shows that democracy at the national level is tenuous and difficult to sustain, even in states where it has become rather institutionalized. He also makes the important point that a state must have capacity and must be able to contain the autonomy of internal elite challengers to popular power (e.g., the military). Though Tilly does not do it, his analysis is usefully applied to the issues of global state formation and global democracy (see below). Tilly rather underplays the "external" factors that have had important consequences for national democracy, and he does not address, in this book, the issues raised by globalization.

A world-systems perspective on national democracy would at least notice that successful core capitalism has been the main support for institutionalizing parliamentary systems in the most developed national societies. The core countries of Europe, the United States, Australia, Canada, New Zealand, and Japan, along with semiperipheral India, have been the most successful and stable cases of national parliamentary democracy. The rest of the world has had a very difficult time institutionalizing parliamentary democracy, though there have been recurrent waves of democratization in the parliamentary sense (Markoff 1996). The main reason for this is that the hierarchical division of labor between the core and the periphery concentrates greater resources in the core, making alliances between potentially competing elites and cross-class alliances more stable because there is a bigger pie to share. In the periphery, struggle to control the state apparatus is more often violent because it is the only game in town. To be sure there are exceptions, and many semiperipheral and peripheral national societies have been able to achieve at least the trappings of parliamentary democracy, especially in the latest wave.

We do not wish to minimize the important differences between formally democratic regimes that operate according to the law versus lawless and arbitrary authoritarian regimes. Achieving formal parliamentary democracy and the rule of law are huge gains for people who have not had them in the past. A visit to any of the contemporary societies in which local elites with their own implements of coercion are the main enforcers of social order is all that it takes to produce great respect for civil rights and the due process of law. But we do wish to point out that formal parliamentary democracy, even in those societies in which it is most heavily institutionalized, is not necessarily the best of all possible worlds.

Within the European Enlightenment discourse, there has long been a contest between representative formal democracy and popular direct democracy. Bill Robinson (1996) characterizes "polyarchy" as a contest managed by contending elites to legitimize regimes based on huge inequalities. The predominant definition of democracy in the West is a definition that separates political rights from economic rights and that legitimizes and sustains private property in the major means of production. More populist and direct versions of the idea of democracy challenge the radical separation between political and economic rights, and the exclusion of economic democracy from the conversation. Thus the kind of democracy that has become hegemonic in the modern world-system is the kind that is most congruent with capitalism. It protects private owners of the major means of production from most claims on their property and profits by narrowly defining the proper terrain of rights.

Polyarchy undercuts direct democracy and defines certain claims as outside the bounds of rational discourse, based on a narrow political philosophy that has evolved from the conservative branch of the European Enlightenment discourse. The leftist versions—anarchism, socialism, and communism—have been vanquished and proclaimed dead in the celebration of the "end of history" and the victory of rational capitalistic democracy.

The critique of Eurocentrism has also challenged the hegemony of the polyarchic definition of democracy. Many peoples of the colonial empires had indigenous forms of small-scale political regulation that allowed people in local communities to have input in decisions that were made in matters that affected their lives. In the contemporary popular resistance to globalizing corporate capitalism, many voices are reasserting the authenticity and value of these tradition political institutions (e.g., Shiva 2005).

Movements that mobilized people around ideas of community self-reliance were frequent responses to the calamities of rural market integration that combined with droughts and famines to produce the huge and disastrous "late Victorian holocausts" during the great wave of capitalist globalization of the late nineteenth century (Davis 2001). These indigenous movements often employed millenarian ideologies in which the good king was to return or the powers of the universe were expected to intervene to destroy the invading railroads and the white devils that were held to be throwing the natural balances of the universe awry. People discovered that they could produce their own food and entertainment without having to subject themselves to global market forces and threatening technologies far beyond their control.

Much of the post-colonial critique of Eurocentrism has assumed that it was the ideology of the European Enlightenment that was a main tool in the colonial subjugation of the Third World by European states. And so the ideologies of rights, the separation of church and state, and other elements of European thought have been rejected as so many relics of domination. It is not liberal ideology that caused so much exploitation and domination. Rather, it was the failure of real capitalism to live up to its own ideals (liberty and equality) in most of the world. That is the problem that progressives must solve.

The first point to make is that democracy is not a European invention and neither has it been a European monopoly. The European discourse of democracy as an invention of the classical Greek city-states is full of contradictions. The economies of most of the Greek city-states were based on slavery (Bollen and Paxton 1997), while the polities of nomadic foragers, which are everywhere on Earth the ancestors of all peoples, were egalitarian systems in which all adults participated in making the important collective decisions of the group.

Over the last twelve thousand years, most of the regions on Earth experienced a process of the emergence of hierarchical social structures in which elites came to dominate and exploit the masses of peasants and workers. But the struggle over control has never ceased, and indeed the cycles of rise and fall that characterize all hierarchical systems stem in part from the basic conflict over control that is the contest of democracy.

This said, we do not agree with those who see all states as equally exploitative, though neither do we agree with those who paint the contemporary national democracies as the best of all possible worlds. Hierarchies have been necessary for the coordination of ever-larger and more complex societies, and societies that are less hierarchical (or smaller) have had to erect their own hierarchies or perish in the struggle with more hierarchical societies. And so nearly all societies on Earth have undergone state-formation or become incorporated into existing states.

But all states are not the same. There are real differences among modern states in the extent to which political and economic rights are extended to all the citizens and the majority participates in consequential political decision-making. While we agree with Robinson that this is partly a sham because it legitimates the rule of capitalist elites, we also find it important to point out that the sham is better than no sham. Truly authoritarian government is worse, and so the problem is to help those who do not yet enjoy national polyarchy to get it and to move beyond polyarchy in those states where that is possible. And we also need to democratize global governance. At the global level, polyarchy would be preferable to the current situation in which the institutions of global governance rely on the institutionalized structure of the interstate system to veil the realities of global power and authority.

But we also agree with Robinson that polyarchy is often used to undercut more radical movements of participatory and direct democracy that are seen as threatening the interests of capitalist elites. And we also wish to raise again the issue of global democracy and to imagine the possible future existence of a democratic and collectively rational global commonwealth.

Capitalist Globalization and Global Governance

We understand the historical development of the modern world-system in terms of the evolution of institutions. These key institutions—commodity production, technology, and techniques of power—have been shaped by struggles among contending powers and between the core and the periphery over the past six centuries as Europe rose to global hegemony.

The story of how global orders have been restructured in order to facilitate capitalist accumulation must be told in deep temporal perspective in order for us to understand how the most recent wave of corporate globalization is similar or different from earlier waves of globalization. Of particular interest here is the phenomenon of world revolutions and increasingly transnational antisystemic movements. In order to comprehend the possibilities for the emergence of global democracy, we need to understand the history of popular movements that have tried to democratize the world-system in the past.

World Revolutions

The evolution that occurred with the rise and fall of the hegemonic core powers needs to be seen as a sequence of forms of world order that evolved to solve the political, economic, and technical problems of successively more global waves of capitalist accumulation. The expansion of global production involved ac-cessing raw materials to feed the new industries and food to feed the expanding populations (Bunker and Ciccantell 2004). As in any hierarchy, coercion is a very inefficient means of domination, and so the hegemons sought legitimacy by proclaiming leadership in advancing civilization and democracy. But the terms of these claims were also employed by those below who sought to protect themselves from exploitation and domination. And so the evolution of hege-mony was produced by elite groups competing with one another in a context of successive powerful challenges from below. World orders were contested and reconstructed in a series of world revolutions that began with the Protestant Reformation (Boswell and Chase-Dunn 2000, 53–64).

The idea of world revolution is a broad notion that encompasses all kinds of resistance to hierarchy, regardless of whether or not it is coordinated. Usually the idea of revolution is conceptualized on a national scale in which new social forces come to state power and restructure social relations. When we use the revolution concept at the world-system level, a number of changes are required. There is no global state (yet) to take over. But there is a global polity, a world order that has evolved as outlined above. It is that world polity or world order that is the arena of contestation within which world revolutions have occurred and that world revolutions have restructured.

Boswell and Chase-Dunn (2000) focus on those constellations of local, regional, national, and transnational rebellions and revolutions that have had long-term consequences for changing world orders. World orders are those normative and institutional features that are taken for granted in large-scale cooperation, competition, and conflict. Years that symbolize the major world revolutions after the Protestant Reformation are 1789, 1848, 1917, 1968, and 1989. Arguably, another one is brewing now. Arrighi, Hopkins, and Wallerstein (1989) analyzed the world revolutions of 1848, 1917, 1968, and 1989. They contend that the demands put forth in a world revolution do not usually become institutionalized until a consolidating revolt has occurred, or until the next world revolution. So the revolutionaries appear to have lost in the failure of their most radical demands, but enlightened conservatives who are trying to manage hegemony end up incorporating the reforms that were earlier radical demands into the current world order.

Of particular relevance here is the story of the nineteenth century and its *tsunami* of capitalist globalization under the auspices of British hegemony. Transnational antisystemic movements, especially the trade union movement and the feminist movement, emerged to contend with global capitalism. Workers and women consciously took the role of world citizens, organizing international movements to contend with the increasingly global organization of an emergent global capitalist class. Political and economic elites, especially finance capitalists, had already been consciously operating on a global stage for centuries, but the degree of international integration of these reached a very high level in the late nineteenth century. Within Europe the British had created the post-Napoleonic "Concert of Europe," an alliance of conservative dynasties and politicians who were dedicated to the prevention of any future French revolutions.

The Royal Navy suppressed the slave trade and encouraged decolonization of the Spanish colonies. The English Anti-Corn Law League's advocacy of international free trade (carried abroad by British diplomats and businessmen) was adopted by most European and American states in the middle of the century. The gold standard was an important support of a huge increase in international trade and investment (Chase-Dunn, Kawano, and Brewer 2000; O'Rourke and Williamson 1999). The expanding Atlantic economy, already firmly attached to the Indian Ocean, was accompanied by an expanding Pacific economy, as Japan and China were more completely and directly brought into the trade and investment networks of Europe and North America. American Ginseng was harvested in the Middle Atlantic states as an important commodity that could be traded for Chinese manufactures rather than having to resort to payment in silver.

The success of this wave of capitalist globalization was not completely uncontested. Within Europe, socialist and democratic demands for political and economic rights of the non-propertied classes, as well as for women, strongly emerged in the world revolution of 1848. The decolonization of Latin America extended the formal aspects of state sovereignty to a large chunk of the periphery. Slave revolts, abolitionism, and the further incorporation of Africa into the capitalist world-system eventually led to the abolition of slavery almost everywhere.

Semiperipheral Development

An important aspect of our model of world-system evolution is the idea of semiperipheral development. We note that institutional development in premodern world-systems has most often occurred because innovations and implementations of new techniques and organizational forms have emerged in societies that are in semiperipheral positions within larger core/periphery hierarchies (Chase-Dunn and Hall 1997, Chapter 5). Thus did semiperipheral marcher chiefdoms conquer older core polities to create larger paramount chiefdoms (Kirch 1984). And semiperipheral marcher states conquered older adjacent core states to create larger and larger core-wide empires (e.g., Chin, Akkad, Assyrian, Achaemenid Persians, Alexander, Rome, Abbasid Caliphate, etc.). Semiperipheral capitalist city-states (Dilmun, Phoenician Tyre, Sidon, Carthage, Venice, Genoa, Melakka, etc.) expanded commercialized trade networks and encouraged commodity production within and between the tributary empires and peripheral regions, linking larger and larger regions together to eventually become the single global economy of today. The modern hegemons (the Dutch Republic of the seventeenth century, the United Kingdom of Great Britain in the nineteenth century, and the United States of America in the twentieth century) were all formerly semiperipheral nation-states that rose to the position of hegemony. They did this by transforming the institutional bases of economic and political/military power in response to challenges from contenders for hegemony and to rebellions and revolutions carried out by popular movements that were contesting the injustices of colonial imperialism and capitalism.

The modern world-system has experienced systemwide waves of democracy rather than separate and disconnected sequences of democratization within individual countries (Markoff 1996). These waves have tended to start in semiperipheral countries, and the institutional inventions that have diffused from country to country have disproportionately been invented and implemented in semiperipheral countries first. And the strongest challenges to capitalism (the communist states) have mainly been concentrated in the semiperiphery.

The workers' movement became increasingly organized on an international basis during the nineteenth century. Organizers were able to make good use of cheap and rapid transportation as well as new modes of communication (the telegraph) in order to link struggles in distant locations. And the huge migration of workers from Europe to the New World spread the ideas and the strategies of the labor movement. Socialists, anarchists, and communists challenged the rule of capital, while they competed with each other for leadership of an increasingly global antisystemic movement that sought to democratize the world-system.

The Direct Democracy of Workers' Councils

In the last 130 years, a number of efforts to constitute direct democracy without capitalists, the state, or a Leninist vanguard party have erupted in the heat of state breakdowns. In some situations these "workers' councils" emerged alongside the state, creating a situation of "dual government." During the Spanish revolution of 1936 through 1939, workers' councils spread over a wide terrain, reaching as much as a third of the country. These councils not only governed without the state, but they sometimes abolished the local currencies and began new systems of exchange. These experiments took place during revolutionary periods when official authorities had lost power. These instances of popular direct democracy were often brief. The Seattle General Strike was a matter of a few days, but the Spanish situation of dual power lasted for three years.

Like most social movements, these councils began by simply reacting to the abuses of the existing order. Workers wanted higher wages, better working conditions, and more justice. But once the authorities lost power, the workers found themselves doing far more than they bargained for. The workers' councils were inventive and festive, producing new forms of collective organization. In Spain, following the failure of Franco's coup attempt, at least one third of the country's firms came under worker self-management. More of the worker-run firms achieved production records than before the coup, despite the chaotic conditions of the civil war.

The organizational forms that emerged in the workers' councils expressed a good deal of creativity with respect to democratic models of economic governance. The central organization of the councils, the main body that took decisions, was the general assembly. Resolutions by the general assemblies were carried out by *mandated* delegates, who had no independent power of their own (unlike representatives who, once elected, have power to make their own decisions). These delegates were instructed to implement decisions made by the assembly. Secondly, these delegates were often *rotated* so that no one would get too comfortable being a permanent authority. Lastly, the delegates were immediately revocable. Any abuse of power was grounds for immediate termination. There was little in the way of bureaucratic procedure that would delay replacement of a delegate who was deemed to be abusing power.

Workers councils emerged in the following locations and times:

- The Paris Commune of 1871
- The St. Petersburg Soviet of 1905
- The Russian Revolution of 1917
- Short-lived experiments in Poland, Italy, Germany, and Bulgaria between 1917–1920
- The Seattle General Strike of 1919
- The Spanish Revolution of 1936 (for most of the first year and then on and off until 1939)
- The Hungarian Revolution of 1956
- The French General Strike of 1968
- The Chilean Revolution 1970–1973
- The Factory committees in Argentina and Venezuela and Peasant councils in Brazil, which are going on now

The Evolution of Global Governance

We conceptualize a global polity that has long been composed of national states in which elites have carried out the jobs of international relations, but that is increasingly becoming an arena of direct popular participation. Cheap and global communications technologies have accelerated a trend toward the formation of transnational social movements that has roots in earlier centuries. Ideas of democracy that are deeply institutionalized in modern societies are being increasingly applied at the global level. Both elite policy-makers and transnational social movements have begun to raise issues about the democratic nature of existing institutions of global governance.

The notion of global civil society imagines a human population of the Earth that is informed about global issues and contemplates action toward the solution of problems that are held to be global in scope. Transnational social movements, understood as both religious and secular, have long contested the institutional structures of global governance, but the participation of large numbers of non-elites has expanded to a new level in the contemporary global justice movement. Demonstrations protesting the G-8, the World Bank, the International Monetary Fund, and the World Trade Organization have become frequent, and hundreds of thousands of people from all the continents have attended the meetings of the World Social Forum. This explosion of global citizenship has been facilitated by the Internet, as local movements easily scale up to become national and then transnational in order to confront issues that appear to have no local or national solutions.

The terminology of "North-South relations" has come to refer to the relations that wealthy powerful countries have with poor and less developed ones (e.g. Reuveny and Thompson 2008). The terms we prefer are *core, periphery, and semiperiphery,* defined as structural positions in a global hierarchy that is economic, political-military, and cultural. The core-periphery hierarchy at the global level is organized spatially, but it is not simply a matter of latitude as implied by the North-South terminology. It is a complex and multidimensional hierarchy of different kinds of interrelated power and dependence relations.

Global governance has long meant "international relations"—the economic, political, military, and cultural interactions among a large number of sovereign states. This is the political system that became institutionalized in Europe with the Peace of Westphalia in 1648, and that was subsequently spread to the whole world as the system of colonial empires became transformed into an Earth-wide interstate system. The system of sovereign states was never purely an anarchy of competition and conflict. Governance took the form of leadership and dominance by a sequence of powerful states—the hegemons—and their allies, but hegemony was intermittent. During the periods of hegemonic rivalry the interstate system came to resemble the model of anarchy that is inscribed in many theories of international relations. Giovanni Arrighi's (1994; 2007) model of systemic cycles of accumulation analyzes the evolution of global governance in a sequence of hegemonies. As Arrighi (2007: 166) says, " ... hegemonic states play governmental functions at the global level."

The interstate system and the rise and fall of hegemonic core powers has been somewhat modified over the past two hundred years (since the end of the Napoleonic Wars) by the emergence of international organizations that operate in between and over the tops of the national states (Murphy 1994; Boli and Thomas 1999). This emergence of multilateral institutions has been called "political globalization" and is seen as a possible precursor to eventual global state formation (Chase-Dunn et al. 2008). Saskia Sassen (2006) and Bill Robinson (2004) have also analyzed the ways in which national states have become reconfigured in the last decades of the twentieth century to serve as institutional instruments of an emerging transnational capitalist class. Thus global governance is structured as a system of allying and competing national states, the rise and fall of hegemons, and an increasingly dense system of public and private institutions that are international and transnational in scope.

Hegemonic rivalry and world wars have been the main mechanism for "choosing" global leadership (Modelski and Thompson 1996). This primitive method of sorting out the consequences of uneven development is what needs to be replaced by a form of global governance that can resolve conflicts peaceably. Some think this has already been achieved by the emergence of multilateral global governance institutions. Others fear that these are not strong enough to withstand the storm of another round of hegemonic rivalry.

At present the main public institutions of global governance are the United States government (the current declining hegemon, but still a military superpower), the United Nations Organization, the Group of 8 most powerful national economies (G-8), and the international financial institutions that were founded at the Bretton Woods Conference in 1944 (the World Bank, the International Monetary Fund, and the World Trade Organization). The main nonpublic institutions are the large transnational corporations and the NGOs and social movement organizations that are taking political action on a global scale. Contemporary global governance is shaped by the complex interactions among all these national, international, and transnational institutions, as well as by transnational NGOs, business firms, and other non-state actors (e.g., transnational social movement organizations). Transnational NGOs and social movements first emerged in the nineteenth century. The number of these, and the sizes of their memberships, has grown greatly in the decades since World War II (Tarrow 2005; Smith 2008).

Waves of Globalization

The decline of British hegemony and the failure of efforts after World War I to erect an effective structure of global governance led to the collapse of capitalist globalization during the depression of the 1930s, culminating in World War II. In our perspective, capitalist globalization is a cycle as well as a trend. The great wave of the nineteenth century was followed by a collapse in the early twentieth century, and then a reemergence in the period after World War II. The global institutions of the post-World War II order, now under the sponsorship of the hegemonic United States, were intended to resolve the problems that were perceived to have caused the military conflagrations and economic disasters of the early twentieth century. The United Nations was a stronger version of a global proto-state than the League of Nations had been, though still a long way from the "monopoly of legitimate violence" that is the effective core of a real state. The Bretton Woods institutions—the World Bank and the International Monetary Fund—were intended to promote Keynesian national development, rather than a globalized market of investment flows. Free trade was encouraged, but the key efforts were about the tracking of international investments and the stabilization of national currencies. The architects of the Bretton Woods institutions were chary about the effects of volatile waves of international capital flows on economic development and political stability because of what they perceived to have been the lessons of the 1920s. The restarting of the world economy after World War II under the aegis of the Bretton Woods institutions and US support for relatively autonomous capitalism in Europe and Japan succeeded tremendously. But the growing power of unions within the core, and the perceived constraints on US financial interests imposed by the Bretton Woods currency regime, along with the oil crisis of the early 1970s, led the United States to abandon Bretton Woods in favor of a free world market of capital mobility. The "Washington Consensus" was basically Reaganism-Thatcherism on a global scale—deregulation, privatizing, and reneging on the "social contract" with core labor unions and the welfare state. The IMF was turned into a tool for imposing these policies on countries all over the world.

This US/British-led neo-liberal regime of global capitalism was a response to the successes of the Third World and the core labor movements, not in achieving true global democracy, but in getting a somewhat larger share of the profits of global capitalism. The attack on the institutions of Keynesian national development (labor unions and the welfare state), was also a delayed response to the world revolution of 1968 in which students, women, environmentalists, Third Worldists, indigenous peoples, democracy movements, and radical parts of the labor movement had critiqued and resisted the inadequacies of the welfare capitalism and business unionism from the Left. The new right appropriated some of the ideology and many of the tactics of the '68ers—demonstrations, civil disobedience, guerilla armies, drug financing, mobilization of subnations, and so forth. These tactics have come back to haunt the powers that be. In the recent wave of blowback some of the organizations and ideologies formerly supported by the US CIA as instruments against the Soviet Union (e.g., al-Qaeda) have turned against their former sponsors, employing dirty tricks to besmirch symbols of global power and to murder innocent bystanders in the heart of the core (Johnson 2000).

We contend that the current historical moment is similar to the later decades of the nineteenth century. Like British hegemony, US hegemony is declining. Contenders for global economic power have been emerging in German-led Europe and in China-led Asia, and post-Soviet Russia has refused to become a playground for Western capital. Popular movements and institutions have been under attack, especially since the rise to ideological hegemony of neo-liberal capitalist globalization across nearly the whole globe. Antisystemic movements are struggling to find new paths for dealing with globalized and hegemonic capitalism. New communications technologies, especially the Internet, seem to be facilitating more coordinated and integrated movements in favor of global democracy. The liberatory aspects of decentered and democratized communications potentials are great. But cheap two-way and mass communications also promote increasing differentiation and specialization of political mobilization, which can undercut efforts to organize intermovement coordination. We hold that the Internet will be, on balance, a liberatory force, but the big gains in movement integration will probably come as a response to the economic, political, and ecological disasters that globalized capitalism is producing now and in the coming decades.

Much of the contemporary resistance to global capitalism is taking the form of local self-reliance, the revitalization of diverse cultural forms, and the rejection of the cultural and technological totems of corporate capitalism. Thus the characterization of the global justice movement protests (Seattle, Genoa, etc.) as "anti-globalization" movements is partially correct, but it is misleading.

Self-reliance may take forms that are progressive or forms that promote divisions among the people based on ethnicity, nation, or race. Self-reliance alone is not an adequate strategy for creating a more humane and sustainable sociopolitical system. Rather, the construction of self-reliant communities needs to engage with a coordinated movement of "globalization from below" that will seek to reform or replace the institutions of global governance with institutions that will promote social justice and environmental sustainability.

Imagining Global Democracy

This means imagining global democracy. What might global democracy look like? And how could we get from here to there? Global democracy needs to address two main issues: huge and growing inequalities within and between countries; and the grave problems of environmental sustainability that capitalist and communist industrialization have produced.

Rather than drawing the blueprint of a global utopia and then arguing the fine points, it makes more sense to understand and learn from the heritage of earlier efforts to do what we are here proposing. Utopias may be useful for those who are unable to imagine any possible improvement over existing institutions. But they also function to delegitimize efforts to make social change because they usually appear to be unattainable. The useful approach is to imagine a historically apt next step, one that the relevant constituencies can agree is a noticeable improvement and that is at least plausibly attainable.

This said, the idea must be sufficiently attractive to motivate risk-taking. So it is possible to err both on the side of caution and on the side of flamboyance. Global democracy means real economic, political, and cultural rights and say for the majority of the world's people over the local and global institutions that affect their lives. Democracy of the national state is part of the solution, but not the whole solution. Global democracy requires that the national states be democratic *and* that the global institutions be democratic. Thus it requires democratic institutions of global governance.

Objections to the Possibility of Global Democracy

Neo-Darwinian authors like Pierre Van den Berge and evolutionary psychologists contend that family and ethnic group loyalties are hardwired into humans by biological evolution, and that this is based on genetic closeness. Humans, like other animals, will always put their own families and ethnic groups first. But there has been a very successful cross-cultural and historical socialization process that has been going for at least the past 500 years that has socialized people to add identification and loyalty to their nation. Some nations are alleged to be based on blood, like families and ethnic groups. But others are constructed around ideas of a common history.

Nationalism is a result of a long process of nation-building. Today most working class soldiers will willingly die for their country. This means that they will put their life in the hands of fellow soldiers in battle, people that they have no kinship with and most of whom they will never see again if they get out of the military alive. And who are these soldiers fighting for? Other Americans. In other words, more strangers whom they will never meet. The very power the slogan "support our troops" has over the average American is a truly powerful indicator of how successful this political socialization undertaking has been. The troops are, after all, strangers. The process of how individuals come to subordinate their ethnic, class, regional, and religious loyalties to a large national community of strangers is the subject of the huge literature on nation-building.

The existence of nationalism as perhaps the most important socially constructed solidarity in the modern world shows that the evolutionary psychologists are at least partly wrong. Identification and altruistic behavior can be reprogramed by human institutions so that people will strongly identify and cooperate with strangers. But this does not prove that there are no limits on the ways in which solidarity may be socially constructed. The fact that many nations have important similarities with kinship ties and ethnic groups might mean that the claims of the evolutionary psychologists are at least partly true (see Gat 2006).

But to what extent does global democracy require that humans identify with and act altruistically toward one another? Is species-being really necessary for global democracy? Do people need to love one another on a global scale in order for global democratic governance to work? As with national states, it would seem that the institutional structures of law, due process, and legitimate authority democratically responsible to the majority, could function in the absence of much in the way of global love if people were to simply acknowledge that, in order for billions of humans to live on Earth, we collectively need some mechanisms for regulating the use of natural resources and for dealing with issues of global inequality.

Ironically, nationalism, which is the best argument against the evolutionary psychologists, is itself somewhat of an obstacle to global democracy. It is nationalism that allows elites to mobilize people to fight one another, and national interests are so strongly institutionalized that transnational social movements have a hard time overcoming national divisions. Ulrich Beck (2005) contends that cosmopolitanism based on the recognition and appreciation of social differences is one of the most valuable outcomes of globalization, and that this emergent cultural feature will play an important role in the democratization of institutions of global governance. Cosmopolitanism is helpful to social movements confronting divisions that stem from nationalism. But how far need we go politically with this? Does it mean that progressive cosmopolitans should not ally and work with nationalists? Should they be excluded from political organizations, as Warren Wagar (1992) suggested? We think this would surely be a mistake. Globalization has not vanquished nationalism, and in fact, the economic and environmental tribulations that are emerging are going to revitalize nationalism as people seek ways to protect themselves from forces over which they have little control. Excluding nationalists is surely a mistake for the movements that want to build global democracy. As with the localists and self-reliance grassroots movements, the job is to find those who will ally with a strategy of globalization from below.

The Global Justice Movement

While transnational social movements in the West date back at least to the Protestant Reformation, the scope and scale of international ties among social activists have risen dramatically over the past few decades, as they have increasingly shared information, conceptual frameworks, and other resources, and coordinated actions across borders and continents (Moghadam 2005; Reitan 2007). In the 1980s and 1990s, the number of formal transnational social movement organizations (TSMOs) rose by nearly 200 percent. While TSMOs are still largely housed in the global north, a rising portion are located in, and have ties to, the global south. This rise in transnational organizing contributed to and helped to produce the global justice movement.

The *global justice movement* is a "movement of movements," that includes all those who are engaged in sustained and contentious challenges to neoliberal global capitalism, propose alternative political and economic structures, and mobilize poor and relatively powerless peoples. While this movement resorts to noninstitutional forms of collective action, it often collaborates with institutional "insiders," such as NGOs that lobby and provide services to people, as well as policy-makers (Tarrow 2005, 55–56; Keck and Sikkink 1998). The global justice movement and its allies includes a variety of social actors and groups: unions, NGOs, SMOs, transnational advocacy networks, as well as policy-makers, scholars, artists, journalists, entertainers, and other individuals.

The World Social Forum (WSF) was established in 2001 as a counter-hegemonic popular project focusing on issues of global justice and democracy.[1] Initially organized by the Brazilian labor movement and the landless peasant movement, the WSF was intended to be a forum for the participants in, and supporters of, grass roots movements from all over the world, rather than a conference of representatives of political parties or governments. The WSF was organized as the open popular alternative to the World Economic Forum, an exclusive gathering of elite business leaders, politicians, and entertainers that takes place annually in Davos, Switzerland. The WSF has been supported by the Brazilian Workers Party and has been most frequently held in Porto Alegre, Brazil, a traditional stronghold of that party. Whereas the first meeting of the

WSF in 2001 reportedly drew 20,000 registered participants from 117 countries, the 2005 meeting of the WSF drew 155,000 registered participants from 135 countries. The WSF is both an institution—with its own leadership, mission, and structure—and an "open space" where a variety of social activists from around the world meet, exchange ideas, participate in multicultural events, and coordinate actions. The WSF is open to all those opposed to neoliberal globalization, but excludes groups advocating armed resistance. Participants vary in terms of their affiliations with particular movements and different types of organizations. Both participants in unconnected local and national campaigns come together with long-time veterans of transnational organizations and internationally coordinated groups (Smith 2008). The WSF has inspired the spread of hundreds of local, national, regional, and thematic social forums (Byrd 2005; della Porta 2005).

North-South Issues

The focus on global justice and north/south inequalities and the critique of neoliberalism provide strong orienting frames for the transnational activists of the World Social Forum. But there are difficult issues for collective action that are heavily structured by the huge international inequalities that exist in the contemporary world-system. Our survey of the attendees of the 2005 World Social Forum found several important differences between activists from the core, the periphery, and the semiperiphery (Chase-Dunn et al 2008).

Those from the periphery were fewer, older, and more likely to be men. In addition, participants from the periphery were more likely to be associated with externally sponsored NGOs, rather than with self-funded SMOs and unions, as NGOs have greater access to travel funds. Southern respondents were significantly more likely than those from the global north to be skeptical about creating or reforming global-level political institutions and to favor the abolition of global institutions.

This skepticism probably stems from the historical experience of peoples from the non-core with colonialism and global-level institutions that claim to be operating on universal principles of fairness, but whose actions have either not solved problems or have made them worse. These "new abolitionists" are posing a strong challenge to both existing global institutions and to those who want to reform or replace these institutions.

Global Party Formation and the
Challenges of Global Democracy

The world-systems perspective holds that the core-periphery global hierarchy is a centrally important structure for understanding and explaining world history and the trajectories of individual countries and regions. The global hierarchy is reproduced over time, in the sense that it is hard to move up or down, although there is some vertical mobility. The semiperiphery, composed of large states and national societies with intermediate levels of development, is an important zone because innovations that transform technologies and forms of organization tend to get implemented (and sometimes invented) in the semiperiphery. It is a fertile location that produces structural and evolutionary change. This is the hypothesis of "semiperipheral development" (Chase-Dunn and Hall 1997: Chapter 5). The struggle of the elites to move up the hierarchy and to stay on top requires hegemonic strategies that incorporate some of the non-elites into developmental projects, but the resistance of those below to domination and exploitation challenges hegemonic projects with new counter-hegemonic strategies of protection and democratization (e.g., Monbiot 2003). We contend that this systemic core-periphery struggle has been a major engine of world historical social change, and that it will shape current and future struggles over global governance.

The national state, for long the most significant locus of political decision-making and focal point of people's identities, has been challenged in these traditional functions by international organizations, especially multinational corporations, regional governing bodies, such as the European Union, and other global governance institutions, such as the World Trade Organization (WTO), the World Bank, and the International Monetary Fund (IMF) (Markoff 1996; Held and McGrew 2002). Both elites and popular social movements seek to influence policy-making at multiple geographic scales; they are increasingly drawing connections between national and local issues with global ones, however, and becoming more active at the global level.

Many observers point out that the institutions of global governance show a notable democratic deficit (e.g., Stiglitz 2002). These institutions lack democratically appointed legislative arms, ombudspersons, and formal policy evaluation mechanisms (Scholte 2004, 211). Scholte points out that, "relationships between national governments and global governance agencies have mainly flowed through unelected technocrats who lack any direct connection with citizens," and that national governments have given "suprastate bodies considerable unchecked prerogative in operational activities" (ibid., 212). Given the widespread perception of this democratic deficit, it is no surprise that social movements and NGOs are making collective efforts to re-gain political influence (Smith 2008; Scholte 2004). Elites, particularly in the semiperiphery, have likewise raised questions about the dominant role played by representatives of core nations within existing global governance institutions and called for their restructuring.

Various scholars and activists argue that global democracy requires restructuring global governance institutions, possibly even the formation of a democratic world government, in order to better regulate the international economy so that it more effectively responds to public needs (Patomaki and Teivainen 2004; Held and McGrew 2002). Others, however, contend that global governance institutions should simply be abolished.

Many see the WSF as an important instrument for preparing the public to actively participate in and influence global governance institutions. For example, Smith (2008, 420) argues that the WSF is a "foundation for a more democratic global polity," since it enables citizens of many countries to develop shared values and preferences, to refine their analyses and strategies, and to improve their skills at transnational dialogue. Patomaki and Teivainen (2004, 151) suggest that the WSF "forms a loosely defined party of opinion" from which global parties might emerge and wield influence on world politics. The last big wave of non-elite global party formation was during and after the world revolution of 1917 when the Comintern, the Third International, brought representatives from national communist parties as well as union, womens', and youth organizations to huge annual congresses held in Moscow during the early 1920s. There have been official international party organizations since then, but they have played only a small role in global governance (Patomaki and Teivainen 2007).

The World Party and Dual Power

As outlined above, we are not satisfied with polyarchy at the national level. We agree with the critics of polyarchy that it is not the best of all possible worlds. We contend that real democracy must address the issue of wealth and property, rather than defining these as beyond the bounds of political discourse. This said, we can also learn much from those experiments with collective property that were carried out in the socialist and Communist states in the twentieth century. State ownership, even when the state is itself truly democratic, creates grave economic problems because of the problem of "soft budget constraints." Large firms need to compete with one another in markets, but even more importantly they should compete for financing by showing that they can make a profit. We admire John Roemer's (1994) model of market socialism, in which ownership shares of large firms are distributed to all adult citizens, who then invest their shares in a stock market that is the main source of capital for large firms. All citizens receive a set number shares at the age of majority and when they die their shares revert to the public weal. So there is no inheritance of corporate property, though personal property can be inherited. Firms, large and small, produce for markets, and labor is rewarded in competitive labor markets. Small firms can be privately owned. This kind of market socialism equalizes income, though some inequalities due to skill differences will continue. The economy will still be a market economy, but the democratic state will guarantee security and property, and oversee the redistribution of corporate shares across generations.

This model of public socialism incentivizes technological change and efficiency without creating and increasing inequalities. It would work well, especially in the core countries for which Roemer has intended it. But when we think about the global economy there are certain problems that are not addressed in Roemer's model. The main problem in the global economy is the existence of huge differences in productivity between core and peripheral labor. This is why labor standards in international economic agreements are anathema to workers and unions in peripheral countries. These function as protectionist agreements for core workers and undercut the ability of peripheral workers to produce commodities and sell them in core markets. The real solution to this is to raise the level of productivity of peripheral labor. So global democracy needs to build institutions that can do this.

This is why we need to democratize and empower the institutions of global governance, including the World Bank and the International Monetary Fund. Movements that seek to abolish these international financial institutions because they are symbols of global capitalism need to either radically reform these, or devise better instruments that can address the issues of core/periphery inequalities. Market socialism in the core will not be enough. A movement for economic democracy in the core needs also to mobilize for economic democracy at the global level.

Support for both more democratic national regimes and global socialist institutions is likely to come from the semiperiphery. We expect that some of the most potent efforts to democratize global capitalism will come out of movements and democratic socialist regimes that emerge in semiperipheral countries. As in earlier epochs, semiperipheral countries have the "advantages of backwardness"—they are not already heavily invested in the existing organizational and political institutions and technologies—and so they have the maneuverability and the resources to invest in new institutions.

Peripheral countries could also do this, but they are more completely dependent on the core and they are not able to mobilize sufficient resources to overcome this dependency. Bolivia, led by Evo Morales, may turn out to be an exception. The semiperiphery, especially the large semiperipheral countries such as Mexico, Brazil, Argentina, India, Indonesia, China, and Venezuela have opportunities that neither core nor peripheral countries have. If a democratic socialist regime is able to come to state power by legal means, and if this regime has the political will to mobilize the popular sectors in favor of democratic socialism, an experiment in market socialism of the Roemerian type could be carried out. Regimes of this kind may already be emerging in the so-called "Red Tide" in Latin America. More are likely to come forth as the option of kowtowing to the megacorporations and the bond traders becomes more obviously bankrupt.

The smaller semiperipheral countries (South Korea, Taiwan, South Africa, Israel) may also opt for democratic socialism, but we expect that these will only be able to do so after earlier efforts have been made in the large semiperipheral countries.

These semiperipheral democratic socialist regimes will be the organizational entities that can forge the links among the global antisystemic movements and produce a network for bringing forth the institutions of global socialism. Globalization from below and the formation of global socialist institutions will need to be facilitated by a loose confederation of world citizens organized as a democratic political network. We have adopted the name given to such a confederation by Warren Wagar (1996)—the World Party. But this is not a party in the old sense of the Third International—a vanguard party of the world proletariat. Rather, the World Party we propose would be a network of people and representatives of popular organizations from all over the world who agree to help create a democratic and collectively rational global commonwealth. The World Party will be open to people of different nations and religions and will seek to create the institutional basis for a culturally pluralistic, socially just and ecologically sustainable world society—a global democracy.

Note

1. World Social Forum Charter, http://wsf2007.org/process/wsf-charter.

References

Amin, Samir. 1997. *Capitalism in an Age of Globalization*. London: Zed Books.
———. 2006. "Towards the Fifth International?" In *Democratic Politics Globally*, edited by Katarina Sehm-Patomaki and Marko Ulvila, 121–144. Network Institute for Global Democratization (NIGD Working Paper 1/2006), Tampere, Finland.
Anderson, E. N., and Christopher Chase-Dunn. 2005. "The Rise and Fall of Great Powers." In *The Historical Evolution of World-Systems*, edited by Christopher Chase-Dunn and E. N. Anderson. London: Palgrave.
Anheier, Helmut K. 2001. "Measuring Global Civil Society." In *Global Civil Society 2001*, edited by Helmut K. Anheier, Marlies Glasius, and Mary Kaldor. New York: Oxford University Press.
Anheier, Helmut K., and Hagai Katz. 2003. "Mapping Global Civil Society." In *Global Civil Society 2003*, edited by M. Kaldor, H. Anheier, and M. Glasius. Oxford: Oxford University Press.
Appelbaum, Richard, and William I. Robinson (eds.) 2005. *Critical Globalization Studies*. London: Routledge.
Arrighi, Giovanni. 1994. *The Long Twentieth Century*. London: Verso.
———. 2007. *Adam Smith in Beijing*. London: Verso.
Arrighi, Giovanni, Terence K. Hopkins, and Immanuel Wallerstein. 1989. *Antisystemic Movements*. London and New York: Verso.

Arrighi, Giovanni, and Beverly Silver. 1999. *Chaos and Governance in the Modern World-System: Comparing Hegemonic Transitions.* Minneapolis: University of Minnesota Press.
Bainbridge, William Sims. 2007. "The Scientific Research Potential of Virtual Worlds." *Science* 317(5837; 27 July 2007): 472–476.
Bamako Appeal. 2006. http://mrzine.monthlyreview.org/bamako.html.
Beck, Ulrich. 2005. *Power in the Global Age.* Malden, MA: Polity Press.
Bello, Walden. 2002. *Deglobalization.* London: Zed Books.
Bergesen, Albert, and Ronald Schoenberg. 1980. "Long Waves of Colonial Expansion and Contraction 1415–1969." In *Studies of the Modern World-System,* edited by Albert Bergesen, 231–278. New York: Academic Press.
Boli, John, and George M. Thomas (eds.). 1999. *Constructing World Culture: International Nongovernmental Organizations Since 1875.* Stanford, CA: Stanford University Press.
Bollen, Kenneth A., and Pamela M. Paxton. 1997. "Democracy Before Athens," In *Inequality, Democracy and Economic Development,* edited by Manus Midlarsky, 13–44. Cambridge: Cambridge University Press.
Borocz, Jozsef. 1992. "Dual Dependency and Property Vacuum: Social Change on the State Socialist Semiperiphery." *Theory and Society,* 21: 77–104.
Bornschier, Volker, and Christopher Chase-Dunn (eds.). 1999. *The Future of Global Conflict.* London: Sage.
Boswell, Terry, and Christopher Chase-Dunn. 2000. *The Spiral of Capitalism and Socialism: Toward Global Democracy.* Boulder, CO: Lynne Rienner.
Boswell, Terry, and Ralph Peters. 1990. "State Socialism and the Industrial Divide in the World Economy: A Comparative Essay on the Rebellions in Poland and China." *Critical Sociology* 17(1): 3–35.
Bunker, Stephen, and Paul Ciccantell. 2004. *Globalization and the Race for Resources.* Baltimore, MD: Johns Hopkins University Press.
Byrd, Scott C. 2005. "The Porto Alegre Consensus: Theorizing the Forum Movement." *Globalizations* 2(1): 151–163.
Carroll, William K., and R. S. Ratner. 1996. "Master Framing and Cross-Movement Networking in Contemporary Social Movements." *Sociological Quarterly* 37(4): 601–625.
Carroll, William K. 2006. "Hegemony and Counter-Hegemony in a Global Field of Action" Presented at a joint RC02-RC07 session on alternative visions of world society, World Congress of Sociology, Durban, South Africa, July 28.
Chase-Dunn, Christopher (ed.). 1982. *Socialist States in the World-System.* Beverly Hills: Sage Publications.
Chase-Dunn, Christopher. 1990. "World State Formation: Historical Processes and Emergent Necessity." *Political Geography Quarterly* 9(2: April): 108–130.
———. 1998. *Global Formation: Structures of the World-Economy* (2nd ed.). Lanham, MD: Rowman and Littlefield.
———. 1999. "Globalization: A World-Systems Perspective" *Journal of World-Systems Research* V(2): 165–185.
———. 2005. "Global Public Social Science." *The American Sociologist* 36(3–4: Fall/ Winter): 121–132. Reprinted in *Public Sociology: The Contemporary Debate,* edited by Lawrence T. Nichols, 179–194. New Brunswick, NJ: Transaction Press.
———. 2007. "Sociocultural Evolution and the Future of World Society." *World Futures* 63(5–6): 408–424.

————. 2008. "The World Revolution of 20xx." In *GSA Papers 2007: Contested Terrains of Globalization,* edited by Jerry Harris. Chicago: ChangeMaker.

Chase-Dunn, Christopher, and Salvatore Babones. 2007. *Global Social Change.* Baltimore, MD: Johns Hopkins University Press.

Chase-Dunn, Christopher, and Terry Boswell. 1999. "Postcommunism and the Global Commonwealth." *Humboldt Journal of Social Relations* 24(1–2): 195–219.

Chase-Dunn, Christopher, and Thomas D. Hall. 1997. *Rise and Demise: Comparing World-Systems.* Boulder, CO: Westview.

Chase-Dunn, Christopher, and Bruce Lerro. Forthcoming. *Social Change.* Boston: Allyn and Bacon.

Chase-Dunn, Christopher, and Bruce Podobnik. 1999. "The Next World War: World-System Cycles and Trends." In *The Future of Global Conflict,* edited by Volker Bornschier and Christopher Chase-Dunn. London: Sage.

Chase-Dunn, Christopher, and Ellen Reese. 2007. "Global Party Formation in World Historical Perspective." In *Global Political Parties,* edited by Katarina Sehm-Patomaki and Marlo Ulvila, 53–91. London: Zed Press.

Chase-Dunn, Christopher, Ellen Reese, Mark Herkenrath, Rebecca Giem, Erika Guttierrez, Linda Kim, and Christine Petit. 2008. "North-South Contradictions and Bridges at the World Social Forum." In *North and South in the World Political Economy,* edited by Rafael Reuveny and William R. Thompson, 341–366. Malden, MA: Blackwell.

Chase-Dunn, Christopher, Yukio Kawano, and Benjamin Brewer. 2000. "Trade Globalization Since 1795: Waves of Integration in the World-System." *American Sociological Review,* February.

Chase-Dunn, Christopher, Andrew Jorgenson, and Thomas Reifer. "The Trajectory of the United States in the World-System: A Quantitative Reflection." *Sociological Perspectives* 48(2): 233–254.

Chase-Dunn, Christopher, Hiroko Inoue, Alexis Alvarez, and Richard Niemeyer. 2008. "Global State Formation In World Historical Perspective." In *World Hegemonic Transformations, The State and Crisis in Neoliberalism,* edited by Yildiz Atasoy. London and New York: Routledge.

Chase-Dunn, Christopher, Christine Petit, Richard Niemeyer, Robert A. Hanneman, and Ellen Reese. Forthcoming. "The Contours of Solidarity and Division Among Global movements." *International Journal of Peace Studies.*

Christian, David. 2003. *Maps of Time.* Berkeley: University of California Press.

Davis, Mike. 2001. *Late Victorian Holocausts.* London: Verso.

Danaher, Kevin (ed.). 2001. *Democratizing the Global Economy: The Battle Against the World Bank and the IMF.* Monroe, ME: Common Courage Press.

della Porta, Donatella. 2005. "Making the Polis: Social Forums and Democracy in the Global Justice Movement." *Mobilization.* 10(1): 73–94.

della Porta, Donatella, Massimilano Andretta, Lorenzo Mosca, and Herbert Reiter. 2006. *Globalization from Below.* Minneapolis: University of Minnesota Press.

Doerr, Nicole. 2006. "Towards a European Public Sphere 'from Below'?: The Case of Multilingualism Within the European Social Forums." In *Alternative Futures and Popular Protest,* Manchester, Conference Paper Series. Metropolitan University.

Engels, Frederic. 1935. *Socialism: Utopian and Scientific.* New York: International Publishers.

Fisher, William F., and Thomas Ponniah. 2003. *Another World Is Possible.* London: Zed.

Florini, Ann. 2005. *The Coming Democracy: New Rules for Running A New World Order.* Washington, DC: Brookings.

Frank, Andre Gunder, and Barry K. Gills (eds.). 1993. *The World System: Five Hundred Years or Five Thousand?* London: Routledge.

Friedman, Jonathan, and Christopher Chase-Dunn (eds.) 2005. *Hegemonic Declines: Present and Past.* Boulder, CO: Paradigm Publishers.

Gat, Azar. 2006. *War in Human Civilization.* New York: Oxford University Press.

Gill, Stephen. 2000. "Toward a Post-Modern Prince?: The Battle of Seattle as a Moment in the New Politics of Globalization." *Millennium* 29(1): 131–140.

Glasius, Marlies, and Jill Timms. 2006. "The Role of Social Forums in Global Civil Society: Radical Beacon or Strategic Infrastructure." In *Global Civil Society 2005/6,* edited by Marlies Glasius, Mary Kaldor, Helmut Anheier, and Fiona Holland, 190–238. London: Sage.

Harvey, David. 2003. *The New Imperialism.* New York: Oxford University Press.

Held, David, and Anthony McGrew. 2002. *Globalization/Antiglobalization.* Cambridge: Blackwell.

Hobsbawm, Eric. 1994. *The Age of Extremes: A History of the World, 1914–1991.* New York: Pantheon.

Johnson, Chalmers. 2000. *Blowback: The Costs and Consequences of American Empire.* New York: Henry Holt.

Kaldor, Mary. 2003. *Global Civil Society: An Answer to War.* Cambridge, UK: Polity Press.

Keck, Margaret E., and Kathryn Sikkink. 1998. *Activists Beyond Borders: Advocacy Networks in International Politics.* Ithaca, NY: Cornell University Press.

Kirch, Patrick V. 1984. *The Evolution of Polynesian Chiefdoms.* Cambridge: Cambridge University Press.

Koenig-Archibugi, Mathias. 2008. "Is Global Democracy Possible?" A paper presented at the annual meeting of the International Studies Association, San Francisco.

Linebaugh, Peter, and Marcus Rediker. 2000. *The Many-Headed Hydra: Sailors, Slaves, Commoners and the Hidden History of the Revolutionary Atlantic.* Boston: Beacon.

Ludlow, Peter, and Mark Wallace. 2007. *The Second Life Herald.* Cambridge, MA: MIT Press.

Mander, Jerry, and Edward Goldsmith (eds.). 1997. *The Case Against The Global Economy: and For a Turn Toward the Local.* San Francisco: Sierra Club Books.

Markoff, John. 1996. *Waves of Democracy: Social Movements and Political Change.* Thousand Oaks, CA: Pine Forge Press.

———. 2006. "Globalization and the Future of Democracy." In, *Global Social Change,* edited by C. Chase-Dunn and S. Babones, 336–362. Baltimore, MD: Johns Hopkins University Press.

Martin, William G., et al. Forthcoming. *Making Waves: Worldwide Social Movements, 1750–2005.* Boulder, CO: Paradigm Publishers.

McMichael, Philip. 1996. *Development and Social Change: A Global Perspective.* Thousand Oaks, CA: Pine Forge.

Modelski, George, and William R. Thompson. 1996. *Leading Sectors and World Powers: The Coevolution of Global Politics and Economics.* Columbia, SC: University of South Carolina Press.

Moghadam, Valentine. 2005. *Globalizing Women.* Baltimore, MD: Johns Hopkins University Press.

Monbiot, George. 2003. *Manifesto for a New World Order.* New York: New Press.

Murphy, Craig. 1994. *International Organization and Industrial Change: Global Governance since 1850.* New York: Oxford.

Netchaeva, Irina. 2002. "E-government and E-democracy: A Comparison of the Opportunities in the North and South." *Gazette* 64(5): 467–477.

Ondrejka, Cory. 2005. "Changing Realities: User Creation, Communication and Innovation in Digital Worlds." Linden Lab White Papers. http://lindenlab.com/whitepapers/Changing_Realities_Ondrejka.pdf.

O'Rourke, Kevin H., and Jeffrey G. Williamson. 1999. *Globalization and History: The Evolution of a 19th Century Atlantic Economy.* Cambridge, MA: MIT Press.

Patomaki, Heikki, and Teivo Teivainen. 2004. "The World Social Forum: An Open Space or a Movement of Movements." *Theory, Culture and Society* 21(6): 145–154.

———. 2007. "Researching Global Political Parties." In *Global Political Parties,* edited by Katarina Sehm-Patomaki and Marko Ulvila, 92–113. London: Zed Press.

Portman, Bridgette. 2008. "Comrades in Arms: Socialists and Communists at the World Social Forum." IROWS Working Paper #38: http://irows.ucr.edu/papers/irows38/irows38.htm.

Rediker, Marcus B. 2007. *The Slave Ship.* New York: Viking.

Reitan, Ruth. 2007. *Global Activism.* London: Routledge.

Reuveny, Rafael, and William R. Thompson (eds.). 2008. *North and South in the World Political Economy.* Malden, MA: Blackwell.

Robinson, William I. 1996. *Promoting Polyarchy: Globalization, US Intervention and Hegemony.* Cambridge: Cambridge University Press.

———. 2004. *A Theory of Global Capitalism.* Baltimore, MD: Johns Hopkins University Press.

Roemer, John. 1994. *A Future for Socialism.* Cambridge, MA: Harvard University Press.

Ross, Robert, and Kent Trachte. 1990. *Global Capitalism: The New Leviathan.* Albany: State University of New York Press.

Rueschemeyer, Dietrich, Evelyn Huber Stephens, and John D. Stephens. 1992. *Capitalist Development and Democracy.* Chicago: University of Chicago Press.

Santiago-Valles, Kelvin. 2005. "World Historical Ties Among 'Spontaneous' Slave Rebellions in the Atlantic." *REVIEW* 28(1): 51–84.

Santos, Boaventura de Sousa. 2006. *The Rise of the Global Left.* London: Zed Press.

Sassen, Saskia. 2006. *Territory • Authority • Rights: From Medieval to Global Assemblages.* Princeton, NJ: Princeton University Press.

Scholte, Jan Aart. 2004. "Civil Society and Democratically Accountable Global Governance." *Government and Opposition* 39(2): 211–233.

Sen, Jai, and Madhuresh Kumar with Patrick Bond and Peter Waterman. 2007. *A Political Programme for the World Social Forum?: Democracy, Substance and Debate in the Bamako Appeal and the Global Justice Movements.* Indian Institute for Critical Action: Centre in Movement (CACIM), New Delhi, India, and the University of KwaZulu-Natal Centre for Civil Society (CCS), Durban, South Africa. http://www.cacim.net/book/home.html.

Shannon, Richard Thomas. 1996. *An Introduction to the World-systems Perspective.* Boulder, CO: Westview.

Shiva, Vandana. 2005. *Earth Democracy.* Boston: South End Press.

Silver, Beverly. 1995. "World Scale Patterns of Labor-Capital Conflict: Labor Unrest, Long Waves, and Cycles of Hegemony." *Review* 18(1): 155–192.

———. 2003. *Forces of Labor.* Cambridge: Cambridge University Press.

Silver, Beverly, and Eric Slater. 1999. "The Social Origins of World Hegemonies." In *Naming the Enemy: Anti-Corporate Movements Confront Globalization,* edited by Arrighi, Silver, Starr, and Amory. London: Zed Press.

Smith, Jackie. 2008. *Social Movements for Global Democracy.* Baltimore, MD: Johns Hopkins University Press.

Smith, Jackie, Marina Karides, et al. 2007. *The World Social Forum and the Challenges of Global Democracy.* Boulder, CO: Paradigm Publishers.

Stevis, Dimitris, and Terry Boswell. 2007. *Globalization and Labor.* New York: Rowman & Littlefield.

Stiglitz, Joseph E. 2002. *Globalization and its Discontents.* New York; Norton.

Tarrow, Sidney. 2005. *The New Transnational Activism.* Cambridge: Cambridge University Press.

Tausch, Arno. 2007. "War Cycles." *Social Evolution and History* 6(2:September): 39–74.

Tetalman, Jerry, and Byron Belitsos. 2005. *One World Democracy.* San Rafael, CA: Origin.

Tilly, Charles. 2007. *Democracy.* Cambridge: Cambridge University Press.

Turner, Jonathan H. 1995. *Macrodynamics.* New Brunswick, NJ: Rutgers University Press.

Urry, John. 1999. "Globalization and Citizenship." *Journal of World-Systems Research* V(2): 311–324.

Wagar, W. Warren. 1992. *A Short History of the Future.* Chicago; University of Chicago Press.

———. 1996. "Toward a Praxis of World Integration." *Journal of World-Systems Research* 2:1. Http://csf.colorado.edu/wsystems/jwsr.html.

Wallerstein, Immanuel. 2004. *World-Systems Analysis.* Durham, NC: Duke University Press.

———. 2007. "The World Social Forum: From Defense to Offense." http://www.sociologistswithoutborders.org/documents/WallersteinCommentary.pdf.

Walton, John, and David Seddon. 1994. *Free Markets and Food Riots: The Politics of Global Adjustment.* Oxford: Blackwell.

Waterman, Peter. 2006. "Toward a Global Labor Charter Movement?" http://wsfworkshop.openspaceforum.net/twiki/tiki-read_article.php?articleId=6.

Wilmer, Franke. 1993. *The Indigenous Voice in World Politics.* Newbury Park, CA: Sage.

Winant, Howard. 2001. *The World Is A Ghetto.* New York: Basic Books.

5

VIOLENCE, THE SACRED, AND THE GLOBAL SYSTEM

USING AN INDIGENOUS IDENTITY FRAMEWORK TO ADDRESS PROBLEMS OF THE WORLD SYSTEM

Michelle M. Jacob

Introduction

Shix páchway!
Howka!

To begin this chapter I wish to greet readers in two indigenous languages. I greet you in both Sahaptin (my tribe, the Yakama Nation's, indigenous language) and Kumeyaay (to honor the indigenous people of San Diego, on whose homeland the Political Economy of the World System conference took place). I begin this way to respect an indigenous understanding of identity. Three important aspects of indigenous identity are articulated through three simple questions: Who are you? Where do you come from? What is your relationship to the land? These are such basic questions, but in our so-called post-modern world, it has become very difficult for many people to answer these questions. From an indigenous perspective, to be able to answer these questions signals a groundedness in one's identity, a sense of peoplehood and humility, as one honors that the land is the basis for our identity. Thus, I shared that I am Yakama, and soon I'll discuss my homeland and traditional culture as a major focus of this chapter, but because I work during the school year at the University of San Diego (USD), I need to honor that I spend much of my time on Kumeyaay homeland. From an indigenous perspective, we believe that if one is solid in one's identity, then one possesses some very valuable knowledge; in short, one knows who one is. And one also knows, to a pretty good extent, how one should act, because being a member of a group teaches this. But, if one doesn't know who one is, then well, we might say a person is much more likely to do really crazy things, like poison the water supply, pollute the air, hurt other people or oneself, harm or waste plants and animals. A sense of identity that can protect us from doing these damaging things is useful as we struggle with the many problems that we face in the world system today.

This chapter teaches readers how to use an indigenous conception of identity to avoid damaging ourselves, each other, and the Earth. Using historical and contemporary Kumeyaay and Yakama cultural examples, I argue that local action is necessary to achieve a more socially just political economy of the world system.

Land as "Commodity" vs. "Basis for Identity"

In my American Indian Studies and Ethnic Studies classes, I teach my students this very basic foundation of Native cultures: the importance of a group-based identity and that identity is rooted in land (Deloria 1994; Jim 1987). Often times, after such discussions students begin to wonder why they were never taught to think of USD as existing on Kumeyaay homeland. This is often times students' first experience grappling with the legacy of colonialism in a personal way, as they can simply "look around" campus and the greater San Diego area and realize all that was taken in the name of missionary, colonist, and settler "progress." Students begin to research their own hometowns and think about the indigenous peoples that they never learned about "back home." Students are able to problematize the capitalist view of "land as commodity" and utilize the indigenous view of "land as a living entity" that is important in a relational sense (Deloria 1994). Indeed, far from being solely an object for economic gain, according to indigenous views, land, and *homeland* in particular, serves as the source of one's identity. College students, many of whom are "away from home" for the first "real" times in their lives, often find this indigenous view of land and identity as empowering, as the "new" and critical indigenous paradigm oftentimes resonates with students' own questions about place and belonging. Although my students are overwhelmingly non-Native, the indigenous view of land as the basis of identity offers the students a way to connect with their educational homeland—beyond the fairly superficial "mascot-wearing, school-color matching" (in USD's case, this means donning "Torero Blue" every Friday) approach to identifying with one's educational home. Students wonder in awe, and sometimes regret, why, in their educational experiences in the K-12+ system, they were denied access to this indigenous way of viewing the world and their own identities. Sometimes, I have students eager to "do something" about this gap in education. For these motivated students I help them brainstorm various public education projects. One such project was a mural that we created my first semester at USD, in 2006.

One of my students, Christy Garcia, worked with an artist from one of the local reservations to sketch ideas for a mural that would honor the Kumeyaay people. The mural served as part of a public education project on our campus, as it was displayed at several different campus functions and served to educate the

Figure 5.1 Kumeyaay mural.

larger campus community about the recognition that USD exists on Kumeyaay homeland. My Ethnic Studies students worked with a local grassroots Indian education organization, the American Indian Recruitment Programs (AIR), to provide afterschool programs for local Native youth.[1] At the AIR sessions, my students tutored and mentored the Native high school students and local tribal cultural traditions were discussed. Several aspects of local cultures are represented on the mural, and our university students, local Native kids, and their families all worked collaboratively on the mural. Many of the community members live on or near the Kumeyaay reservations, which extend from Northern San Diego County to South County and across the border to the four Baja Kumeyaay reservations.[2] Thus, not only did my students help create a project that educates our campus community about our relationship with the land, but the project itself served as a way of connecting with and honoring the local tribal peoples on whose homeland we study and work. This project was especially helpful for my students, who are overwhelmingly from suburban communities and are often lacking a strong sense of identity. Projects such as the Kumeyaay mural help students process their personal connection to the legacy of colonialism.

Another example of "making visible" the history of this land upon which our university sits, was the dedication of a Native plants garden at USD, at which

Figure 5.2　Map of Kumeyaay Reservations, as painted on the Kumeyaay mural.

another group of students added signage and basic information to the garden area, replacing neglected signage that was there previously and renaming the space the "Kumeyaay garden." This space is directly behind the University Center, a main dining and social gathering place on campus. The garden overlooks Tecolote Canyon, Mission Bay, and the Pacific Ocean. It is a special and quiet place where one can reflect on the beauty of this homeland of the Kumeyaay people. Importantly, this is the only publicly accessible space on campus that recognizes the indigenous history of the land upon which our campus is built.

Many other spaces and places on campus recognize the *colonial* history of the land; especially notable are the statue of violent missionary Father Junipero Serra, placed in front of Serra Hall, and the Spanish colonial architecture that persists throughout the campus. Additionally, recognizing and celebrating "history and tradition" are key to annual campus celebrations, but most often, the "history" celebrated begins in 1949, the year USD was founded as a Catholic university. Indigenous views of history are ignored and silenced in this hegemonic, modernist narrative.

While a sign in a garden or a mural painted with community members may not be the ultimate answers to problems in the world system, I offer these real-life educational examples as simple ways that we can all work towards addressing the roots of the problems we face in the world system. The goal of my chapter is to analyze the theme of our PEWS conference panel, "Violence, the Sacred, and the Global System," through a lens that uses an indigenous perspective and a decolonized methodology. Rather than *telling* you about what I mean by an indigenous perspective and a decolonized methodology, I wanted to provide some introductory examples that *showed* you what I mean by that. Given that most people who read this volume will be educators, I hope that my discussion of identity and the examples from my classes have helped, in a real practical way, to accomplish this.

In other research projects, I focus on questions of colonialism and how indigenous peoples can be empowered to heal from wounds inflicted by colonialism. I believe that centering indigenous perspectives about violence, the sacred, and the global system can help lead us to a useful place. From an indigenous perspective, this is the entire point of scholarship and education: to arrive at a place in which our teaching and learning can be *applied* in order to do "good work." In my case, that means supporting sovereignty struggles, thinking and acting sustainably, and knowing and respecting Native cultures.

Violence

Native peoples are perhaps some of the greatest experts on violence, due to the many forms of violence which have swept through and continue to impact our communities. As indigenous scholar Eduardo Duran (2006) theorizes, contemporary social problems in indigenous communities are rooted in colonial violence inflicted on our peoples. Disease, warfare, genocide, missionization, boarding schools, termination, relocation, and an onslaught of assimilation policies, institutional discrimination, and discouragement led to many forms of social breakdown in our communities. Not all of the damages of colonial violence can be quantified, but some can. Andrea Smith reports, "On reservations, American Indians have a life expectancy of 47 years. The tuberculosis rate for Natives is 533 percent higher than the national average; the accident mortality rate 425 percent higher ... the alcoholism rate 579 percent higher; the diabetes rate 249 percent higher ... than the national average" (2005, 116).

Perhaps the best way of understanding the ongoing impact of colonial violence in Native communities is to think about this problem using a framework that Duran (2006) provides. In his work as a counselor among Native peoples, he uses the concept of "colonial bureaucratic violence" to discuss the many ways in which institutions continue to alienate, isolate, and oppress Native peoples. A major part of the effectiveness of "colonial bureaucratic violence" lies in the ways in which institutions ignore and deny the importance of Native cultures. In this discussion, Gayatri Spivak's (1990) notion of "epistemic violence" is useful. The "institutional dysfunction" that colonial bureaucratic violence creates is harmful because it encourages or mandates an erasure of cultural practices and identities. Colonial bureaucratic violence is harmful for Native peoples, in that it alienates one from one's traditional culture. An obvious example is the boarding school era, in which Native children were stolen from their homes by government and religious personnel and exposed to a curriculum intent on "killing the Indian and saving the man," but other examples include contemporary educational systems that refuse to offer indigenous language classes, or schools that use textbooks that neglect or misrepresent indigenous cultures and histories. Such examples are a form of colonial bureaucratic violence that ultimately harms Native peoples. But these examples are also harmful to non-Natives, who could learn much about themselves, their histories, and the lands upon which they live and work, which are oftentimes Native homeland. That any person should be alienated from the rich histories and traditions of the land is severely dysfunctional from an indigenous perspective.

The Sacred

Next, I want us to consider ideas of "the sacred" from an indigenous perspective. I teach a seminar on American Indian Health and Spirituality. In my class, we problematize the concept of "religion," which is often conflated with "the sacred." In doing this critique, we draw from indigenous studies scholars such as Vine Deloria, Jr. (1994, 1–2), who argued that one needs to "emphasize the role that spaces and places play in our human religious perceptions," that a Native "religious view of the world [is one that] seeks to locate our species within the fabric of life that constitutes the natural world, the land and all its various forms of life," and that "at the deepest philosophical level our universe must have as a structure a set of relationships in which all entities participate." Such arguments destabilize the hegemonic view that places Western thought and tradition at the center of moral thought, a main objective of much of Deloria's work in texts such as *God is Red* and *Custer Died for Your Sins.* In my view, Deloria's analysis fits nicely with some of the comments that Immanuel Wallerstein made at the Political Economy of the World System conference. Wallerstein encouraged us to work towards a relatively democratic and relatively egalitarian world system. These are indeed good aspirations. My work in this chapter attempts to show how traditional Native cultures can help us in our efforts to think through how we can work towards our democratic and egalitarian goals. However, in putting an indigenous view of identity at the center of my analysis, I offer a counterpoint to Wallerstein's work, in that I am urging readers to begin their critique of the world system by looking at their connection to indigenous homeland and peoples.

Indigenous views of the sacred are rooted in people's relationship with the land. As Deloria called for, in *God is Red,* "It is time for the people to gather and perform their old ceremonies and make a final effort to renew the earth and its peoples—hoofed, winged, and others" (1994, 3). Such arguments fly in the face of modernist theories that point to indigenous cultures and traditions as "backwards" and a "source of poverty" in the global capitalist market. Indeed, indigenous scholars such as Vine Deloria, Jr, Winona LaDuke, and Taiaiake Alfred all argue that indigenous cultural traditions are a source of protection in the violent, consumer-driven global economy (Deloria 1994; LaDuke 2005; Alfred 2005). Central to indigenous cultures is a "rootedness in place," as Deloria argues. Perhaps tribal-specific examples will help to illuminate this important point.

From my own tribal perspective, we as Yakama people are taught from a very young age about our sacred foods. While all foods that the Earth and our Creator provide are considered blessings, some foods, due to our own spiritual traditions, are considered sacred. One of these foods, for Yakama people, is *núsux,* or salmon. Salmon has long sustained us as a people. Indeed, without salmon, we would not have survived to exist as a people today. Salmon has been at the center of our economic, dietary, spiritual, and social order for countless generations. Indeed, my people's relationship with salmon is sacred, as prayers are offered at the fishing sites, fishing seasons depend upon the advice and counsel of traditional spiritual leaders, and religious ceremonies mark the official opening of annual fishing seasons.[3] This is how it has always been, according to our elders: "The People's survival from year to year, generation to generation, was assured. Their way of life was in rhythm with nature. Earth and life were sacred. The land taught material and spiritual values" (Yakama Indian Nation 1977).

Connecting Violence, the Sacred, and the Global System

I want to now move to connecting ideas of violence and the sacred to the final theme of this chapter: the global system. In discussing the global system, I want to focus most on a case study of historical trauma and healing for Yakama peoples. In doing so, I will make explicit connections between the important parts of Yakama history and culture: Celilo Falls, the Hanford B reactor, the nuclear bomb dropped on Nagasaki, the Dalles Dam, the Celilo Falls mural on the Yakama Reservation, and children enjoying the 2008 Yakama Nation Treaty Days parade. To tell the story of how these important sites and events are tied together in the world system, I will draw from ethnographic and historical sources of information.

Thinking about the material for this chapter took me back to my childhood, when I was about the same age as my nephews and niece are today, who enjoy celebrating at our annual Yakama Nation Treaty Days parade. It was at that time when a beautiful mural depicting our most sacred salmon fishery was unveiled on our reservation. One of my aunties rounded up a bunch of us children and we went to bless the mural and do traditional dances to welcome and honor it, and perhaps most importantly, we were honoring the memory of our sacred Celilo Falls. We were honoring the *memory* of our sacred and most plentiful fishery because it was buried under the backwaters of the Dalles Dam, constructed on the Columbia River with its floodgates closing in 1957.

Part of the modern-era fever to further industrialize and develop the Northwest, the Dalles Dam project promised economic bounties for many: the rural poor Whites of the Northwest, the private investors who controlled the electricity grid, the growing industries who relied on big energy, the Northwest Indians who could take settlement monies in exchange for the destruction of the fishing site, and perhaps *most* of all, the burgeoning economy that grew from and around massive federal investment in the Hanford Nuclear Reservation (Barber 2005).

Hanford, located on our homeland, traditional wintering grounds of the Yakama people, was the apple of many of our national leaders' eyes. Hanford was considered a tremendous success due to its contribution in producing the plutonium used in the bomb that was dropped on Nagasaki (Makhijani 1995). Let me quickly and explicitly connect the dots to explain these important parts of Yakama historical trauma:

1. Land is stolen from Yakama peoples through the Treaty process.
2. This stolen land is used to develop a 586 square mile nuclear facility.
3. This facility pollutes our rivers with nuclear contamination; these are the same rivers where we fish for our salmon, one of our sacred foods.
4. In doing this mad science, Hanford refines the plutonium used to destroy Nagasaki.

5. In the modernist euphoria that celebrates Hanford's success, the Dalles Dam project is finally pushed through, despite tremendous opposition from Yakama leaders.
6. With the building of the Dalles Dam, our most sacred fishery is destroyed.

By the way, Hanford has never been cleaned up. It is the most contaminated nuclear site in the United States. In 2009, there remained 53 million gallons of radioactive and toxic waste in underground tanks, some of which the Department of Energy has acknowledged has leaked into the aquifer and Columbia River. More bad news, when campaigning in the Northwest in 2008, then-Senator Barack Obama was asked how his policy to clean up Hanford's nuclear pollution would differ from President George Bush's. In his response, Obama confessed that he did not even know what Hanford was (Democracy Now! 2009).

Currently, the Department of Energy is working on plans for a facility that will supposedly clean up the radioactive waste. The Department of Energy (DOE) regularly issues press releases about the Hanford facility, including one from April 10, 2009, which stated that the department was working on making an efficient plant that will be "the best value for the American taxpayer." Annually, at least $2 billion is spent on such research and testing efforts. In several decades of substantial public tax dollar investment, there has been no big bang for the buck in cleaning up Hanford. This environmental disaster is not only a form of violence upon the Yakama Nation, but also upon all those who are connected to the water, land, and air that surrounds the Hanford nuclear reservation and the polluted Columbia River. Despite years of study, proposals, and review, DOE has now pushed back the startup date on this efficient clean up plant. The earliest we can expect it to begin is now 2019. I guess we can all wait ten more years for that big clean up bang.

Indigenous Resilience: Honor the Past, Give Hope for the Future

With all of the terrible things I have shared in this chapter, I want readers to remember as well something very positive: the tremendous resilience of our people. We are still here, and that is something to celebrate. To demonstrate some of this resilience, I want to talk next about the lasting power and memory of Celilo Falls as a source of strength. A coalition of Native and non-Native peoples painted a beautiful mural of Celilo Falls.

When I was a child, we danced in this parking lot to honor Celilo, our traditional fishermen, and the spirit of núsux and our people. We danced then, and continue to dance today, to honor the past and to give us hope for the future. I believe the best academic work does this, too: it honors the past, and gives hope for the future.

Figure 5.3 Celilo Falls mural.

We must remember and honor the many people who, in the era after Celilo was destroyed, fought and keep fighting to protect our indigenous fishing rights: the fish-ins of the 1960s, the court battles of the 1970s, 1980s, 1990s, and 2000s, the contemporary Native warriors and our non-Native allies who support our struggles for self-determination (Nagel 1996). They are our heroes and role models.

And that is how I want to conclude: by pointing out the importance of social *action*. I want to leave you with the questions: What can *you* do? How can you use the information in this chapter to inform your action? At the heart of indigenous cultural teachings is often a call to action, thus I will share a few basic ideas that you can apply that may help achieve a greater, more socially just world system. Knowledge of self and one's relationship to the land can provide one with a powerful ethnical analysis of one's own subjectivity as well as the world system. Staying true to indigenous beliefs, local concerns are placed at the center of these recommendations. Remember the defining questions of identity that I provided at the beginning of this chapter: Who am I? Where do I come from? What is my relationship to the land? One simple thing we can do is to recognize the fact that we are on indigenous homeland; this recognition helps define one's identity, and it situates an individual in relation to the history of colonization. That recognition of history, violence, and conquest is important for establishing a good relationship with the land. We can nurture that relationship by supporting sovereignty struggles of indigenous peoples. We can reach out, learn from, and build relationships with the indigenous peoples of the land upon which we find ourselves. We can think and act sustainably in our own individual lives and in the collectives to which we belong, as this is an important way to nurture our relationship with the land. And finally, we can, in combination with these acts, make an effort to respect and know Native plants, foods, and peoples. We can ask ourselves: how are Native peoples and cultures represented in the institutions in which I work?[4] If Native peoples are represented in your institution, good! Build that relationship and strengthen it. If indigenous peoples and cultures are not represented, or are done so poorly, then figure out how you can better advocate for Native peoples and cultures. Building on traditional teachings, relationships must be established and fostered. Get to know indigenous peoples by attending public events, offering to help in grassroots efforts, eat together, host one another at the institution as well as in the community.

We all stand to gain by engaging in this relationship building and pushing for greater representation. We all live and work on indigenous homeland of some kind. So in these simple ways, we can more solidly know who we are, where we come from, and foster a healthy relationship with the land. From an indigenous perspective, if we do these things, we are less likely to damage ourselves, each other, and the earth. Then, it may be possible to bring into reality Deloria's vision of "a set of relationships in which all entities participate."

Notes

1. See the AIR website for a more detailed description of the youth programs provided: www.airprograms.org.
2. The Kumeyaay are one of the indigenous groups that had the US-Mexico border cross them. For a more detailed discussion of Kumeyaay history, see Connolly's *Kumeyaay: A History Textbook.*
3. For a more detailed description of the First Salmon ceremony, see Brown (2005) and Geffen and Crawford (2005).
4. Please note: tokens don't count. If your institution is tokenizing indigenous peoples and cultures, then shame on you for standing by when a form of colonial bureaucratic violence is happening.

References

Alfred, Taiaiake. 2005. *Wasase: indigenous pathways of action and freedom.* Peterborough: Broadview Press.

Barber, Katrine. 2005. *Death of Celilo Falls.* Seattle: University of Washington Press.

Brown, Jovana J. 2005. "Fishing Rights and the First Salmon Ceremony." In *American Indian Religious Traditions, Vol. 1,* edited by Suzanne J. Crawford and Dennis F. Kelley. Santa Barbara: ABC-CLIO.

Deloria, Vine. 1994. *God is Red.* Golden, CO: Fulcrum Publishing.

Democracy Now! 2009. "Hanford Nuclear Reservation: A Look at the Nation's Most Polluted Nuclear Weapons Production Site." April 21, 2009. http://www.democracynow.org/2009/4/21/hanford_nuclear_reservation_a_look_at. Accessed: June 25, 2009.

Duran, Eduardo. 2006. *Healing the Soul Wound: Counseling with American Indians and Other Native Peoples.* New York: Teachers College Press.

Geffen, Joel, and Suzanne J. Crawford. 2005. "First Salmon Rites." In *American Indian Religious Traditions, Vol. 1,* edited by Suzanne J. Crawford and Dennis F. Kelley. Santa Barbara: ABC-CLIO.

Jim, Russell. 1987. "The Nuclear Waste Issue in the State of Washington and a Tribal Response." *Wicazo Sa Review* 3(1): 26–30.

LaDuke, Winona. 2005. *Recovering the Sacred: The Power of Naming and Claiming.* Boston: South End Press.

Makhijani, Arjun. 1995. "A Readiness to Harm." In *Nuclear Wastelands: A Global Guide to Nuclear Weapons Production and Its Health and Environmental Effects,* edited by A. Makhijani, H. Hu, and Katherine Yih, 1–9. Cambridge, MA: MIT Press.

Nagel, Joane. 2006. *American Indian Ethnic Renewal: Red Power and the Resurgence of Identity and Culture.* New York: Oxford University Press.

Smith, Andrea. 2005. *Conquest: Sexual Violence and American Indian Genocide.* Boston: South End Press.

Spivak, Gayatri. 1990. "Can the Subaltern Speak?" In *Marxism and the Interpretation of Culture,* edited by C. Grossberg and N. L. Grossberg, 271–313. Urbana: University of Illinois Press.

Yakima Indian Nation. 1977. *The Land of the Yakimas.* Toppenish, WA: Yakima Indian Nation Tribal Council.

6

FARM LABOR AND THE CATHOLIC CHURCH IN CALIFORNIA

THE TORTILLA PRIEST AND THE PEOPLE OF THE CORN

Alberto López Pulido

> I have suddenly developed a craving for corn tortillas.
> *Rev. Victor Salandini, 1971*[1]

The impact of Christian spirituality and in particular Roman Catholic social teachings regarding the rights of working people and labor issues represents an important and consistent theme in twentieth century Chicana/o labor history. It is a history that focuses on the rights and struggles of agricultural workers, beginning with the bracero program in the 1940s and reaching a crescendo in the 1960s and '70s with the unionizing efforts of César Chávez.

This essay provides a brief introduction to this church-labor encounter as it contextualizes Chicana/o farm worker legacy and its intersections with the Roman Catholic Church, in an attempt to reflect on the momentous history of farmworkers and its encounter with the church in the making of California's powerful agricultural history. Particular focus is placed in this essay on the events that transpired during the 1970s in Southern California, when a sympathetic priest chose to celebrate a Roman Catholic mass with a corn tortilla to bring attention to the plight of striking farmworkers seeking social justice.

Transitory, Non-Organized, Non-White Farm-workers: Made in California

Early twentieth century California history is marked by an economic and de-mographic expansion that had begun in the mid-nineteenth century with US occupation and east-to-west movement into northern Mexico motivated by the pretext of manifest destiny.[2] By 1940, California's population had burgeoned to a total population of 7 million—a total eight times its original number of 865,000 people, during a sixty-year period from 1880 to 1940. The profit-centered capitalist corporate expansion that typified the eastern United States influenced the development of the newly acquired west coast where industry and profit were carved out of the vast agricultural landscape that characterized the region.

Unlike a major part of the United States, where farm practices were largely a family endeavor undertaken by small farms worked by family mem-bers and a few hired hands with crops being grown for their own use and not for sale in the market, California agriculture was transformed and marked by the large corporation structure of agribusiness specializing in seasonal crops. Technological advances such as the refrigerated railroad car being introduced into the agricultural sector by 1877 enabled growers to rapidly expand their markets, and they were now able to sell their products throughout the en-tire country. The agricultural economy of the New West required both the mobility of capital matched by the mobility of people. California would be-come the leading agricultural producer that shaped, formed, and eventually dominated corporate agribusiness, distinguished by an industry that sought to keep production costs low and profits high. Such an economic equation framed an industry that sought out cheap labor, molded as an unstable, migratory, non-white, non-organized, and foreign labor force. It first began with Native American migrant workers soon after the US occupation, to be followed by Asian (Chinese and Japanese) immigrants, then East Indian and Filipino workers in the early twentieth century. Mexican/Chicano farmworkers began to dominate the agricultural sector by WWI and into the contemporary period.

The Role and Encounter with the Roman Catholic Church

These "undesirable," unorganized, transitory foreign workers that were shaped by the hegemonic forces of agribusiness in California during the late nineteenth and twentieth centuries were always understood as possessing souls by religious communities, who sought them out to provide guidance and direction via organized religion. Mexican farmworkers of California in the twentieth century expressed sacred practices and observances that were woven and integrated into their everyday life. Eyewitness accounts from the period report braceros farmworkers kneeling before a community-generated shrine of Our Lady of Guadalupe after a long day of work.[3]

Though this essay identifies the 1940s as the critical historical moment where the encounter between the Catholic Church in California and Mexican/ Chicanos as farmworkers occurs, it is critical for us to complicate this history by recognizing that the Roman Catholic Church had established a relationship with indigenous and mestizo populations hundreds of years earlier through the elaborate California mission system, which played a decisive role in shaping the agricultural order of California. During the eighteenth century, Spanish colonists, with justifications from the Roman Catholic Church, established a conversion and mission labor system as a prelude to so-called self-reliance and eventual freedom for indigenous people. These indigenous communities cleared the land and erected the buildings. They cultivated the crops, tended herds, tanned hides, manufactured soap and candles, ground flour, and worked in leather and iron. Women spun, wove, and cooked, in addition to guarding stock and felling timber. Indian labor is what enabled the Spanish mission system to flourish as it undergirded an economic empire of impressive dimensions. By the 1820s, twenty-one missions stretched from San Diego to Sonoma, with an Indian population of some 64,500. Their assets ran into the millions and their annual returns were enormous.[4]

The establishment of the Mexican northern frontier in the 1820s brought forward strong nationalistic sentiments and secularization laws aimed at removing Spanish clerics by the 1830s. Secularization of the missions meant that missions would be turned over to diocesan clergy or lay administrators if clergy were unavailable. State-supported missionaries from religious orders who ran the missions were replaced with parish-supported priests, known as secular clergy or *curas,* responsible for the propagation of the faith.[5] This marked the end of the mission system as established by Spanish colonists.

The Church in the Fields: Encountering
Mexican Farmworkers

The bracero program began in 1942, through a joint agreement between the United States and Mexican governments, in response to the severe labor shortage and high demand in the agricultural sector brought on with the advent of the Second World War. It represents the first significant encounter between Mexican farmworkers and the Roman Catholic Church in the twentieth century. In describing the program, cheap foreign labor was considered advantageous to owners of large-scale farms who employed "stoop" labor in great quantities, according to the US President's Commission on Migratory Labor.[6] The movement of Mexican farmworkers into the agricultural sectors of the United States represented both a spiritual and moral concern for the American Catholic Church.

In 1943, the Social Action Department of the National Catholic Welfare Conference organized a conference to address the socioeconomic problems of the Mexican workers. More extensive meetings, held in Denver, followed in 1944, where policies and actions were recommended to American Catholic bishops. These meetings underscored the "ill qualities" of the Mexican population—ill-fed, ill-cared-for, ill-dressed, and ill-educated as a result of their low paying jobs. Such individuals were considered to be in danger of losing their faith if they came into contact with intense Protestant proselytism. Recommendations came forward to establish regional organizations to take care of migrant workers. Roman Catholic bishops of the local dioceses were instructed to secure funds for the Spanish-speaking from the American Board of Catholic Missions and the Catholic Extension society.[7]

As a result, a grant program for the bishops of Los Angeles, Santa Fe, and San Antonio was approved in 1944 at the annual meeting of the American Catholic hierarchy, to study the question of the Spanish-speaking.[8] Out of this came forth the very first meeting of the bishops of the American southwest in January of 1945, out of which was established the Bishops Committee for the Spanish Speaking (BCSS). BCSS was designed initially to work strictly with braceros in the San Antonio region. This would eventually change to address the needs of the Spanish speaking in other "missionary dioceses" of the southwest. BCSS began with a budget of $15,000 to analyze and attack the problems and impact of industry, agriculture relief, housing, and race discrimination among the Mexican community. By 1948, BCSS expanded its activities to address more directly the problems of migratory labor. In the state of Texas, for example, a priest was appointed from each Roman Catholic diocese to work with the migrant population through the creation and establishment of migratory centers. With data from priests compounded with information from the Texas employment commission, BCSS was successful in providing a fairly accurate snapshot of the patterns of migratory workers. Letters would be sent to the pastors of churches and missions located in the areas where migrants could be found. Such data helped to provide transportation services for migrants to attend religious services and to acquire the sacraments.[9]

Within months of the initiation of the BCSS, the American Catholic hierarchy had made contact with the Mexican Catholic Church, who began to send Mexican missionary priests to minister to migrants. By the early 1950s, Mexican missionary priests had established a plan of ministering to their flock guided by Pope Pius XII's Apostolic Constitution of *Exsul Familia* that guided clergy to take interest in the spiritual welfare of displaced people. This critical document is noteworthy as it incorporated teachings of "social justice" regarding the spiritual care of workers. Mexican priests worked collectively to promote strategies of social justice for migrant workers, resulting in a manual on pastoral care that guided clergy to instruct braceros on human rights.[10]

Labor Organizing and Tortillas: The Sacred World of Farmworkers: A Guide for Action

Upon reflection, from the Bishop's Committee for the Spanish speaking in response to the threat of effective Protestant ministries and religious conversions of Mexican farmworkers, to the awakening of César Chávez with regards to Roman Catholic encyclical teachings in the form of the *Rerum Novarium* that supports the rights of workers to organize, the integral role of the sacred represents a critical guide in orienting the daily lives and historical struggles of working-class farmworkers.

An examination of sacred myths and rituals in the construction, reproduction, and orientation of the lives of farmworkers represents a necessary and fruitful area of study and analysis in Chicana and Chicano religions. Consider the transformation of highways and dirt roads into the sacralized landscapes that became sites of penance for *peregrino* farmworkers, led by the *Virgen de Guadalupe,* who sacrificed their bodies in exchange for equitable wages and decent working conditions, or the work of Protestant ministries and Protestant expression by Mexican farmworkers, of which very little is known. The relationship between the role of religion and farm labor history represents a critical area in need of serious scholarly consideration. In addition to acts of pilgrimage and Protestant expression, I wish to introduce another sacred and religious symbol into the mix in relation to the daily lives of farmworkers, in particular during the 1970s in southern California. I offer up the impressionable, enduring, omnipotent, and potentially sacred object known as the tortilla, both flour and corn to be exact, and of no particular brand name or logo, that took a central and prominent place in farm labor history during the 1970s.

In July of 1971, during a four-month-old strike by farmworkers at the Egger-Ghio tomato farms in San Ysidro, California, the priest, Father Victor Salandini, decided to celebrate a Roman Catholic mass utilizing a corn tortilla (it is not certain whether it was handmade or store bought) to serve as the "Holy Eucharist," which Roman Catholics believe is transformed into the "Body of Christ" as a result of the mass. This spontaneous religious ceremony occurred along the roadside in solidarity and in honor of striking farmworkers, utilizing an old ironing board transformed into a religious altar, with Father Salandini positioned behind it, adorned in Roman Catholic vestments consisting of a burlap *sarape* emblazoned with the black thunderbird of the United Farmworkers. The events that would transpire as a result of Father Salandini's actions are the focus of the remainder of this chapter.

From a broader perspective, this chapter represents part of a much larger research project that seeks to examine the history of contact between nations and empires in relation to the production, consumption, and interpretation of food and nutrition in the Americas. In addition to the framework offered at the outset of this essay, the overarching focus of this project is on the history of maize in Mexico and the American Southwest. As a scholar of American religions, this research is informed by two major questions: 1) What are the cultural, moral, and political taboos and restrictions around food and food consumption? That is, how does the consumptions of specific foods go from being sacred and normative to profane and deviant acts, and how are such actions challenged or reinforced by religious bureaucracies and institutions? 2) In what sociological and historical contexts does food become a political act and a form of political resistance and why? My preliminary research has identified two major historical moments for exploring these critical questions. The first period is the sixteenth and seventeenth centuries of colonial Mexico, and the second, which is the focus of this chapter, occurs in the twentieth century in the American southwest. This project offers an interdisciplinary interpretation of maize in the history of the Americas. It incorporates anthropological, sociological, and religious studies interpretations of how the utility and memory of maize was and is transformed over time.

Consider that maize is a gigantic domesticated grass, known as *teosinte,* of tropical Mexican origin, with a presence in the Americas that is over seven-thousand years old. The cultivation of maize and the elaboration of its food products are inextricably bound with the rise of pre-Columbian civilizations in the Americas. As a species that does not exist naturally in the wild and must be sown and protected by humans for purposes of survival and reproduction, maize has been identified by the anthropologist Arturo Warman as a thoroughly cultural artifact.[11] Consequently, the domestication and improvement of maize is strongly correlated with the development of cultural complexity and rise of sophisticated civilizations in Mesoamerica.

The sacred dimension or sacrality of maize is evident in the creation myths of Mesoamerican societies. The Mayans tell of three gradual improvements of creation, where humanity is first made of mud, followed by wood, and "corn dough" successively, with maize proving to be the ideal human flesh. The *Mexica* or Aztec people build on this creation myth and put forward a similar narrative where imperfect people were created and therefore devoured during previous eras or "suns," until the fourth sun where the gods make maize dough and mixed it with their own blood to produce the best possible beings known as "maize people." This explains why in the Nahuatl language of the Mexica the word for maize dough is *toneuhcayotl,* meaning "our flesh."[12]

A radical change with regards to the sacralization of maize was imminent with the arrival of the conquering Spanish in the early sixteenth century. New agricultural techniques such as extensive plantation agriculture and new plant species such as sugarcane, olive trees, and wheat were introduced into Mesoamerica. The Spanish utilized maize as a food product and introduced it into Europe and their other locations of contact, *but* they tended to regard maize as an inferior grain that produced "coarse" food stuff best suited for animal consumption. The Spanish did all in their power to introduce wheat and wheat food products into the newly conquered lands in both its production and consumption in the Americas. Spanish Colonial ideological and religious institutions were utilized to reinforce these new cultural food customs and to redefine the sacred utilization, consumption, and interpretation of maize in the new society.

On July 14, 1971, soon after Father Salandini's historic tortilla mass, he was notified by Bishop Leo T. Maher that he was suspended from his duties as a Roman Catholic priest in the diocese of San Diego because he chose to use corn tortillas (described as "leavened bread"), rendering the mass as "invalid" from the perspective of the presiding bishop. According to Canon Law 924.2, the Eucharistic bread "must be only wheat." In fact, instructions by the Sacred Congregation for the Discipline of the Sacraments in 1929, taught that bread made of any substance other than wheat is "invalid matter," as are breads to which has been added such a great quantity of another substance that it can no longer be considered wheat bread.[13] As introduced above, in the ancient tradition of the Latin Church, the priest is to use unleavened bread in the Eucharistic celebration, as this has become the custom for Western Churches since the eighth and ninth centuries. In addition to codifying Father Salandini's religious tortilla celebration as unspiritual, the bishop of San Diego found Father Salandini guilty of "scandalous disobedience" because he chose to use corn tortillas, making the mass "invalid" in the words of the bishop.[14] This act by Father Salandini was a derogation of Canon Law 805, which states that "the local Ordinary has the right to appoint or approve teachers of religion and even to remove them or demand that they be removed if a reason of religion or morals requires it."[15] Also, the bishop's actions to remove Father Salandini were "due entirely to his disobedience in refusing to use mass vestments." was a violation of Canon Law 929, which states "in celebrating and administering the Eucharist, priests and deacons are to wear the sacred vestments prescribed by the Ornaments Rubric."[16] Finally, Father Salandini was officially accused of "using his religious status as a political weapon and harassing the owners of the picketed farm operations by holding daily mass in defiance of a court injunction."[17]

With regards to the larger farmworker struggle, Father Salandini's actions brought exposure to the reality as stated by Bishop Maher that "Good Catholics are involved on both sides of this dispute, and I have stressed repeatedly my intentions to remain neutral and my readiness to mediate for the benefit of both sides." He continues: "I strongly support the right of the farmworkers to organize although not necessarily through the United Farmworkers Organizing Committee."[18]

Father Salandini's initial suspension lasted a total of one week and was officially lifted by the Bishop on July 21, when Father Victor agreed to discontinue use of the tortilla, to remove the black eagle from his vestment, and to stay away from the Egger-Ghio farms. This agreement was honored for approximately two months, until, in September of this same year, Father Salandini informed his followers that he was prepared to resume using the corn tortilla for the Sacrament, unless Bishop Maher abided by a promise to collect food from the 167 parishes in the San Diego Catholic diocese and deliver it to the striking workers and their families. Father Salandini's actions were a direct result of his allegations that the diocesan charity office had withheld food-stuffs from seventy-five striking workers that had been on strike since March, with twelve of these workers being dismissed for wearing UFW buttons.[19] The bishop responded by denying these allegations. with the statement that all of the needy in San Diego were being provided with food assistance "including, but not exclusively those who were on strike and on the picket line."[20]

In his autobiography, *The Confessions of the Tortilla Priest,* Salandini writes that the idea of using a tortilla to celebrate a Catholic Mass came when he had run out of hosts and had announced that he would have to cancel mass. He explains that he had gone to the neighborhood church where the grower Egger was an active parishioner, and Salandini was not given any hosts. The farmworkers responded by suggesting to the priest that he utilize a tortilla for the mass; this was originally a flour tortilla (which would have been acceptable because it consists of "leavened bread"), but later Salandini chose to use corn tortillas and consistently used them to bring publicity to issues of social justice and the plight of farmworkers.[21] As he stated, "If the Bishop is going to continue to oppose us in our struggle for social justice, then the corn tortilla to which he has such strong objections will signify our determination and our conviction that there is law above ecclesiastical law."[22] Furthermore, Salandini understood the symbolic power embodied in the tortilla; in his words, it represented the "Mexican's staff of life."[23]

Victor Salandini was born in Port Angeles, Washington, of Italian im-migrant parents and entered the migrant farmworker's world at the age of nine. He grew up in Escondido, California, where, as he states, "his father grew grapes for the wine industry."[24] In his mind, he should have evolved into a "grower, a man of means who ran squads of braceros and Chicanos," but as he reflects, something went wrong in the Orange orchards where he spent so much of his time. Throughout his youth during the 1940s, he actively picked oranges during the summer months. At the age of eighteen, he considered himself the fastest orange picker in the region which earned him the name *El Bicicleta* or "the bicycle" by his Chicano coworkers, who admired his form, speed, and dedication.

In 1952, Salandini was ordained as a Catholic priest for the San Diego diocese. He was heavily influenced by Father Leo Davis, the diocesan seminary rector, who instructed Salandini to examine the economic roots of social problems in society. He taught Father Victor that the root of all of our social ills could be resolved through an economic perspective. Along with Father James R. Anderson, Salandini and Davis would become the nucleus for the Cardijn Center, named after Rev. Joseph Cardijn from Belgium, who was responsible for starting the Young Christian Workers Movement (YCWM) in the early twentieth century. The focus of the YCWM was to show young workers how to Christianize their work and their fellow workers. This movement became effective due to its small group strategies that sought to create and build leadership skills within its membership.

It was Father Davis who, during the early sixties, encouraged Father Victor to team up with César Chávez. Once Salandini entered the world of Chávez and the United Farmworkers, it would become a spiritual home he would never leave. In addition to the historic actions by the tortilla priest discussed here, Father Victor would become both the spiritual leader and research director for the United Farmworkers. He would also be the first Roman Catholic priest to ever go to jail, with César Chávez in the early 1960s. As Chavez would later reflect on this critical event, not only would Father Victor Salandini become the now-famous Tortilla priest, but he would also be known as the "priest of the workers," admired and loved by farmworkers throughout California during the 1960s and '70s.[25]

We are left with some important inquiries and questions for additional research. It is important that we uncover a deeper connection between maize in Mesoamerican societies and the Chicano experience in the twentieth century. It is clear that, as a Roman Catholic priest, Father Salandini understood the deep significance of maize in the hearts and minds of Mexican and Chicano farmworkers, but what additional insights might we unearth? Another critical issue is the rejection of maize as a sacred and honored staple by the European Christian Church, in contrast to the deeper historical significance of wheat within the sacred worldview of Roman Catholics. Parallel to the maize connection over time in the Americas, it would be important to examine if similar trajectories exist for the evolution of wheat in Europe and in the Americas. The hope is that additional research will provide us with some answers to these important questions.

Notes

1. "Notes on People." *The New York Times,* Saturday, July 17, 1971.
2. Ernesto Galarza, *Farmworkers and Agri-business in California, 1947–1960.* Notre Dame: University of Notre Dame Press, 1977; Mario Barrera, *Race and Class in the Southwest: A Theory of Racial Inequality.* Notre Dame: University of Notre Dame Press, 1979; Tomás Almaguer, *Racial Fault Lines: The Historical Origins of White Supremacy in California.* Berkeley: University of California Press, 1994.
3. Antonio R. Soto, "The Chicano and the Church in Northern California, 1848–1978: A Study of an Ethnic Minority within the Roman Catholic Church." Unpublished dissertation, UC Berkeley, 1978, pp. 163–164.
4. David F. Selvin, *A Place in the Sun: A History of California Labor.* San Francisco: Boyd and Fraser, 1981; Richard Steven Street, *Beasts of the Field: A Narrative History of California Farmworkers, 1769–1913.* Stanford: Stanford University Press, 2004.
5. Francis J. Weber, *The Writings of Francisco García Diego Y Moreno: Obispo De Ambas Californias.* Los Angeles: Los Angeles Catholic Diocese, 1976.
6. Alberto López Pulido, "Race Relations within the American Catholic Church: An Historical and Sociological Analysis of Mexican American Catholics." Unpublished Dissertation. University of Notre Dame, 1989.
7. Soto, 168.
8. López Pulido, 64.
9. López Pulido, 66.
10. Rosemary E. Smith, "The Work of the Bishops' Committee for the Spanish Speaking on Behalf of the Migrant Worker." M.A. Thesis. The Catholic University of America, 1958.
11. Arturo Warman, *La Historia de un Bastardo: Maiz y Capitalismo: Obras de Historia,* Mexico D.F: Fondo de Cultural Economica, 1988.
12. R. J. Salvador. "Maize." *Encyclopedia of Mexico: History, Society and Culture.* Michael S. Werner, (ed.). Chicago: Fitzroy Dearborn, 1997.
13. John P. Beal, James A. Coriden, and Thomas J. Green, *New Commentary on the Code of Canon Law.* New York: Paulist Press, 2000: 1116.
14. Everett R. Holles, "'Tortilla Priest' Aids Strikers on Coast." *The New York Times,* Sunday, September 12, 1971.
15. Canon Law Society of America, *Code of Canon Law: Latin English Edition.* Washington DC: Canon Law Society of America, 1998: 263.
16. Beal et al., 959.
17. Holles.
18. Holles.
19. Holles.
20. Holles.
21. Victor Salandini, *The Confessions of the Tortilla Priest.* San Diego: San Diego Review, 1992: 75–76.
22. Holles.
23. Holles.
24. Salandini, 1.
25. Salandini, vi, vii.

7

TREADMILLS, RIFTS, AND ENVIRONMENTAL DEGRADATION

A CROSS-NATIONAL PANEL STUDY, 1970–2000

Andrew K. Jorgenson and Brett Clark

Introduction

The human dimensions of global environmental change are among the most pressing issues facing the world today. PEWS (i.e., political-economy of the world-system) scholarship has much to contribute to the study of society/nature relationships, and recent studies in environmental sociology have successfully adopted a world-systems approach (e.g., Bunker and Ciccantell 2005; Jorgenson and Kick 2006; Roberts and Parks 2007). Related to this, many structural perspectives in environmental sociology are quite complementary to world-systems analysis, offering additional insights concerning the characteristics of and unequal relationships within the stratified interstate system. This abbreviated study is illustrative of the latter. We draw from multiple theories in environmental sociology to assess the extent to which economic development and national militaries contribute to environmental harms. In particular, we engage treadmill of production and destruction theories as well as the metabolic rift perspective, and we evaluate their specific assertions in cross-national fixed-effects panel analyses of per capita carbon dioxide emissions and the per capita ecological footprints of nations.

We begin with a discussion of the treadmill of production and metabolic rift approaches, both of which focus on the environmental consequences of economic development. Next, we introduce readers to the treadmill of destruction perspective, a relatively new approach that highlights the environmental impacts of militaries. Prior to summarizing the findings for the study and their relevance for the engaged theoretical orientations, we describe the modeling techniques, samples, and variables included in the analyses. Following the results section, we briefly conclude with a call for PEWS scholars to pay closer attention to the world's growing environmental crisis and to employ rigorous quantitative methods in future comparative research.

The Treadmill of Production and the Metabolic Rift

Humans have transformed the world in a multitude of ways—many of which were unfathomable just two hundred years ago—in order to meet "social needs." Through these processes, humans forge their history in relation to the physical world. Increasingly, the economy has become one of the most important social structures that influence how society interacts with nature, through the extraction and processing of natural resources. This involves the organization of labor, transportation, trade, and production—not to mention disposal of waste within an international economic system (Frey 1994; Hornborg 2006). The ecological ramifications of these socioeconomic relationships are one of the key areas of study within environmental sociology. We draw from two complementary orientations to assess such associations in comparative perspective.

The treadmill of production perspective (e.g., Gould, Pellow, and Schnaiberg 2008) focuses on how an economic system driven by endless growth, on an ever-larger and intensive scale, generates widespread ecological degradation (Schnaiberg and Gould 1994). The economy is driven by an "insatiable appetite" to expand profit due to the "the inherent nature of competition and concentration of capital" (Schnaiberg 1980, 230). Joseph Schumpeter (2000, 206), the great economist, notes that the capitalist economic system cannot stand still—it must expand if it is to survive. New technologies are employed to expand production and to reduce labor costs. Such growth requires raw materials and energy to operate, given that nature is used to fuel industry and to produce the commodities for the market (Gould et al. 2008). As a result, economic growth and the environment are caught in an "enduring conflict" (Schnaiberg and Gould 1994). An economy premised on constantly increasing the scale and intensity of production to expand profits runs up against a finite world, not to mention the problems associated with the generation of pollution. It increases the degradation of the environment as its bounty is consumed at a faster rate, potentially undermining the reproductive capacities of ecosystems (Clark and York 2005).

Attempts to dematerialize society and decouple the economy from energy and material consumption have been caught in the "Jevons paradox"—as greater efficiency in resource use often leads to *increased* consumption of resources (Jevons 1906). In other words, gains made in improving the efficiency of energy use tend to be outstripped by the expansion and intensification of production, and the actual use of a raw material tends to expand (Clark and Foster 2001; Jorgenson 2009; York 2006). Thus, the treadmill of production perspective asserts that economic growth generates environmental problems, given the ceaseless demands placed upon nature. Resource consumption grows and environmental degradation worsens as development continues while the scale and intensity of production increases.

The metabolic rift perspective considers the interpenetration of nature and society in order to ecologically embed socioeconomic systems and to understand the interchange of matter and energy between nature and society (Foster 1999). Metabolic research, within environmental sociology, incorporates an analysis of natural cycles and systems—illuminating both quantitative and qualitative dimensions of socio-ecological relationships—and a critique of political economy. Capitalism imposes a particular social metabolic order that shapes the productive interchange, as it subjects the natural world to the logic of capital, reducing it purely to an object to facilitate the accumulation of wealth, regardless of whether such demands conflict with natural processes that help sustain ecosystems (Mészáros 1995). As a result, the social metabolism of capitalism is increasingly separated from natural metabolism, producing metabolic rifts in natural cycles and processes that violate the nature-imposed regulative laws of social production and lead to ecological degradation.

Marx's metabolic analysis emerged out of his studies of agriculture and the depletion of soil (Foster 1999; 2000). He noted that the soil required specific nutrients—nitrogen, phosphorus, and potassium—to maintain its ability to produce crops, because as crops grow they take up these nutrients. The enclosure movement and the concentration of land created a division between town and country, causing the urban population to grow. Food and fiber were shipped to distant markets, transferring the nutrients of the soil from the country to the city where they accumulated as waste, rather than being returned to the soil. Marx explained that this type of production "disturbs the metabolic interaction between man and the earth, i.e., it prevents the return to the soil of its constituent elements consumed by man in the form of food and clothing; hence it hinders the operation of the eternal natural condition for the lasting fertility of the soil" (Marx 1976, 637). As a consequence, a rupture is created in the nutrient cycle.

The transfer of nutrients was tied to the accumulation process and increasingly took place at the national and international level, as the bounty of the countryside and distant lands was transferred to urban centers of economically developed nations. Intensive agricultural practices to increase the yield of food and fiber only intensified this process, squandering the riches of the soil, eventually leading to the mass importation of guano and eventually the development of artificial fertilizers, but the metabolic rift was not mended, given the town-and-country relationship and the drive to accumulate capital (Clark and Foster 2009; Foster 1999).

Metabolic rift analysis suggests that an economic system predicated on constant growth leads to environmental degradation through the intensification of the social metabolism, which undermines natural cycles and processes. This analysis has been employed to study how economic growth relies upon the burning of fossil fuels to power and expand production, leading to increased emissions of carbon dioxide. At the same time, the absorption capacity of carbon sinks is being compromised due to deforestation, accelerating the concentration of carbon in the atmosphere. Thus, the carbon metabolism of the economy is contributing to global climate change (Clark and York 2005).

We posit that higher levels of economic development increase the consumption-based environmental impacts of nations (i.e., per capita ecological footprints) as well as their per capita carbon dioxide emissions. Both the treadmill of production and metabolic rift theories would suggest such relationships. We now turn to a discussion of treadmill of destruction theory, which highlights the potential environmental impacts of nations' militaries.

Environmental Degradation and the Military

Prior sociological studies focus on how the military influences levels of domestic income inequality (Kick, Davis, and Kentor 2006), economic development (Kentor and Kick 2008), and other social outcomes (Jenkins and Scanlan 2001). Despite its potential influence on the environment, there has been scarcely any, with few exceptions, theorization or research in sociology regarding the environmental impacts of militarism. Hooks and Smith (2004; 2005) are perhaps the most notable exceptions. Drawing upon the treadmill of production argument, they study the relationships between the military and environmental degradation. While recognizing that the military and economy are related, they contend that the former is somewhat independent of the latter. In this, they explain that the military has its own expansionary dynamics, which involve significant environmental and ecological costs. Given the logic of militarism and the emphasis on national security, the military produces a treadmill of destruction, which undermines environmental protection.

York (2008) notes that while the effects of warfare on the environment expose the potentially serious environmental harms that military institutions, technologies, and behaviors can produce, it does not capture the full extent of their overall ecological impacts (see also Jorgenson 2005). The treadmill of destruction perspective argues that militaries as social structures generate environmental degradation regardless of whether they are engaged in armed conflicts or not (Hooks and Smith 2005). Even outside of war, military institutions and their activities consume massive amounts of nonrenewable energy and other resources to sustain their overall infrastructures and hardware (Dycus 1996). Research and development as well as general maintenance of equipment also contribute to the environmental impacts of militaries. What is more, military operations and infrastructure require the use of land for bases, other forms of installations, and training exercises. The land employed to these ends has steadily increased over the last century (United Nations' Center for Disarmament 1982). A network of military bases encompasses the globe, requiring a vast amount of resources to staff, operate, and transport equipment and personnel between destinations.

As part of the treadmill of destruction, the military stockpiles fuels and other materials. This also partially fosters the treadmill of production. To some extent, many industries are geared to meeting the material requirements of the military, including transportation equipment and communications technologies. A whole support economy exists to keep the military stocked with various supplies, including food for military personnel as well as large quantities of various organic and synthetic materials for uniforms and other specialized forms of clothing. In other words, the treadmill of destruction extends and further fuels the treadmill of production, given that social surplus is directed to supporting the military.

In addition to consuming resources, the military generates different forms of waste, even during peacetime activities. In testing, supporting, and sustaining an arsenal of weapons, large amounts of toxic substances are known to pollute the land and water surrounding military bases and the immediate communities (LaDuke 1999; Shulman 1992; Thomas 1995). Additionally, the armed forces consume large amounts of fossil fuels that directly contribute to carbon dioxide emissions and the emission of other greenhouse gases known to impact global warming and climate change. Renner (1991) indicates that land vehicles, aircrafts, sea vessels, and other forms of machinery burn 75 percent of all energy used by armed forces worldwide. The Pentagon, it is argued, is quite possibly the largest consumer of nonrenewable energy resources, especially fossil fuels, in the United States (Santana 2002). The global reach of the military through the network of military bases increases the natural resources consumed to sustain such an infrastructure. The treadmill of destruction highlights how militarization and related technological and infrastructural changes trump environmental concerns.

We argue that the treadmill of destruction theory provides a useful avenue for understanding the relationships between the military and environment. While developing this perspective, Hooks and Smith (2004; 2005) focused on the US military and domestic environmental conditions. Here, we situate the theoretical orientation in an international comparative perspective. Geopolitical competition often drives arms races, as well as concomitant technological advances, infrastructural development, and growth in troop size—not to mention the role that international trade has in distributing heavy military equipment in various countries. For developed nations, especially, the environmentally damaging capabilities of militarism are partly a function of technological developments with weaponry and other machinery. These capital-intensive militaries employ advanced weaponry and utilize state of the art transportation systems to facilitate the rapid movement of troops and to enhance the strike capabilities of nations, which often involve an extensive system of vehicles and infrastructure to aid in the deployment of equipment and personnel. Further, capital-intensive militaries are likely to increase their material infrastructure or become more spatially dispersed (Kentor and Kick 2008). In a related vein, world-systems scholars have emphasized that nations with relatively larger and more technologically advanced militaries utilize their global military reach to gain disproportionate access to natural resources (e.g., Chase-Dunn 1998; Jorgenson 2003; Kentor 2000).

Overall, we posit that military personnel and high-tech equipment require extensive infrastructures that are highly resource consumptive and waste generating. In the subsequent panel analyses we assess the above propositions by analyzing the effects of military expenditures per soldier and military personnel on per capita carbon dioxide emissions and the per capita ecological footprints of nations. Treadmill of destruction theory would propose that both military factors contribute to increases in the per capita consumption-based environmental impacts of nations (i.e., their ecological footprints) as well as increases in the intensity (i.e., per capita) of their anthropogenic carbon dioxide emissions.

The Analyses

Fixed Effects Models

We use a pooled-time series of cross-sections panel dataset design to estimate ordinary least squares (OLS) fixed effects (FE) models. This is one of the most commonly used methods in the comparative social sciences, because it addresses the problem of heterogeneity bias (see Halaby 2004). Heterogeneity bias in this context refers to the confounding effect of unmeasured time-invariant variables that are omitted from the regression models. To correct for heterogeneity bias, FE models control for omitted variables that are time invariant but that do vary across cases. This is done by estimating unit-specific intercepts, which are the fixed-effects for each case. FE models are quite appropriate for this type of cross-national panel research because time-invariant unmeasured factors such as natural resource endowments and geographic region could affect environmental outcomes. The FE approach also provides a stringent assessment of the relationships between independent variables and the outcomes, given that the associations between them are estimated net of unmeasured between-country effects. Overall, this modeling approach is quite robust against missing control variables and closely approximates experimental conditions. Results of Hausman tests also indicate that FE models are more appropriate than random effects (RE) models for the current analyses. In all OLS FE models we include a correction for first-order autocorrelation (i.e., AR[1] correction). Not correcting for autocorrelation can often lead to biased standard error estimates.

Dependent Variables

Carbon dioxide emissions per capita are employed as the study's first dependent variable. These data are obtained from the World Resources Institute (WRI) (2005). Anthropogenic carbon dioxide emissions represent the mass of carbon dioxide produced during the combustion of solid, liquid, and gaseous fuels, as well as from gas flaring and the manufacture of cement. They do not include emissions from land use change or emissions from bunker fuels used in international transportation. More specifically, the data come from the World Resources Institute's Climate Analysis Indicators Tool (CAIT), which is an information and analysis tool on global climate change. CAIT provides a comprehensive and comparable database of greenhouse gas emissions data (including all major sources and sinks) and other climate-relevant indicators. The values were converted to the actual mass of carbon dioxide from original values showing the mass of elemental carbon; the World Resources Institute multiplied the carbon mass by 3.664, which is the ratio of the molecular mass of carbon dioxide to that of carbon. Carbon dioxide emissions per capita represent the mass of carbon dioxide emitted per person for a country in metric tons as a result of the same production and flaring processes as for the measures of total emissions. WRI calculate per capita emissions from total emissions using population estimates from the United Nations Population Division. We use the natural logarithm for these data to minimize skewness. For analogous reasons, we take the natural logarithm for other variables.

The second dependent variable is the *ecological footprint per capita (ln)*, which we obtained directly from the Global Footprint Network. We treat these data as relatively comprehensive indicators of consumption-based environmental demand. The recently updated national footprint estimates measure the bioproductive area required to support consumption levels of a given population from cropland (food, animal feed, fiber, and oil); grassland and pasture (grazing of animals for meat, hides, wool, and milk); fishing grounds (fish and seafood); and forest (wood, wood fiber, pulp, and fuelwood). They also include the area required to absorb the carbon dioxide released when fossil fuels are burned, and the amount of area required for built infrastructure (e.g., roads, buildings). Regarding the former, the carbon dioxide portion of the footprint deals explicitly with natural sequestration, which involves the biocapacity required to absorb and store the emissions not sequestered by humans, less the amount absorbed by the oceans. A relatively new addition to the comprehensive footprint measure is the nuclear footprint subcomponent. Due to lack of conclusive and available data, the nuclear energy portion of the footprint is assumed to be, and thus estimated as the same as, the equivalent amount of electricity from fossil fuels. However, this subcomponent accounts for less than 4 percent of the total global footprint in the year 2000, and this percent is even lower for earlier years. The ecological footprint is measured and reported in global hectares and is calculated by adding imports to, and subtracting exports from, domestic production. In mathematical terms, consumption = (production + imports) – exports. This balance is calculated for more than 600 products, including both primary resources and manufactured products that are derived from them. Each product or category is screened for double counting to increase the consistency and robustness of the measures. To avoid exaggerations in measurement, secondary ecological functions that are accommodated on the same space as primary functions are not added to the footprints.[1]

Independent Variables of Particular Interest

We include gross domestic product per capita (*GDP per capita*) as a measure of a nation's level of economic development, affluence, and capital intensity. These data, for which we use the natural logarithm, are measured in 2000 constant US dollars and obtained from the World Bank (2007). The treadmill of production and metabolic rift perspectives would posit positive associations between both outcomes and level of economic development.

To assess the arguments of treadmill of destruction theory, we employ two military measures: *military expenditures per soldier* and *military participation.*[2] Military expenditures data (SIPRI 2000) include all current capital expenditures on the armed forces, including peacekeeping forces; defense ministries and other government agencies engaged in defense projects; paramilitary forces, if these are judged to be trained and equipped for military operations; and military space activities. More specifically, such expenditures include operation and maintenance; procurement; military research and development; military and civil personnel, including retirement pensions of military personnel and social services for personnel; and military aid (in the military expenditures of the donor country). Military expenditure per soldier (ln) is calculated by dividing total military expenditures by total military personnel. Total military personnel estimates are gathered from the World Bank (2007) and total military expenditures are obtained from the Stockholm International Peace Research Institute (SIPRI) (1977; 1984; 1987; 1991; 2000). This predictor measures the high-tech nature, or capital intensiveness, of national militaries (e.g., Kentor and Kick 2008; Jorgenson 2005).

Military participation (ln) is a ratio of the number of military personnel per 1,000 population. Military personnel are active duty military personnel as well as paramilitary forces if the training, organization, and equipment suggest they may be used to support or replace regular military forces. We obtained the military participation data from the World Bank (2007). Like others, we treat this variable as an indicator of the relative labor intensity of nations' militaries (see also Kick, Davis, and Kentor 2006; York 2008).

Additional Independent Variables Included in the Reported Analyses

Manufacturing as percentage of total GDP controls for the extent to which a domestic economy is manufacturing-based. These data are gathered from the World Bank (2007). Most perspectives in the social sciences posit that all else being equal, nations with relatively larger manufacturing sectors will use larger and more intensive amounts of fossil fuels and consume other forms of resources, which contribute to increases in both carbon dioxide emissions and overall consumption-based environmental impacts.

Urban population as percentage of total population controls for a country's level of urbanization. We obtain these data from the World Bank (2007). Prior cross-sectional and panel analyses reveal positive associations between urbanization and a variety of environmental outcomes, including the total and per capita ecological footprints of nations (e.g., Jorgenson and Burns 2007; York et al. 2003) as well as the emission of carbon dioxide and other noxious gases (Jorgenson 2007; York and Rosa 2006). While perhaps the most common measure of urbanization for cross-national research in the environmental social sciences, we acknowledge its relative limitations.

Percent population aged 15–64 controls for the extent to which a nation's population is adult and non-dependent. These data are accessed from the World Bank (2007). Structural human ecology (e.g., Dietz and Rosa 1994) posits that all else being equal, nations with relatively larger non-dependent adult populations will consume more fuels and natural resources, which increases both the carbon dioxide emissions and ecological footprints of nations.

Due to space limitations, descriptive statistics and bi-variate correlations are not reported. However, they are available from the authors upon request.

Countries Included in the Analyses

We analyze two balanced cross-national panel datasets consisting of five-year increments from 1970 to 2000 (i.e., 1970, 1975, 1980, 1985, 1990, 1995,

2000). The first dataset, which is for the per capita carbon dioxide emissions analyses, includes seven observations on seventy-two nations, with a total of 504 observations. The second dataset, for the analyses of per capita ecological footprints, consists of seven observations on thirty-seven nations, totaling 259 observations. The countries in each dataset consist of those where observations of the dependent variable(s) and all independent variables are available for the seven time points. Table 7.1 lists all countries included in each of the two datasets.

Table 7.1 Countries Included in the Current Study

Algeria*	Kuwait*
Argentina*	Luxembourg
Australia	Madagascar
Austria*	Malawi
Bangladesh	Malaysia
Belgium*	Mexico*
Bolivia	Morocco
Brazil*	Nepal*
Burundi	Netherlands*
Cameroon*	New Zealand
Canada*	Nicaragua
Chile	Nigeria
Colombia*	Norway
Cyprus	Oman
Denmark	Pakistan*
Dominican Republic	Panama*
Ecuador	Peru
Egypt*	Philippines
El Salvador	Portugal*
Finland*	Rwanda*
France*	Senegal*
Ghana	South Africa*
Greece	Spain
Guatemala	Sri Lanka
Hungary*	Sweden*
India*	Syrian Arab Republic*
Indonesia*	Thailand*
Iran*	Togo
Ireland*	Tunisia*
Israel	Turkey*
Italy*	United Kingdom*
Jamaica	United States*
Japan*	Uruguay
Jordan	Venezuela*
Kenya*	Zambia
Korea	Zimbabwe

Notes: all listed countries are included in the carbon dioxide emissions analysis;
* denotes countries included in the analysis of the per capita ecological footprints

Results

The findings for the panel analyses are reported in Table 7.2. For all predictors we provide unstandardized coefficients, the absolute values of t-statistics, and standardized coefficients, and for each tested model we report values for r-square overall. The same model is tested for both dependent variables and consists of all predictors described above.

Before discussing the results of interest, we briefly summarize the associations between the outcomes and the additional predictors. The effects of manufacturing as percent GDP and urban population on per capita carbon dioxide emissions are positive, indicating the importance in controlling for both when investigating anthropogenic emissions measured by intensity. However, their effects on per capita ecological footprints are non-significant. The effect

Table 7.2 Coefficients for the regression of per capita CO_2 emissions and per capita ecological footprints on selected independent variables: fixed effects model estimates with AR[1] correction for 7 observations on 72 countries and 37 countries, 1970–2000

	CO_2 Per Capita	Footprint Per Capita
GDP per capita (ln)	.54***	.14***
	(8.28)	(5.40)
	[.52]	[.43]
Military Expenditures	.21***	.11***
per soldier (ln)	(3.80)	(4.56)
	[.08]	[.14]
Military Participation (ln)	.42***	.16***
	(5.20)	(5.39)
	[.15]	[.18]
Manufacturing	.02***	.01
as % GDP	(5.50)	(1.38)
	[.08]	[.02]
Urban Population	.03***	.01
as % Total Population	(8.15)	(1.29)
	[.38]	[.01]
Percent Population Aged	.01	.01*
15 to 64	(.67)	(2.10)
	[.02]	[.06]
Constant	3.80***	-.06
	(8.87)	(.31)
R2 overall	.86	.87
Overall Sample Size	504	259
Number of Countries	72	37

Notes:
*p<.05 **p<.01 ***p<.001 (two-tailed tests); unstandardized coefficients flagged for significance; absolute value of t statistics in parentheses; standardized coefficients in brackets

of population age structure in the context of percent population aged 15 to 24 is non-significant for per capita carbon dioxide emissions. Conversely, per capita footprints are positively associated with relative levels of non-dependent populations. While not the focus of the current study, these differing effects on the two dependent variables highlight the importance in assessing the extent to which the impacts of various political-economic and human ecological factors differ across unique environmental outcomes.

Both outcomes are positively associated with level of economic development (GDP per capita), and the relative magnitude of the associations is quite pronounced. In fact, these outcomes are quite consistent with prior research on per capita environmental outcomes, as the positive effect of development is much more pronounced than all other predictors in the analyses. These findings lend clear support to the complementary arguments of treadmill of production theory and the metabolic rift approach in environmental sociology. Further, in analyses conducted elsewhere the quadratic for GDP per capita (with GDP per capita squared) is also positive and significant in models of both dependent variables, which suggests that heightened economic development does not lead to a relative decline in environmental impacts or a decoupling between the economy and environmental harms. Even though valid comparative evidence from rigorous research is lacking to support such assertions (see Jorgenson and Kick 2006; York and Rosa 2003), the latter are common propositions in environmental economics (e.g., Grossman and Krueger 1995)—often referred to as the environmental Kuznets curve—as well as ecological modernization theory in contemporary sociology (e.g., Mol 2001).

Military expenditures per soldier and military participation both positively affect per capita carbon dioxide emissions, and the relative magnitudes of their effects on per capita emissions are far beyond trivial. In a similar vein, the per capita ecological footprints of nations are positively associated with both military participation and military expenditure per soldier, and the magnitude of the impacts are moderate in strength. Thus, we find substantial support for treadmill of destruction theory. As articulated by the theory, labor intensive and technologically advanced militaries of nations require enormous amounts of resources for their complex infrastructures, to support ongoing research and development, and to maintain their relative size and power. The amount of land used by armed forces for bases and other forms of installations has increased steadily over the last century, which partly accounts for the positive associations between both aspects of militaries and the consumption-based environmental demands of nations. The armed forces consume large amounts of fossil fuels in a variety of ways, and this is likely to increase as high-tech militaries continue to develop and implement newly developed transportation vehicles and machinery for national security purposes, with the latter generally taking great precedence over environmental sustainability concerns. While these continual changes contribute to the use of fossil fuels and subsequent anthropogenic carbon dioxide emissions, the intensity of the latter is also impacted by labor intensive militaries, given the amount of fuels used for the movement, training, and protection of troops and support personnel.

Conclusion

Here we presented a modest slice of our ongoing research agenda that engages multiple perspectives to study the environmental impacts of human activities in their different manifestations. While the current study does not adopt an explicit world-systems orientation, the tested theories are indeed complementary to the major works of many leading scholars in the PEWS community (e.g., Bunker 1984; Chase-Dunn 1998; Wallerstein 1974). Consistent with the articulations of both treadmill theories and the metabolic rift perspective, our results show that economic development and nations' militaries both contribute significantly and independently to different forms of environmental degradation. In essence, more economically developed nations and those with more powerful, capital-intensive militaries are highly resource consumptive and waste generating, and like other associations and processes, these society/nature relationships are embedded in the core/periphery hierarchy.

In addition to its substantive importance, this research illustrates the utility in employing rigorous quantitative comparative methods to study macro phenomenon of interest to PEWS scholars. The perspective is rich with fine comparative-historical works as well as in-depth case studies and theoretical debates, and we wouldn't claim that sociologists have excluded quantitative methods in PEWS-oriented research.[3] However, we suggest that the application of more rigorous panel model techniques like those used here—when appropriate—would lead to more valid and reliable results, which would undoubtedly contribute to the advancement of PEWS scholarship and its increased integration with other complementary areas in sociology and our sister disciplines.

While other contributors to this collection have given ample and very justified attention to debates about the existence of and temporality for economic crises in the contemporary world-system, and other scholars have highlighted the role of militaries in maintaining the stratified interstate system, we would like to conclude by reminding readers that the world is caught in a multifaceted ecological crisis with potentially devastating consequences for all of humanity as well as non-human species. Inattention to the global ecological crisis and its political-economic causes is not just intellectually and academically shortsighted. As our esteemed colleague, Peter Grimes, poignantly asserted over a decade ago when highlighting the global ecological crisis, "we live today in a time of unprecedented crises on a global scale ... the crisis is real, urgent, and global," and "the crisis of the biosphere, (political-) economy, and political legitimacy are mutually interactive, the unraveling of their causal links is similar to teasing apart a knot in thread—all the parts are connected" (Grimes 1999, 13–14). Thus, it is our hope that the current study will encourage other scholars to seriously consider the environmental impacts of large-scale political-economic institutions and global social change in future investigations.

Notes

1. The footprint calculations also use (1) equivalence factors to take into account differences in world average productivity among different land types, and (2) yield factors to take into account national differences in biological productivity. The ecological footprint includes only those aspects of resource consumption and waste production for which the Earth has regenerative capacity and where data exist that allow this demand to be quantified in terms of bio-productive area.

2. To minimize collinearity, we regress both military measures on GDP per capita and employ the residuals in the reported panel analyses as measures of unique aspects of national militaries, independent of economic development.

3. Notable exceptions include (but aren't limited to): Chase-Dunn, Kawano, and Brewer 2000; Dixon and Boswell 1996; Jorgenson and Kuykendall 2008; Kentor 1998; Roberts and Parks 2007.

References

Bunker, Stephen G. 1984. "Modes of Extraction, Unequal Exchange, and the Progressive Underdevelopment of an Extreme Periphery: The Brazilian Amazon, 1600–1980." *American Journal of Sociology* 89: 1017–1064.

Bunker, Stephen G., and Paul S. Ciccantell. 2005. *Globalization and the Race for Resources*. Baltimore, MD: Johns Hopkins University Press.

Chase-Dunn, Christopher. 1998. *Global Formation: Structures of the World-Economy*. Lanham, MD: Rowman & Littlefield.

Chase-Dunn, Christopher, Yukio Kawano, and Benjamin Brewer. 2000. "Trade Globalization since 1795: Waves of Integration in the World-System." *American Sociological Review* 65: 77–95.

Clark, Brett, and John Bellamy Foster. 2001. "William Stanley Jevons and *The Coal Question*: An Introduction to Jevons's 'Of the Economy of Fuel.'" *Organization & Environment* 14(1): 93–98.

———. 2009. "Ecological Imperialism and the Global Metabolic Rift: Unequal Exchange and the Guano/Nitrates Trade." *International Journal of Comparative Sociology* 50(3–4): 311–334.

Clark, Brett, and Richard York. 2005. "Carbon Metabolism: Global Capitalism, Climate Change, and the Biospheric Rift." *Theory and Society* 34(4): 391–428.

Dietz, Thomas, and Eugene A. Rosa. 1994. "Rethinking the Environmental Impacts of Population, Affluence and Technology." *Human Ecology Review* 1: 277–300.

Dixon, William, and Terry Boswell. 1996. "Dependency, Disarticulation, and Denominator Effects: Another Look at Foreign Capital Penetration." *American Journal of Sociology* 102: 543–562.

Dycus, Stephen. 1996. *National Defense and the Environment.* Hanover, NH: University Press of New England.

Foster, John Bellamy. 1999. "Marx's Theory of Metabolic Rift: Classical Foundations for Environmental Sociology." *American Journal of Sociology* 105(2): 366–405.

———. 2000. *Marx's Ecology.* New York: Monthly Review Press.

Frey, R. Scott. 1994. "The International Traffic in Hazardous Wastes." *Journal of Environmental Systems* 23: 165–177.

Gould, Kenneth, David Pellow, and Allan Schnaiberg. 2008. *The Treadmill of Production: Injustice & Unsustainability in the Global Economy.* Boulder, CO: Paradigm Publishers.

Grimes, Peter. 1999. "The Horseman and the Killing Fields: The Final Contradiction of Capitalism." In *Ecology and the World-System,* edited by Walter Goldfrank, David Goodman, and Andrew Szasz, 13–42. Westport, CT: Greenwood Press.

Grossman, G., and A. Krueger. 1995. "Economic Growth and the Environment." *Quarterly Journal of Economics* 110: 353–377.

Halaby, Charles. 2004. "Panel Models in Sociological Research: Theory into Practice." *Annual Review of Sociology* 30: 507–544.

Hooks, Gregory, and Chad L. Smith. 2004. "The Treadmill of Destruction: National Sacrifice Areas and Native Americans." *American Sociological Review* 69(4): 558–575.

———. 2005. "Treadmills of Production and Destruction: Threats to the Environment Posed by Militarism." *Organization & Environment* 18(1): 19–37.

Hornborg, Alf. 2006. "Footprints in the Cotton Fields: The Industrial Revolution as Time–Space Appropriation and Environmental Load Displacement." *Ecological Economics* 59: 74–81.

Jenkins, Craig, and Steve Scanlan. 2001. "Food Security in Less-Developed Countries, 1970–1990." *American Sociological Review* 66: 714–744.

Jevons, W. Stanley. 1906. *The Coal Question; An Inquiry Concerning the Progress of the Nation, and the Probable Exhaustion of our Coalmines.* London: Macmillan and Company.

Jorgenson, Andrew K. 2003. "Consumption and Environmental Degradation: A Cross-National Analysis of the Ecological Footprint." *Social Problems* 50: 374–394.

———. 2005. "Unpacking International Power and the Ecological Footprints of Nations: A Quantitative Cross-National Study." *Sociological Perspectives* 48: 383–402.

———. 2007. "Does Foreign Investment Harm the Air We Breathe and the Water We Drink? A Cross-National Study of Carbon Dioxide Emissions and Organic Water Pollution in Less-Developed Countries, 1975–2000." *Organization & Environment* 20: 137–156.

———. 2009. "The Transnational Organization of Production, the Scale of Degradation, and Ecoefficiency: A Study of Carbon Dioxide Emissions in Less-Developed Countries." *Human Ecology Review* 16: 63–73.

Jorgenson, Andrew K., and Thomas J. Burns. 2007. "The Political-Economic Causes of Change in the Ecological Footprints of Nations, 1991–2001: A Quantitative Investigation." *Social Science Research* 36: 834–853.

Jorgenson, Andrew, and Edward Kick (Eds.). 2006. *Globalization and the Environment.* Leiden, The Netherlands: Brill.

Jorgenson, Andrew, and Kennon Kuykendall. 2008. "Globalization, Foreign Investment Dependence, and Agriculture Production: A Cross-National Study of Pesticide and Fertilizer Use Intensity in Less-Developed Countries, 1990–2000." *Social Forces* 87: 529–560.

Kentor, Jeffrey. 1998. "The Long Term Effects of Foreign Investment Dependence on Economic Growth 1940–1990." *American Journal of Sociology* 103: 1024–1046.

———. 2000. *Capital and Coercion*. New York: Garland.

Kentor, Jeffrey, and Edward Kick. 2008. "Bringing the Military Back In: Military Expenditures and Economic Growth 1990 to 2003." *Journal of World-Systems Research* 14: 142–172.

Kick, Edward L., Byron Davis, and Jeffrey Kentor. 2006. "A Cross-National Analysis of Militarization and Inequality." *Journal of Political and Military Sociology* 34(2): 319–337.

LaDuke, Winona. 1999. *All Our Relations: Native Struggles for Land and Life*. Boston: South End Press.

Marx, Karl. 1976. *Capital*, vol. 1. New York: Vintage.

Mészáros, István. 1995. *Beyond Capital*. New York: Monthly Review Press.

Mol, Arthur P. J. 2001. *Globalization and Environmental Reform*. Cambridge: MIT Press.

Renner, Michael. 1991. "Assessing the Military's War on the Environment." Pp. 132–152 in *State of the World*, edited by Linda Starke. New York, NY: WW Norton & Company.

Roberts, J. Timmons, and Bradley Parks. 2007. *A Climate of Injustice: Global Inequality, North-South Politics, and Climate Policy*. Cambridge, MA: MIT Press.

Santana, Deborah. 2002. "Resisting Toxic Militarism: Vieques versus the U.S. Navy." *Social Justice* (Spring-Summer), 37–48.

Schnaiberg, Allan. 1980. *The Environment: From Surplus to Scarcity*. New York: Oxford University Press.

Schnaiberg, Allan, and Kenneth A. Gould. 1994. *Environment and Society: The Enduring Conflict*. New York: St. Martin's Press.

Shulman, Seth. 1992. *The Threat at Home: Confronting the Toxic Legacy of the U.S. Military*. Boston: Beacon Press.

Schumpeter, Joseph. 2000. *Essays: On Entrepreneurs, Innovations, Business Cycles, and the Evolution of Capitalism*. New Brunswick, NJ: Transaction Publishers.

Stockholm International Peace Research Institute [SIPRI]. 1977, 1984, 1987, 1991, 2000. *SIPRI Yearbook: World Armaments and Disarmament*. New York: Oxford University Press.

Thomas, William. 1995. *Scorched Earth: The Military's Assault on the Environment*. Philadelphia, New Society Publishers.

United Nations' Center for Disarmament. 1982. *The Relationship Between Disarmament and Development* (Disarmament Study Series No. 5). New York, NY: United Nations.

Wallerstein, Immanuel. 1974. *The Modern World-System I: Capitalist Agriculture and the Origins of the European World-Economy in the Sixteenth Century*. New York: Academic Press.

World Bank. 2007. *World Development Indicators* (CD ROM version). Washington, DC: World Bank.

World Resources Institute. 2005. *Earth Trends Data CD-ROM: The Wealth of the Poor*. Washington DC: World Resources Institute.

York, Richard. 2006. "Ecological Paradoxes: William Stanley Jevons and the Paperless Office." *Human Ecology Review* 13:143–147.

———. 2008. "De-Carbonization in Former Soviet Republics, 1992–2000: The Ecological Consequences of De-Modernization." *Social Problems* 55: 370–390.

York, Richard, and Eugene A. Rosa. 2003. "Key Challenges to Ecological Modernization Theory: Institutional Efficacy, Case Study Evidence, Units of Analysis, and the Pace of Eco-efficiency." *Organization & Environment* 16(3): 273–288.

———. 2006. "Emissions of Sulfur Dioxide and Nitrogen Oxides in the Modern World-System." Pp. 119–132 in *Globalization and the Environment,* edited by Andrew Jorgenson and Edward Kick. Netherlands: Brill.

York, Richard, Eugene Rosa, and Thomas Dietz. 2003. "Footprints on the Earth: The Environmental Consequences of Modernity." *American Sociological Review* 68: 279–300.

8

ISLAM, IMMIGRATION, LAÏCITÉ, AND *LEITKULTUR*

Bahar Davary

"The treatment of aliens, foreigners, and others in our midst is a crucial test case for the moral conscience as well as political reflexivity of liberal democracies ... the lines separating we and you, us and them, more often than not rest on unexamined prejudices, ancient battles, historical injustices, and sheer administrative fiat."[1]

The dawn of the new millennium was to witness a world with neither boundaries nor frontiers. The triumph of capitalism and its declaration as the only remaining legitimate ideology was assumed to bring about the mental liberation of humanity and the end of history.[2] This making of the world as one homogeneous whole by swallowing the so-called "elixir of liberal capitalism" has now long been considered a premature euphoria.[3] The world of the twenty-first century remains divided and burdened by violence, war, and instability, and by cultural and ethnic hierarchies, as well as the perceived superiority of the West over the rest. The meaning and end of globalization remain unclear. Is the end of globalization greater cultural interaction among people leading to understanding and harmonious relation, or is it to become a means of further establishing Western secular values—often considered as the "default" values—for every nation and every society?

The contemporary rhetoric—with its heavy focus on terrorism, drug trafficking, and national security—provides an opportune distraction from the prevalent underlying cultural and racial superiority and inferiority complexes that continue to shape perceptions on issues of citizenship, political and civil rights, as well as immigration rights, and the much broader concepts of belonging and identity.[4]

This chapter will focus on the question of whether or not the progress of a civilization depends on creating racial, national, linguistic, or religious homogeneity, as some states and strategists suggest. Does racial and cultural homogeneity ensure progress? Does that mean that multiculturalism and the cultural autonomy of various ethnic, linguistic, and religious groups within a nation are a threat to a civilization's stability or prosperity?

In her book *The Origins of Totalitarianism* (1951) Hannah Arendt wrote: "something much more fundamental than freedom and justice, which are rights of citizens, is at stake when belonging to a community into which one is born is no longer a matter of course and not belonging no longer a matter of choice ... we become aware of the existence of a right to have rights. . . . The right of every individual to belong to humanity, should be guaranteed by humanity itself."[5] Arendt concludes that "It is by no means certain whether this is possible."[6]

A hundred years prior to Arendt's writing, in the early nineteenth century, the French aristocrat Joseph Arthur Comte de Gobineau developed the racialist theory in his book *On the Inequality of the Human Race* (1853–1855). The rise of nationalism in Europe in the nineteenth century was concurrent with the establishment of the concepts of race and nation as fundamental necessities in understanding of human societies and their development. This was especially prominent in the work of Gobineau, who first articulated the widely accepted discourse on race in France.[7] According to Gobineau, the world consists of races that are unequal (like various breeds of dogs) and antagonistic towards one another. For him, characteristics of race are inherent, hereditary, and permanent. Every race entails its psychological, physical, and intellectual characteristics.[8] He declares the Aryan race as the most excellent because it is the most well-shaped, the most beautiful, and the most capable of creating civilization. In his view, civilization is associated with race.[9]

Arendt astutely observes in her "Race-Thinking Before Racism" that Gobineau's opinion was already widely accepted among the French nobility. He simply articulated the accepted racialist opinion into a full-fledged historical doctrine while "claiming to have detected the secret law of the fall of civilization."[10] He defined race as a people with common origin, common blood, common identity, and the ability or inability to create civilization. Civilization is, according to Gobineau, a product of a specific race and the expression of its genius. Hence civilizations are naturally antagonistic because races are antagonistic towards each other. Therefore, their combination results in degeneration. He writes: "civilization is incommunicable, not only to savages, but also to more enlightened nations. This is shown by the efforts of French good will and colonization in the ancient kingdom of Algiers at the present day, as well as the experience of the English in India, and the Dutch in Java."[11]

What Comte de Gobineau called the good will of civilizing in Algiers is summed up quite differently by Frantz Fanon. He writes: "It is not easy to conduct, with a minimum of errors, the struggle of a people, sorely tried by a hundred and thirty years of domination, against an enemy as determined and as ferocious as French colonialism."[12] The conquest of Algeria, which began in 1830, was a conquest but even more so a deformation of the social order.[13] He adds that France's civilizing mission in North Africa and especially in Algeria produced "the most perfidious case of depersonalization in history, a case of cultural asphyxia."[14]

The central goal of some contemporary political theories with striking similarities to the views of Gobineau is no longer to only ensure racial purity but to preserve cultural, religious, and linguistic purity. In this new form of racialism, cultural and ethnic differences and group boundaries are perceived to be unbridgeable and insurmountable. As in other racist ideologies, in order to establish and inflate the differences between people, negative values are attributed to some traits and positive values to others. The same method used historically as a means to justify the creation of racial, ethnic, and cultural hierarchies is applied today. One culture is assumed to be superior to another. What follows is justification of the discriminatory treatment of the presumed "inferior."[15] This new racism has replaced and/or infused the idea of "racial difference" with that of "cultural difference." The minority groups who, simply by the nature of their race, religion, culture, language, or national origin, are considered to be "inferior" are demanded, required, and/or encouraged to assimilate into the cultural norm. In these cases, assimilation is perceived as desirable "for their own good," but it is also perceived as not attainable.[16]

Following Bernard Lewis's coining the phrase, "clash of civilizations," Samuel Huntington described cultures as mutually exclusive and incompatible and therefore at the brink of conflict. His aim is the sustenance of cultural purity.[17] The essential problem with any form of purism, be it ethnic, linguistic, religious, or national, is that it is a myth which is disconnected from reality. Huntington defines the core component of US identity in terms of race, ethnicity, culture, and religion. He looks to the seventeenth- and eighteenth-century Americans to find his ideal society. He concedes that the early immigrants to America, the pilgrims, were religiously, ethnically, and linguistically the same as the British. How could one make the assertion that American identity is centered around Protestantism, whiteness, or the English language? If these are the essential, core components of the American identity, why did the colonies revolt against the British (with whom they shared all of those traits)? Why gain independence from the British? There must be something else upon which the early American settlers based their identity. And surely enough, many famous figures of the revolution failed to fit Huntington's strict definition of American (eight of the fifty-six signatories of the Declaration of Independence having been foreign born; from Britain, Ireland, Scotland, and Wales).

Huntington fears that the "persistent inflow of Hispanic immigrants ... [will] divide the United States into two peoples, two cultures, and two languages."[18] His justification for seeing Hispanic immigrants as a threat is grounded in his claim that "Mexicans and Latinos have not assimilated into mainstream US culture, forming instead their own political and linguistic enclaves ... and rejecting the Anglo-Protestant values that built the American dream."[19] This fear bears an uncanny resemblance to those of many right-wing politicians in France who claim that Muslim immigrants are not assimilating. I will come back to this point later in this chapter.

Huntington sees a threat in "the popularity of the doctrines of multiculturalism and diversity," and believes that it will lead to "the rise of group identities based on race, ethnicity, and gender over national identity."[20] It is interesting, however, that he himself defines national identity along racial, ethnic, and religious lines by emphasizing the role of Anglo Protestants in establishing the United States and explicitly favoring them as the "original" Americans. His emphasis on national identity is, in reality, defined by perceptions of race and ethnicity, rather than values and ideas.

Some consider his views to be unabashedly racist and xenophobic, pointing to his shoddy research, questionable analysis, and noticeable leaps in logic, as well as in hermeneutics and methodology.[21] Others praise him as one who has paid no court to fashion or political correctness and see at the core of his worldview an old-fashioned patriotism.[22] In expressing his fear of what he calls the "Americano dream," he can be counted in the good company of the founding fathers such as Benjamin Franklin, who once said: "I have great misgivings about these immigrants because of their clannishness, their little knowledge of English, their Press, and the increasing need of interpreters. I suppose in a few years [interpreters] will also be needed in the [congress] to tell one half of our legislators what the other half say."[23] However, Franklin was not referring to Mexicans (who had yet to establish themselves as a major immigrant demographic in the United States), but to Germans. Huntington reiterates what many white nativists before him had expressed, the difference being that past nativists' criticisms were directed toward other whites. Nineteenth-century nativists, who were suspicious of Catholic immigrants, the Germans and Irish, had similar fears. Again, it was the young Benjamin Franklin who had said that those immigrants were "oozing slowly but ceaselessly out of central Europe,"[24] querying as to why "Pennsylvania, founded by the English" should "become a Colony of *Aliens,* who will shortly be so numerous as to Germanize us instead of us Anglifying them, and will never adopt our Language."[25] What Huntington adds to this nativist phobia are the ethnicity, race, and religion factors. In domestic policy, he strategizes immigration policy, while in international affairs he becomes the strategist of a clash in which Islam and the West become the contenders.

In response to Huntington's flawed dichotomy, Barbara Ehrenreich creatively writes: "In a world that contains Christian Wahabists like Ashcroft and Islamic Calvinists like Bin Laden," it makes little sense to talk about culturally monolithic civilizations such as "Islam" and the "West." That is because "there are no clear-cut, and certainly no temperamentally homogeneous, civilizations to do the clashing."[26] Every civilization has within it many opposing worldviews and ideologies. Communities and cultures interact both in subtle and in explicit ways and are therefore constantly evolving. These interactions and influences bring about changes in the respective communities' languages, customs, and religious traditions and rituals. To accept these changes is not a pre-deterministic pessimism but a realistic acceptance of social and cultural evolution, transformation, continuity, and change.

Like Gobineau, Huntington did not bring about a new idea: he simply presented the prevalent opinion as a strategy. The strategist of the 'clash of civilizations' defines the core component of US identity in terms of race, ethnicity, culture, and religion, and looks to the seventeenth and eighteenth century Americans to find his ideal society. Huntington's fear is that the "persistent inflow of Hispanic immigrants ... [will] divide the United States into two peoples, two cultures, and two languages."[27] Huntington's justification in seeing Hispanic immigrants as a threat is grounded in his claim that, "Mexicans and Latinos have not assimilated into mainstream US culture, forming instead their own political and linguistic enclaves ... and rejecting the Anglo-Protestant values that built the American dream."[28]

In Europe, this same fear is expressed in the policies of the right-wing politicians, who are concerned that the Muslim immigrants are not assimilating. In this case the linkage between all Muslims despite their nationalities shape some of the debate against Muslims who are "in" but not "of" Europe.[29]

According to the 2004 figures of the National Institute for Statistics and Economic Studies, the French government estimates the Muslim population to be five or six million (8–10 percent of the total population). This is the largest Muslim population in Western Europe. About 70 percent of these people are of North African ancestry, mainly from the former French colonies and protectorates of Algeria, Morocco, and Tunisia.[30] In Germany, the Federal Ministry of the Interior estimates the Muslim population to be about 3 million (3.6 percent of the population). The majority of the Muslim population of Germany is Turkish.[31]

Large waves of immigration to Europe began in the late nineteenth century, when Germany, France, and England began imports of labor that opened and welcomed the entry of guest workers. During World War II, laborers were brought in from the then colonies as in the case of France. After the war things changed, with many of these workers who were now French citizens remaining in France with their families.[32] The state still assumed these workers were temporary (and disposable) and housed them in tenements in poor suburbs isolated from the French mainstream. At the end of the Algerian War of independence, the French colonists and soldiers returned home bitter from the defeat. Along with them, many Algerians migrated to escape the aftermath of the bloody war, loss of jobs, and the uncertainties of the newly independent Algeria. The loss of Algeria was followed by a recession and scarcity of jobs in France. Algerian workers in France were viewed not only as colonial subjects but were also charged with taking jobs away from the French. The issue of assimilation of the colonized Algerians, according to Mohammed Arkoun, started far earlier in the 1930s when the third Republic launched the idea of assimilation and integration of the "indigenes" Algerians in the political space.[33] Previously, according to Adolphe Cremieux's decree, Algerian Jews were given collective French citizenship.[34] For the rest of Algerian communities it was World War II that marked the efforts to integrate them in the Republic.[35]

In Germany, immigration trends were similar but smaller in numbers. Banning Islamic groups continues to be relatively uncontroversial, and fear of visibly Muslim men is often legitimized and goes unexamined, in the name of constitutional patriotism. The threat of the visibly Muslim woman with her headscarf is even stronger than that of a Muslim man.[36] Among the main principles in the debates about assimilating immigrants, especially practicing Muslims and "traditional Turks," is a renewed sense of German identity and what constitute German-ness.[37] The concept of *leitkultur,* defined as the dominant culture or the guiding culture, is the leading principle for decisions regarding immigrant integration. On October 18, 2000, Freidrich Merz, the leader of CDU parliamentary group, proposed in Bundestag that immigrants who want to live in Germany permanently must adopt the language and *leitkultur von Deutschland.* There are other German politicians of course who have denounced the very idea of asserting Germanness as an identity because of its association with Germany's traumatic past.[38] For the supporters of *leitkultur,* however, it is only natural to propose and accept that the process of citizenship entails what is called "the Muslim Test." The purpose of this test is to make sure that would-be citizens will defend the constitution and will accept Germany's democratic values.[39]

Katherine Pratt Ewing states that: "[I]n addition to political questions that probe attitudes toward Israel, Jews, and terrorists acts, a number of the questions focus on the private domain of gender and family relations."[40] Sampling the questionnaire, Ewing reveals that the test assumes a gender relationship in which the rights of women are violated, focusing on the most extreme manifestation of Turkish practice taken as normative, juxtaposed with the ideals of a democratic society, which are also read as normative.[41] Although within a month a motion was introduced to stop the implementation of such a test and despite the condemnation of most politicians, the ban failed.[42]

The *leitkultur* of Germany is the *laïcité,* of France, that is, the sacred indivisible, secular Republic. Throughout Western Europe, the xenophobic rhetoric of the extreme right is "increasingly anti-Islamic rather than simply anti-immigrant."[43] Much like Huntington targets the Hispanic immigrants, many in Europe target Muslim immigrants. Fetzer and Soper's research data supports this observation, indicating that Martiniquais Catholics, who have very dark skin and are a racial minority in France, "are more free to practice their religion and probably encounter slightly less public hostility than lighter-skinned Maghrebins Muslims."[44]

The disaffected Arab immigrants often referred to as the *Beurs*[45] marched across France in 1983, a march that was modeled on a 1963 demonstration led by Dr. King.[46] They demanded equal rights, hoping that they would achieve what the Polish and the Italians have achieved before them, that is, citizenship. Instead, they were beaten, and two were killed. The standard immigration story did not occur, mainly due to the difference between the French natives and the "new strangers," who were not only visibly different, but also were Muslims.[47]

Strict and militant *laïcité* to which the French system subscribes is hostile to religion in general and to Islam in particular. In the case of Muslims, religion becomes the basis for legitimacy of discrimination against them. *Laïcité* suggests that the state can only protect the private expressions of religion, implying the legitimacy of the state in banning the *hijab* in public schools for its supposed violation of French-style church-state separation. This issue is neither a struggle between tradition and modernity, nor about the separation of church and state; it is fueled by postcolonial guilt, fear, racism, and nationalism.[48] One of the main disadvantages of French Muslims is that they do not have a prominent Muslim authority. Not a single member of the National Assembly is a Muslim, and up until 2005 neither were any of the *ministres* followers of Islam.[49] Azouz Begag became France's first cabinet minister of North African origin in June 2005. He insists on the need to understand the roots of the social and ethnic tensions leading to disturbances.[50] Quite differently, Hanifa Cherifi, the most visible Muslim in the French government, is known as the "*hijab* czar." Cherifi's main responsibility is to convince French Muslim girls not to wear the *hijab* in public. "For most practicing Muslims, then, she is far from a hero."[51] Integration of an immigrant Muslim—second and third generations—means full submission to and adoption of Western secular values. That is, as Tariq Ramadan has pointed out, to be "Muslim without Islam."[52] To be "too much" of a Muslim means not to be integrated into the Western way of life and its values. The claim is that *laïcité* will remove the differences so that the nation can emerge.[53] According to Fetzer and Soper, "this reading of *laïcité* is disastrous for Muslim integration in France." What these *laicards* breed is to "propel already disaffected and ghettoized communities further from the political mainstream and into the arms of radical Islamists."[54]

The reality of transnational migration and movement of peoples across the state borders brings about the question of changing patterns of solidarity and national, ethnic, and religious loyalties. What are the boundaries of the globalized political communities? What are the requirements of such political membership? Should citizenship in America, Europe, and elsewhere include the uniformity of religion, language, and culture? Should it require subscription to *laïcité,* the secular culture or the *leitkultur,* the cultural norm? If the response to the latter two questions is affirmative it entails ethnic and cultural amnesia. It implies that the presence of cultural, religious, and/or racial minorities is a threat to the sustainability of a community. It assumes that the communal and cultural breakdown of a country is the indispensable result of defending the rights of minorities. And finally, it can be deduced that the holders of these views find it necessary to deny the rights of minorities in order to ensure the vitality of a unified tradition.[55] This ideology overlooks the complexity of group identities and religious, ethnic, and linguistic loyalties. It would be interesting to look at a work which is considered a classic by both Muslim and Western non-Muslim scholars, a work composed seven centuries ago on the rise and fall of civilizations.

Fourteenth-century Arab historian Ibn Khaldun (born Tunis 1332; died Cairo 1406), the forerunner of modern historiography and economics, has been described as a man who took "diplomacy for his profession and the world for his province."[56] Often known as a precursor to Western figures such as Machiavelli, Bodin, Gibbon, Montesquieu, Herder, W. James, and Max Weber, Khaldun was first and foremost a theologian[57] and philosopher for whom metaphysics was the noblest of all sciences.[58]

His *Muqaddimah,* written in 1377, was meant to be a preface to his book on world history. Instead, it became the introduction of a new science and the scientific method, and a detailed and objective theory of the state, where he analyzed the political, social, and economic factors underlying the establishment of political units and the evolution of the state.[59]

One of the central concepts in Khaldun's theory of human society is the concept of '*asabiyya, (asab,* to bind together) or social cohesion, group solidarity. It is a social cohesion that spontaneously arises in tribes and other small kinship groups and can be intensified and strengthened by religious ideology. It is '*asabiyya,* which marks the greatness or the weakness of civilizations. '*Asabiyya,* in Ibn Khaldun's view, was not invested in blood and genes. Differences among people were not innate, but rather a product of climate, diet, and social conditions. Ibn Khaldun's interpretation of history bears "a striking disregard to established prejudices."[60] The comment that his theories are parallel to those of Comte de Gobineau reveals a misunderstanding, which is rooted in mistranslation of Ibn Khaldun's work.

Abdelmajid Hannoum, in his "Translation and the Colonial Imaginary," discusses the language of the translators and the transformation of

Ibn Khaldun's text into a colonial narrative.[61] In the colonial narrative re-written by translators, the *Muqaddimah* of Ibn Khaldun is transformed into "the history of two races: a conqueror race coming from the Orient, and a conquered one, indigenous to North Africa." They are described as not only two races but two nations as well. This explanation is not in tune with Khaldun's understanding of the two important terms. It creates a racialist theory, one that does not exist in the original work, and imposes a meaning other than the text's own. With the prevalence of Gobineau's racialist theories of the nineteenth century, it is not surprising that de Slane's translation of Ibn Khaldun carried with it the colonial semantics of the terms "race" and "nation." He translated Ibn Khaldun's terms *jil* (generation), *ummah* (community), and *tabaqa* (class) interchangeably as race and nation. Ibn Khaldun does believe that religion magnifies *'asabiyya*, but religious sentiment cannot bring about change unless it is based on *'asabiyya*.[62]

Within the global village of the twenty-first century, religion remains a strong line of demarcation and separation. Potentially, it can become a powerful symbol of unity and struggle for what Arendt calls: "the right of every individual to belong to humanity," a right that "should be guaranteed by humanity itself."

Diana Eck speaks in her book *A New Religious America* about an astonishing new reality, that is, how a "Christian Country" has now become the world's most religiously diverse nation.[63] Eck is not alone in celebrating the present time as an age of multiculturalism. Yet we are constantly reminded by daily news and current events that this religious and cultural pluralism is threatened by imperial projects that rely not only on re-Christianization of the nation, but also on the demonization of Islam.[64] This polarization has made it difficult for Muslims to use religion in their pursuit of immigrant civil rights.[65]

By contrast, Christian and Jewish clergy exercise their religious rituals and use their symbols more freely to promote the labor rights of Latino immigrant workers, especially in the service industries. Many of them are influenced by the strategies and experiences of the civil rights movement and of César Chávez and the United Farm Workers of America and have rich sources of religious symbolism, ethics, and ritual, and they do not hesitate to invoke those.[66] Christian ethics in general, Catholic social thought, and the Catholic Bishops' Pastoral letter "Economic Justice for All" in particular, aid those who are convinced that a Christian society is a society based on justice for all. Community is indeed central to the concept of a Trinitarian God and the focus of Christian belief. Bishop Nicholas DiMarzio has clearly stated the consistent teaching of the Church on immigration. He sums it up as "true welcoming." He explains that people have the right to migrate to sustain their lives and families, that a country has a right to regulate its borders and control immigration, and that the country must regulate its borders with justice and mercy.[67] This helps those involved both at an individual level and the communal level. They come to social activism motivated by their religious beliefs, and they constantly reassure and reassert it to one another in their meetings and forums.[68] How can Muslims contribute to this struggle for justice? What is their narrative?

The story of Islam begins about fourteen hundred years ago with about 200 people: men, women, and children and their migration, the *hijra.* These early Muslims were persecuted in their own city of Mecca, so they left their homeland and migrated to what was shortly after called *Medinat-u Nabi,* the City of the Prophet. Delegations from the conflicting tribes had invited Muhammad, who was known for his aptitude in conflict resolution, to live amongst them with his people and bring an end to their endless quarrels. So important is this migration, *hijra,* that it marks the beginning of the Muslim calendar. The revelation of the Qur'an and the birth of its Prophet, revered as he is, are not the markers of Islamic history, but migration is.[69] It was the *hijra* that led to the creation of the *umma,* the Islamic community and the most significant expression of Islamic solidarity—a nation without boundary, a community constituted on the brotherhood and sisterhood of its members, under God. Hasan Hanafi, in his definition of civil society, speaks of the *umma* as a unit in which all human beings are its ontological members.[70] This does not negate the existence of multiple *umam* (moral communities), yet they are within the framework of Islamic morality which, "upholds the essential similarities that link all human beings with mutual obligations of respect and decent behavior."[71] "The growing de-territorialization of Islam," as Olivier Roy has pointed out, has led to the political reformulation of an imaginary *umma,* with *Al-Qaeda* claiming to be the vanguard of the *umma.*[72]

Judaism, Christianity, and Islam are examples of the great monotheistic traditions that form trans-national and trans-ethnic communities. They embrace diversity "in the name of a single-commanding God, who bears a single message for a humanity that is one in Heaven's sight."[73] The meaning of the word monotheistic, "*tawhidi*" from the Islamic viewpoint, can help in understanding of the contribution of Abrahamic values for our societies. Belief in the unity of God has a central place in Islam. This refers to the understanding that there is no "other" before God. Muslim scholars have made the analogy between the relation between God and the universe and likened it to the relation between an author and her text. Just as every word has the same relation with its author and there is no priority between the first word and the last, Islamic theological tradition "does not allow the notion of 'otherness' within its basic horizon of faith."[74] Clearly, Islamic thought accepts difference between different religions, and between belief and disbelief. The Qur'an advises Muslims to get to know different people and societies (Qur'an: 49:13). This "difference," however, should not be confused with the notion of "other" as delineated by modern Western philosophies. The difference between the two lies in the fact that, while Islamic thought understands "difference" between human beings based purely on their actions (*'amal*), modern philosophies of "other" base their theories on ontological presuppositions.[75] An understanding of the *umma* as the community of all humans, all beings, with an urge to understanding of our differences in practice would lead us to a borderless compassionate world. The *umma* is not a static and inert unit, but an entity in the making.

In conclusion, I am not endorsing religious, ethnic, or cultural Esperanto, but simply calling for attentiveness to the complex, multifaceted characters of cultural, religious, ethnic, and national identity, both individual and collective, and to the interplay among these characteristics of identity. It is not only a call for just distribution of resources but for equal membership. Humanity cannot thrive if Hispanic, Muslim, Christian, African, Asian, or other immigrants undergo a cultural, linguistic, religious, and ethno-historical amnesia. We cannot reach a more authentic self if we cut off part of ourselves. Identity with its many aspects can neither be reduced to one single affiliation nor can it be compartmentalized.[76] Otherwise, as Richard Rodriguez pointed in his autobiography, they will find themselves strangers to their parents, and a stranger to their memory of themselves.[77] Cultural-ethnic-linguistic and religious amnesia do not produce better individuals nor a better society, but realization of past unjust practices, and an end to the present wrongful stereotypes and perceptions, followed by forgiveness, can help lead the way to harmonious multicultural societies. As Michael Henderson has pointed out, "national pride" and "national shame" regarding historical events must coexist. When there is no room for both, there can be no national soul.[78]

Finally, in the world of the twenty-first century, if our faith is to lead us to salvation and liberation, it cannot speak in one language and with the symbols of one culture. It cannot be an isolated affair, but it must be a community enterprise. It is *en cojunto,* sharing and togetherness, that ultimately lead us to salvation. This statement is not an alteration of the Christian or Islamic orthodoxy, but an affirmation of the significance of orthopraxy.

Notes

1. Carl Schmitt, *The Crisis of Parliamentary Democracy,* trans. by Ellen Kennedy (Cambridge, MA: MIT Press, [1923] 1985). Quoted in Seyla Benhabib, *The Rights of Others: Aliens, Residents, and Citizens* (UK: Cambridge University Press, 2004), 178.

2. Francis Fukuyama, *The End of History and the Last Man* (New York: Perennial, 2002.)

3. Mehrzad Boroujerdi, "Iranian Islam and the Faustian Bargain of Western Modernity," *Journal of Peace Research,* Vol. 34, No. 1. 1997, 1–5.

4. Michael Blake and Mathias Risse's study is interesting. They suggest not a redistribution of the world's territory but contend that: "the collective ownership status of the earth may limit acceptable regimes of property, including regimes of immigration." Michael Blake and Mathias Risse, "Immigration and Original Ownership of the Earth," *Notre Dame Journal of Law, Ethics, and Public Policy,* vol. 23, Issue No. 1, 2009. 133–165.

5. Hannah Arendt, *The Origins of Totalitarianism* (New York: Harcourt, Brace and Jovanovich, [1951] 1968), 296–297.

6. Ibid., 297.

7. Abdelmajid Hannoum, " Translation and the Colonial Imaginary: Ibn Khaldun Orientalist" in *History and Theory,* Vol. 42, No. 1 (February 2003), 73.

8. Gobineau, *Essai sur l'inégalité des races humaine,* trans. *Inequality of Human Races,* by Adrian Collins (New York: H. Fertig, 1967), 133.

9. Ibid.

10. Hannah Arendt, "Race-Thinking Before Racism," *Review of Politics,* 6 (January 1944), 47.

11. Gobineau, 171.

12. Frantz Fanon, *A Dying Colonialism* (London: Writers and Readers, 1980), 26.

13. Malek Alloula, *The Colonial Harem* (Minnesota: University of Minnesota Press, 1986), viii.

14. Alloula, xvii–xviii.

15. See Martin Sheinin and Reetta Toivanen, eds., *Rethinking Non-Discrimination and Minority Rights* (German Institute for Human Rights, Berlin, 2004), 166.

16. As Marjorie Proctor-Smith has pointed out, the ordering of relationships into patterns of dominance and submission is essential to maintenance of structures of patriarchy, racism, classism, and ageism. She writes: "The corollary is that those less valued are expected to submit to "their betters." By applying punitive and restrictive means of control, both overt and subtle, the dominant person or group is empowered to extract submission from others. In the case of women, children, and people of color, Procter-Smith notes that the dominant structure assumes "that it is in their nature to submit, even to desire it—they are "natural slaves." See Marjorie Proctor-Smith, *In Her Own Rite: Constructing Feminist Liturgical Tradition* (Nashville: Abingdon Press, 1990), 18.

17. See Timo Makkonen, *Identity, Difference and Otherness: The Concepts of People, Indigenous People and Minority in International Law* (Helsinki: Eric Castren Institute Research Reports 7/2000, Helsinki University Press, 2000).

18. Samuel Huntington, "The Hispanic Challenge," http://www.foreignpolicy.com/story/cms.php?story_id=2495.

19. Ibid.

20. Ibid.

21. See Mehrzad Boroujerdi, "Iranian Islam and the Faustian Bargain of Western Modernity" *Journal of Peace Research,* Vol. 34, No. 1. 1997, 1–5. Also see Raul Yzaguirre, "Huntington and Hispanics," *Foreign Policy,* No.142 (May-June, 2004), 4. See also Oliver Roy's work on the conundrum of clash and dialogue. Roy's critique of Huntington is based on the fact that Huntington defines cultures as objects with "a set of permanent and objective patterns that determine the collective behaviour of actors." Olivier Roy, *Globalized Islam: The Search for a New Ummah* (New York: Columbia University Press, 2004), 328–329.

22. Fouad Ajami, "Huntington and Hispanics" *Foreign Policy,* No. 142 (May-June 2004), 8.

23. http://query.nytimes.com/mem/archivefree/pdf?_r=2&res=9D06E3DD1E30E13ABC 4A52DFB6678382609EDE.

24. Ibid.

25. Ibid.

26. Barbara Ehrenreich, "Christian Wahabists" in *Nothing Sacred: Women Respond to Religious Fundamentalism and Terror,* ed. by Betsy Reed (New York: Thunder's Mouth Press/Nation Books, 2002), 257.

27. Samuel Huntington, "The Hispanic Challenge," http://www.foreignpolicy.com/story/cms.php?story_id=2495.

28. Ibid.

29. Talal Asad, *Formations of the Secular: Christianity, Islam, Modernity. Cultural Memory in the Present* (Stanford: Stanford University Press, 2003) 166.

30. www.insee.fr/en/ffc/docs_ffc/cs117e.pdf.

31. http://www.zuwanderung.de/cln_115/nn_1070222/EN/ImmigrationPast/Statistics/ statistics_node.html?_nnn=true.

32. See Jacques Simon, *L'immigration Algerienne en France: De 1962 a Nos Jours* (Paris: L'Harmattan, 2002).

33. Mohammed Arkoun, "Les Reponse A l'immigration en Europe: Integration, Assimilation, Intercreative" in *Traduccion, Emigracion y Culturas,* coordinadores, Miguel Hernando de Larramendi and Juan Pablo Arias (Cuenca: Editiones de la Universidad de Castilla-La Mancha, 1999), 17.

34. The 1870 *Décret Crémieux* secured full citizenship for the Jews in French-ruled Algeria. It also set in motion an anti-Jewish countermovement among the non-Jewish French colons in Algeria.

35. Mohammed Arkoun, 17.

36. Katherine Pratt Ewing, *Stolen Honor: Stigmatizing Muslim Men in Berlin* (Stanford, California: Stanford University Press, 2008), 211.

37. Ibid.

38. Ibid.

39. Ibid., 181.

40. Ibid., 182.

41. Ibid., 183.

42. Charles Hawley, "A German State Quizzes Muslim Immigrants on Jews, Gays and Swim Lessons." Spiegel Online, January 31. http://www.spiegel.de/international/0,1518,397482,00 .html.

43. Joel S. Fetzer and J. Christopher Soper, *Muslims and the State in Britain, France, and Germany* (Cambridge University Press, 2005), xi.

44. Fetzer and Soper, 21.

45. The term *beur* is, according to the rules of *verlan* (French slang), the reversal of the word *arabe*. It refers to second-generation maghrebis. This term is one among almost "thirty different appellations reflecting the unease of the republic vis-à-vis 'citizens' who are not like 'us.'" Terms such as *jeunes des banlieues* (ghetto youths), *jeunes des quartiers* (guys in the 'hood), *jeunes de ZEPS* (problem school youths), are a few among others. See Azouz Begag, *Ethnicity and Equality: France in the Balance,* trans. by Alec G. Hargreaves (Lincoln and London: University of Nebraska Press), 19–21.

46. Azouz Begag, 17.

47. John Bowen, *Why the French Don't Like Headscarves: Islam, The State, and Public Space,* (Princeton: Princeton University Press, 2007), 66–67.

48. Joan Wallach Scott, *Politics of the Veil* (Princeton and Oxford: Princeton University Press, 2007).

49. Fetzer and Soper, 93.

50. Azouz Begag, vii.

51. Fetzer and Soper, 93.

52. Tariq Ramadan, *To Be a European Muslim* (Leicester, UK: Islamic Foundation, 1999), 184–185.

53. From the statement of Ernest Cheniere, principal of a public junior high school in Creil, explaining his decision of suspending three Muslim girls for wearing the *hijab*. See Michel Gonod, "La riposte: Pourquoi ce principal de college s'oppose a l'offensive des religieux." *Paris-Match,* (November 9, 1989), 60–63.

54. Fetzer and Soper, 155.

55. Bahar Davary, "Matter of Veil: A Muslim Response" in *Ethics and World Religions: Cross Cultural Case Studies,"* eds. Regina Wentzel Wolfe and Christine E. Gudorf (Maryknoll, New York: Orbis Books, 1999), 154.

56. Cedric Dover, "The Racial Philosophy of Ibn Khaldun," *Phylon,* 1952, 107.

57. Franz Rosenthal, "The Muqaddimah by Ibn Khaldun," *Philosophy,* Vol. 36, No. 137 (April–July, 1961), 255–256.

58. Antony Black, *The History of Islamic Political Thought: From the Prophet to the Present* (New York: Routledge, 2001), 165.

59. H. A. R. Gibb, "The Islamic Background of Ibn Khaldun's Political Theory," *Bulletin of the School of Oriental Studies,* University of London, Vol. 7, No. 1 (1933), 23–31.

60. Ibid.

61. Abdelmajid Hannoum, "Translation and the Colonial Imaginary: Ibn Khaldun Orientalist," *History and Theory,* Vol. 42, No. 1 (February 2003), 61–81.

62. Antony Black, 173.

63. Diana Eck, *A New Religious America: How a "Christian Country" Has Become the Most Religiously Diverse Nation* (New York: Harper Collins, 2002).

64. Pierrette Hondagneu-Sotelo, *God's Heart Has No Boundaries: How Religious Activists Are Working For Immigrant Rights* (University of California Press, 2008), 174.

65. Mohamed Arkoun questions the fact that religion has come to be associated with issues of immigration in Europe. He writes: "Pourquoi, demandera-t-on, mettre un tel accent sur le religieux des qu'il est question de l'immigration en Europe? Ne doit-on pas donner la priorite a l'insertion politique, economique, culturelle?" Mohamed Arkoun, "Les Reponse a l'immigration en Europe: Integration, Assimilation, Intercreative" in *Traduccion, Emigracion y Culturas,* co-ordinadores, Miguel Hernando de Larramendi and Juan Pablo Arias (Cuenca: Editiones de la Universidad de Cstilla-La Mancha, 1999), 21.

66. Ibid., 175.

67. Nicholas A. DiMarzio, " A Welcoming Church" in *From Strangers to Neighbors: Reflections on the Pastoral Theology of Human Migration* (New York: St. John's University, Vincentian Center for Church and Society, 2004), 19–31.

68. Pierrette Hondagneu-Sotelo, 174.

69. Later theologians and jurists discussed the issue of migration in a binary context, that is, *dar al-harb* (lands of war) to *dar al-Islam* (Lands of peace). Such binary division of the world was, according to some Muslim scholars, created in a situation of hostility initiated by non-Muslim countries towards Muslim countries. Accordingly, they argue, such division no longer exists in a time when Islamic law is not practiced or enforced in Muslim countries and Muslims may have more freedom to practice Islam in non-Muslim countries. Wahbah Al-Zuhayli, *Al-'ilaqat al-duwaliyyah fil-islam muqaranatan bil-qanun al-duwali al-hadith,* 4th edition, Mu'assassat al-rissalah, Beirut, 1989, 195–196.

70. Hasan Hanafi, "Alternative Conceptions of Civil Society: A Reflective Islamic Approach" in *Islamic Political Ethics: Civil Society, Pluralism, and Conflict,* ed. Sohail H. Hashmi (Princeton: Princeton University Press, 2002). 58.

71. Hanafi, 58.

72. Olivier Roy, *Globalized Islam: The Search for a New Ummah* (New York: Columbia University Press, 2004), 47.

73. Miroslov Volf, "Distance and Belonging" in *Abrahamic Faiths, Ethnicity, and Ethnic Conflicts,* ed. Paul Peachey, http://www.crvp.org/book/series01/1-7/chapter_xiv.htm (8.8.27).

74. Burhanettin Tatar, "Our Nation—Can We Grow Together?" Conference paper. n.p.

75. Tatar, 8.

76. Amin Maalouf, *In the Name of Identity: Violence and the Need to Belong,* trans. by Barbara Bray (New York: Penguin Books, 2003), 2–5.

77. Richard Rodriguez, *Hunger and Memory: The Education of Richard Rodriguez* (New York: Bantam Books, 1983), 161.

78. Roy L. Brooks, *Atonement and Forgiveness: A New Model for Black Reparations* (Berkeley: University of California Press, 2004), 154.

9

A CRITICAL VIEW OF WALLERSTEIN'S UTOPISTICS FROM DUSSEL'S TRANSMODERNITY

FROM MONOEPISTEMIC GLOBAL/ IMPERIAL DESIGNS TO PLURI-EPISTEMIC SOLUTIONS

Ramon Grosfoguel

This chapter discusses Immanuel Wallerstein's Utopistics in light of Enrique Dussel's transmodernity. The attempt here is not to throw away Wallerstein's Utopistics, but to radicalize it using Enrique Dussel's transmodernity as a decolonial intervention. The first part is a discussion about Wallerstein's concept of Utopistics in light of his world-system analysis and his prediction of a forthcoming bifurcation towards a new historical system. The second part is a discussion about epistemic racism and Eurocentric fundamentalism. The third part is a critical discussion of Utopistics in light of the critique to epistemic racism and Eurocentric fundamentalism.

Wallerstein's Utopistics

Immanuel Wallerstein (1995; 1998) characterizes the first decades of the twenty-first century as a transitional moment, a moment of bifurcation leading toward the end not only of US hegemony but of the current historical-system. In agreement with Wallerstein, the recent events of the early twenty-first century confirms the first part of this prediction, that is, the fall of the US hegemony. While the end of capitalism as a world-system is yet not confirmed, it is obvious that it is in serious crisis with high probabilities of a terminal crisis (Wallerstein 1995; 1998; 2003). The current historical-system (the capitalist world-system) has lasted more than 500 years. Using the "chaos theory" developed by Nobel Prize–winning chemist Ilya Prigogine and the Brussels school, Wallerstein speaks of a coming period of uncertainty and bifurcation (Wallerstein 1991a). Depending on the success or failure of our social agency and the interventions of anti-systemic social movements at this moment of bifurcation, the transition toward a new historical-system could lead to a better or a worse system than that which presently exists. Nothing will predetermine or guarantee the future. This is a period of uncertainty. There could arise a new historical-system which is more just and egalitarian or one which is more exploitative and oppressive. If Wallerstein (1998) is correct in his analysis of the current historical situation, it is urgent to tackle the problem of our action as collective subjects and rethink our utopias in order to create alternative worlds.

As Wallerstein has demonstrated in his historical sociology, the transition between feudalism and the modern world in Europe did not take place as Marxist and liberal narratives have described: a bourgeois class that emerges in the cities and through reforms or revolutions displaces the feudal aristocracy (Wallerstein 1974; 1979). To the contrary, it was this same feudal aristocracy, which—in search of solutions for the crisis of the old system—created a new historical-system, the "modern/colonial, capitalist/patriarchal, European/Euro-North-American world-system" (Grosfoguel 2006). Wallerstein's provocative thesis is that the new historical-system that emerged toward the end of the fifteenth century, when European colonial expansion has been worse, that is, less egalitarian, more destructive to life (human and non-human), and more discriminatory than the old historical-system that it replaced (Wallerstein 1991b). As was the case with this transition between the old historical-system and the current "modern/colonial, capitalist/patriarchal world-system" at the end of the fifteenth century, today we are confronting a moment of bifurcation. The transnational capitalist elites of the twenty-first century could follow the same strategy of the feudal aristocracy at the end of the fifteenth century and reinvent themselves by creating a new historical-system—worse than the one we live in—in order to preserve their privileges. They enjoy a degree of wealth and military power never before seen in any other historical-system in human history. As a result, Wallerstein emphasizes that the dominant classes on the level of the world-system are not going to hand over their power or renounce their privileges without a struggle. Another possible scenario is that subaltern groups develop a global struggle that will permit the construction of a new or several new and diverse historical-systems that are better than the system in which we find ourselves today.

For Wallerstein, during the long periods of systemic reproduction, historical-systems operate with relative stability despite the cyclical crises that obstruct them and the anti-systemic movements that challenge them. The struggles of anti-systemic movements have very limited possibilities to destroy the historical-system during the long centuries of stable reproduction, although they can modify some mechanisms of reproduction in the long term. It is only during moments of terminal crisis—precisely at the same moment that the crudest expressions of the weakness and crisis of the structural mechanisms that reproduce the system appear—that the actions of collective subjects acquire a decisive importance for the transformation toward a new historical-system. These are the moments of opportunity for social transformation that Wallerstein calls "kairos" or "transformational TimeSpace." They are moments in which, to use Wallerstein's expression, the free-will factor of groups and individuals have the potential to create an impact at a world-scale. It is precisely in these periods of terminal systemic crisis that the struggles of anti-systemic movements can make a difference in the creation of a new historical-system that is more just and egalitarian than the previous one. Hence the importance that Wallerstein ascribes to Utopistics during this moment of bifurcation.

Wallerstein insists that the creation of a program toward a new and alternative historical-system could never be the result of the ideas of an individual, but that instead it must necessarily result from a global debate. This is why he limits himself to suggesting some elements that he considers indispensable to take into consideration in this debate, without intending to give an exhaustive or final response to the matter. The World Social Forum is one of those spaces that Wallerstein identifies as fundamental for this debate. For Wallerstein, the global debate centers on the "spirit of Porto Alegre" versus the "spirit of Davos." The former is the spirit of the anti-systemic social movements, while the latter is the spirit of the dominant privileged classes in the world-system.

For Wallerstein, one of the central elements of this debate is to think about a "substantive rationality" which, while setting out from the existing world-system, can conceive the potential for a new, alternative historical-system that will be more egalitarian, more just, and more democratic than the present system. This is why he insists that the task is not to create utopias but rather

Utopistics. Utopias, for Wallerstein, are "dreams of heaven that could never exist on the earth" (Wallerstein 1998, 1). Utopistics, on the other hand,

> ... is the serious assessment of historical alternatives, the exercise of our judgment as to the substantive rationality of alternative possible historical systems. It is the sober, rational, and realistic evaluation of human social systems, the constraints of what they can be, and the zones open to human creativity. Not the face of the perfect (and inevitable) future, but the face of an alternative, credibly better, and historically possible (but far from certain) future. It is thus an exercise simultaneously in science, in politics, and in morality. (Ibid., 1–2)

After a critical evaluation of the disasters of the twentieth-century socialist experience (Wallerstein 1995; 1998, 66–69), Wallerstein proposes—as one of the principal elements for a global debate toward the creation of a new and alternative historical-system—that instead of the "ceaseless and endless accumulation of capital," the primary logic of social and political decisions should be to create structures which give primacy to the maximizing of the quality of life for everyone at the same time, and the limitation of forms of collective violence, so that everyone has the broadest space for individual options and decisions insofar as these do not threaten the survival and the equal rights of others. The idea would be to extend to all humanity—not merely to a minority, defined in racial terms as Euro-descended/white or in gender terms as men, which is what occurs in historical capitalism (see Wallerstein 1983)—the liberal ideals of democracy, equality, and individual, civil, and social rights within an egalitarian system, without labor exploitation or classist/racist/sexist domination, that provides radical institutional forms for democratic decision-making beyond the traditional, bourgeois, liberal forms of democracy. To be able to accomplish this, it would be necessary to create a historical system in which everyone feels satisfied with the work they do, in which, in the case of an unexpected need, assistance would be socially available for all, and in which the resources of the biosphere would be sufficiently preserved so that there would be no losses between the present and future generations and no exploitation from one generation to the next. For this, it would be absolutely necessary to change the relations of power in production, and as a result, to transform work incentives from the primacy of material remuneration toward the primacy of a combination of moral and honor incentives and, above all, the control over labor time. Control over labor time, so that people will be more free in terms of time for living, is something that Wallerstein emphasizes as a central element in the debate regarding the shape of a new, alternative historical-system. Against the formal capitalist rationality of the present, for Wallerstein, efficiency is not incompatible with structures that are not subordinated to the logic of profit; indeed, there could be even more productive efficiency in structures that use other kinds of incentives and satisfaction in the labor process, such as would fulfill the basic necessities for all on the global level, create more free time, reproduce the biosphere, and enjoy moral/social recognition. So the primary productive structure proposed by Wallerstein for an alternative historical-system beyond historical capitalism would take the form of the creation of decentralized units which would represent the predominant manner of producing within the new system and which would be driven by logics very different from the earning of profits and accumulation of capital. There would need to be a workers' democracy both within these units and between them in order to avoid the transformation of their administrative personnel into a new ruling class.

To summarize, once we dismiss the developmentalist idea that social change centers on the "seizure of power" at the level of the nation-state, and once we understand that states are inserted within broader structures like the international division of labor and the global interstate system—the two central power structures of the current capitalist world-system for Wallerstein—the struggle must be focused on the creation of a new historical system whose spatial-temporal coordinates are broader than nation-states. This means concentrating out struggle on the process that take place below and above nation-states; that is to say, following the Zapatista example, to link local struggles to global ones without making the national struggle or the "seizure of state power" the center of the struggle. This view does not rule out interventions at the level of states and the national level of countries, it simply decenters and deflates the nation-state as the neuralgic center of political intervention for social transformation as was the case with the old anti-systemic movements of the twentieth century. If some anti-systemic movement comes to power in a nation-state, it should not repeat the developmentalist illusion of "socialism in a single country," that is, the illusion that a system can be changed from the administration of a single national state. This illusion was crucial in leading the socialist and national liberation movements to become conservative developmentalist movements, administrators of the nation-state, instead of radical agents for anti-systemic transformation (Wallerstein 1991a; 1995). For Wallerstein, who during the 1970s spoke of creating a world socialist government, today it is necessary to abandon the socialist utopia, which was always rooted in bureaucratic statist ideas. The new, alternative, non-capitalist historical-system cannot center on socialist statism—national or global—that in practice meant during the greater part of the twentieth century the institutionalization of "state capitalisms." If capitalism is a world-system and not a national system, anti-capitalist struggle and the creation of a new, alternative historical-system must equally be carried out as a process on the global scale beyond the borders of nation-states and beyond states themselves (be they national or global). This was an old idea of the anti-systemic movements which was abandoned in the twentieth century alongside Leninist "developmentalism" and Stalinist "socialism in a single country." The new Utopistics must consider the creation of socialized/collective/

democratic forms of administration and management of the production and reproduction of life on the global scale beyond capitalism and socialist statism.

Having discussed Wallerstein's conception of Utopistics, I would like to do a friendly critique to his concept. But before, we need to first have a discussion about epistemic racism and Eurocentric fundamentalism.

Epistemic Racism and Identity Politics

Epistemic racism is one of the most hidden racisms in our "modern/colonial capitalist/patriarchal world-system" (see Grosfoguel 2006). Social, political, and economic racisms are much more visible and recognized than epistemological racism. The latter operates through the privileging of the identitarian ("identity") politics of Western whites male elites; that is, the tradition of thought of Western men (almost never including women) is considered to be the only legitimate form for the production of knowledges and the only one with access to "universality" and "truth." Epistemic racism considers non-Western knowledges to be inferior to Western knowledges. If we look at the canon of thinkers privileged within academic disciplines, we can see that without exception these privileged Western thinkers and theories are above all those of European and Euro-North-American men. This hegemonic "identity politics" is so powerful and so normalized through the discourse of "objectivity" and "neutrality" of the "ego-politics of knowledge" of the human sciences that when we think of "identity politics" we immediately assume as if by "common sense" that we are talking about racialized minorities. In fact, without denying the existence of "identity politics" among sectors of racialized minorities, the hegemonic "identity politics"—that of Eurocentric discourse—uses this identitarian, racist discourse to discard all critical interventions rooted in "other" epistemologies (Maldonado-Torres 2008). The underlying myth of the academy is still the scientist discourse of "objectivity" and "neutrality" which hides the "locus of enunciation," that is, who it is that speaks and from what body and epistemic space within the relations of power (Grosfoguel 2006). Through the myth of the "ego-politics of knowledge" (which in reality always speaks through a white, male body and a Eurocentric geopolitics of knowledge) those critical voices coming from individuals and groups inferiorized and subalternized by this hegemonic epistemic racism are denied. If epistemology has color—as African philosopher Emmanuel Chukwudi Eze (1997) points out so well—then the Eurocentric epistemology that dominates the social sciences also has a color. The construction of the latter as superior and the rest of the world as inferior forms an inherent part of the epistemological racism which prevails in the world-system since more than 500 years ago.

The epistemic privilege of whites was consecrated and normalized through the colonization of the Americas since the end of the fifteenth century. From renaming the world with Christian cosmology (Europe, Africa, Asia, and later, America) and characterizing all non-Christian knowledge as a product of the devil, to assuming in their own European provincialism that it was only within the Greco-Roman tradition, passing through the Renaissance, the Enlightenment, and Western sciences, that "truth" and "universality" are achieved, the epistemic privilege of white, Eurocentric "identity politics" was normalized to the point of invisibility as a hegemonic "identity politics." In this way, all "other" traditions were deemed inferior (characterized in the sixteenth century as "barbarians," in the nineteenth century as "primitives," in the twentieth century as "underdeveloped," and at the beginning of the twenty-first century as "anti-democratic"). Hence inferiorized ethnic/racial groups have always been the objects of attack by the epistemic racism of the West, which argues for inferiority, partiality, and the lack of objectivity in their knowledge-production.

Against this hegemonic "identity politics" that always privileged white, European, Christian, and Western beauty, knowledge, traditions, spiritualities, while inferiorizing and subalternizing the non-white, non-European, non-Christian, and non-Western, those subjects rendered inferior and subalternized by these hegemonic discourses developed their own "identity politics" as a reaction to the racism of the former. This process was necessary as a part of a process of self-valorization in a racist world that renders them inferior and disqualifies their humanity. However, this process of identitarian affirmation has its limits if it leads to fundamentalist proposals that invert the binary terms of the hegemonic white/Eurocentric racism. For example, if what is done is to assume that the subalternized (non-white) ethnic/racial groups are superior and that the dominant (whites) are inferior, we are merely inverting the terms of hegemonic white racism without overcoming its fundamental problem: racism, that is, the rendering of some human beings inferior and the elevation of others to the category of superior on cultural or biological grounds (Grosfoguel 2003). Another example is if we accept—as do some Islamic and Afrocentric fundamentalists—the hegemonic Eurocentric discourse that the European tradition is the only one that is naturally and inherently democratic, whereas the non-European "others" are naturally and inherently authoritarian, denying democratic discourses and forms of democratic institutionality to the non-Western world (which are, of course, distinct from Western liberal democracy), and as a result, supporting political authoritarianism. This is what all Third Worldist fundamentalists do when they accept the Eurocentric premise that the only democratic tradition is the Western one, and therefore assume that democracy does not apply to their "culture" and their "societies," defending monarchic or dictatorial forms of political authority. This merely reproduces an inverted Eurocentrism.

The "Balkanization" that results from these identitarian politics ends up reproducing, in an inverted form, the same essentialism and fundamentalism of the hegemonic Eurocentric discourse. If fundamentalism assumes its own cosmology and epistemology to be superior and the only source of truth, inferiorizing and denying equality to any other, then Eurocentrism is not merely a form of fundamentalism but the hegemonic fundamentalism in the world today. Those Third Worldist fundamentalisms (Afrocentric, Islamist, Indigenist, etc.) that emerge in response to the hegemonic Eurocentric fundamentalism are subordinate forms of that Eurocentric fundamentalism insofar as they leave intact the binary and racial hierarchies of Eurocentric fundamentalism (Grosfoguel 2006). In the world-system today, there lamentably exists a vociferous minority of Afrocentric, Indigenist, Asian-centric, and Islamic fundamentalists who put in question the validity and legitimacy of their claims. But fortunately these groups represent an insignificant minority, although unfortunately white supremacists exaggerate their influence in order to discredit and undermine critical agendas for active anti-racist and anti-Eurocentrist critique.

A foundational basis for contemporary discussions on political Islam and on the so-called "War on Terrorism" is "epistemic racism." Epistemic racism is the inferiorization of non-Western epistemologies and cosmologies to privilege Western epistemology as the superior form of knowledge and as the only source to define human rights, democracy, citizenship, and so forth. This is grounded in the idea that reason and philosophy lies in the West while non-reason lies in the "rest." As Lewis Gordon said:

> The notion that philosophy was a peculiarly European affair logically led to the conclusion that there was (and continues to be) something about European cultures that makes them more conducive to philosophical reflection than others.... The notion of Europeans' intrinsic connection to philosophy is, in other words, circular: it defines them as philosophical in the effort to determine whether they were philosophical.... To conclude that the kinds of intellectual activity that were called philosophical in the past and have joined the fold in the present were thus limited to one group of people, most of whom were artificially lumped together to create false notions of unity and singular identity, requires a model of humanity that does not fit the facts. (Gordon 2008, 6)

Epistemic racism is a foundational and constitutive logic of the modern/colonial world. European humanists and scholars in the nineteenth century such as Ernest Renan " ... argued that Islam was incompatible with science and philosophy. He based his reasoning on the claim that Islam was an essentially Arab religion and that Arabs belong to the Semitic race, which has an 'atomistic' mentality that is incapable of philosophical synthesis ... Renan remained firmly convinced that Semites (meaning Arabs and Jews) did not have this capacity" (Ernst 2003: 20–21).

This epistemic racism is manifested in discussions about human rights today. Non-Western epistemologies that define human rights and human dignity in different forms from the West, are simply excluded from the conversation. This is linked to the contemporary discussions about "fundamentalism." According to "born again Neo-con," Christopher Hitchens: " . . . the very definition of a 'fundamentalist' is someone who believes that 'holy writ' is . . . the fixed and unalterable word of God" (Hitchens 2009, 74). This specific definition, which is the hegemonic definition used in the West today, hides what is fundamental of all fundamentalisms, that is, the belief in the superiority of their own epistemology and the inferiority of the rest. The first premise of Hitchens's definition is that a fundamentalist has to be necessarily religious. In this definition, so-called secular views are excluded a priori from being fundamentalist. The problematic secular/religious Western binary is reproduced here. Accordingly, a secular perspective cannot be fundamentalist under the logic of this definition. Second, the premise that the only possible fundamentalism is about any doctrine that does a "literal," "dogmatic" interpretation of a "sacred text." The premise is that a "sacred text" can only be a religious text. To treat a secular text as "sacred" is not considered as part of the definition of fundamentalism. Secular forms of fundamentalism, such as Stalinism as a Marxist fundamentalism or Positivism as form of scientific fundamentalism, are excluded from the hegemonic definition.

In sum, this definition hides the most important form of fundamentalism in the world-system from the sixteenth century until today: Eurocentric fundamentalism. It is so powerful that it is used as the "norm" and the hegemonic "common sense" to define what is democracy, what is "terrorism," what is "economy," what are human rights, what is the environment, and who is a fundamentalist. Eurocentric fundamentalism is the "sacralization" of the Western tradition of thought and the inferiorization of non-Western epistemologies and cosmologies. It is founded on epistemic racism. Its Universalism is equivalent to one particular defining for the rest as a global/imperial design. If we break with the secular/religious binary split, what is shared by all fundamentalisms in the modern/colonial world is "epistemic racism." A major consequence of the European colonial expansion and its epistemic racism is what Boaventura de Sousa Santos (2007) has called "epistemicide" against non-Western epistemologies. The invisibility and even extermination of other epistemologies is at the root of Eurocentric fundamentalism. Moreover, the hegemonic role of Eurocentric fundamentalism is manifested in that many of what are called today Third World fundamentalisms, such as Islamic fundamentalism, Afrocentric fundamentalism, and indigenous fundamentalism, are inverted forms of Eurocentric fundamentalism.

If the West defines itself as inherently and naturally democratic, in favor of women's rights, human rights, democracy, freedom, and so on, the non-West is defined as inherently and naturally authoritarian, patriarchal, and the like. This Eurocentric binary, which is at the foundation of epistemic racism, is not displaced but inverted by what are called third world fundamentalisms. So, what I want to emphasize here is that third world fundamentalisms such as Islamic fundamentalism or Afro-centric fundamentalism are derivative forms of Eurocentric fundamentalism. They just invert the Eurocentric binary and affirm the opposite side of the binary and leave intact the hegemonic binary itself. For example, they will affirm patriarchy or authoritarian forms of political authority, leaving in the hands of Eurocentrism the image of being democractic and feminist. Hitchens's definition of fundamentalism hides the underlying assumption of all fundamentalisms: the ethnocentric idea that only one's own epistemology is superior and the rest are inferior.

Utopistics Beyond Eurocentrism

Once we have discussed the concepts above, I want to return to our early discussion on Utopistics. The perspective known as the "world-system approach" that Immanuel Wallerstein has developed during the last four decades is one of the most critical, suggestive, and provocative theoretical contributions that has existed up to the present. Wallerstein as an intellectual committed to the "wretched of the earth" has radically questioned the epistemology of the social sciences, Eurocentrism, the myths of Western historiography regarding the rise of the West, the evolutionist view of social systems, developmentalism, and the liberal conceptualization of the capitalist system and statist socialism. His contributions in analytic and conceptual terms have been enormous. His historical-sociological analysis regarding the formation of the current modern/capitalist world-system—one which stretches from 1450 to 1914—is required reading for anyone who seeks to grasp and transform the complex historical-social processes of domination and exploitation that we have been experiencing for the last 500 years. We do not have the space here to deal with all of this. I simply want to take advantage of these brief comments to indicate a series of questions with regard to his most recent work on the approaching bifurcation and his proposed "Utopistics."

If Wallerstein's prediction that the capitalist world-system will come to an end in the next 50 years is proved incorrect and, instead, the system ends in 25 years or in 150 years, this is a secondary concern to his more fundamental assertion regarding the terminal and irreversible crisis of the mechanisms of systemic reproduction which have reached an "asymptotal" point. The systemic contradictions that Wallerstein identifies are crucial for understanding the processes of collapse in the present system and the opening of a bifurcation toward a historical-system that could be better or worse than the current system. No historical system is eternal. Hence the importance that he ascribes to Utopistics in this transitional moment.

The fact that no war, revolution, or rebellion has managed to overthrow the capitalist world-system during the long centuries of its reproduction gives empirical validity to Wallerstein's thesis that the action of social subjects and anti-systemic movements lacks anti-systemic effectiveness until the moment of terminal crisis and bifurcation of the system. However, I am left with a doubt: to what point is this less the effect of the efficiency of the mechanisms of systemic reproduction and more the result of the failure of anti-systemic movements, or a combination of the two? If Wallerstein's thesis is correct, then the system would operate according to a powerful structural determinism during the long centuries of more or less stable systemic reproduction and expansion, and the action of subjects—their free will—will only have transformative effects at the moment of systemic bifurcation. While this thesis might seem to make sense and correspond to historical facts, it seems problematic to me because it attributes such a powerful structural determinism to the system that it would seem as though the actions of social agents have no effect upon social reality or that they were impotent to transform it except in periods of systemic bifurcation. I ask myself to what point, if Napoleon or Hitler had triumphed in their expansionist wars, would the capitalist world-system have been transformed into a world-empire at the beginning of the nineteenth century with the first or in the mid-twentieth century with the second? Similarly, to what degree, if the sixteenth-century indigenous uprisings had succeeded in the Americas, would capitalism have been able to constitute an international division of labor, a global market, and as a result a world-system? Equally, if the proletarian revolutions at the end of the nineteenth and early twentieth century had succeeded in Europe, to what point was it possible that the terminal crisis of the system might have occurred earlier? In my opinion, social actors always have the potential to destroy the system. The problem is that in political power-struggles, nothing is predetermined or guaranteed, and variables like violence and ideology enter into the equation to neutralize the possibility for anti-systemic mobilization.

Finally, I have other questions directed at those elements that Wallerstein offers for the proposed global debate and related to the previous discussion we had on transcending the epistemic racism of the present system. I suspect that his proposals—which on principle seem important to consider—remain trapped within a Eurocentric, Western epistemology. Why should we continue thinking about creating a single alternative historical-system and not a diversality of alternative historical-systems? Why should we continue thinking of a single historical system defined from the premises of the West? Aren't the Zapatista slogan about "a world in which other worlds are possible" and the slogan of much of the World Social Forum of "not one but other worlds are possible" calling for a multiplicity of alternative historical-systems or for a single historical system that is defined from the non-Western epistemologies? Doesn't the proposal of monosystemic and mono-epistemic alternatives result in the reproduction of a Eurocentric scheme? On the other hand, doesn't the idea of extending to all humanity the liberal ideals of democracy, equality, fraternity, and liberty reproduce a Western-centric epistemic premise? When indigenous groups like the Zapatistas claim that "we are equal because we are different," this is a notion of "concrete equality" which interrogates the liberal imaginary of "abstract equality," which since the French Revolution has erased the faces of non-Western people. An indigenous person does not want to be "integrated" into the Western world or its liberal ideals, he or she wants their world to be treated equally without erasing its difference and its alternative forms of existence. The same occurs with Islamic feminists, Afro-Caribbean movements, Buddhist parties in Asia, and with all those anti-systemic movements that set out from "other" epistemologies.

Is it not fundamental to decolonize, that is, to criticize Western values from the perspective of "other" epistemologies and open up the epistemic and cosmological diversity of the planet? For example, the West has always treated nature as a means to an end. Setting out from this cosmology, the West ended up developing technologies that destroyed nature. Those non-Western cosmologies which have always treated nature as an end in itself have a great deal to offer this discussion. That is, to imagine possible worlds, we need to overcome the pretension of creating a single, universal, alternative historical-system as the solution to the current system. If we continue to set out from Western cosmology and epistemology to imagine possible worlds—reproducing a profound deafness toward other, non-Western epistemologies—we run the risk of reproducing from the left those western global designs that were imposed by persuasion and/or force on the non-Western world through imperial/colonial expansion. Wasn't twentieth-century socialism precisely a global/western/colonial design that was imposed as the only possible alternative model to capitalism? We need to think from an epistemic pluriversality that allows us to imagine multiple possible alternative worlds against the capitalist mono-world. As Enrique Dussel (2001) would say: the recognition of the epistemic diversity of humans leads to a world, beyond the modern/colonial world, that he calls "transmodernity."

A pluri-epistemic world or an "ecology of knowledge" (Sousa Santos 2007) beyond the current mono-epistemic one leads us toward an anti-capitalist, decolonial, transmodern world, in opposition to a Eurocentric, post-modern world which would represent a continuation of the modernity/coloniality of the current capitalist world-system. Transmodernity is the utopian project proposed by Latin American philosopher of liberation Enrique Dussel to transcend the Eurocentric version of modernity (Dussel 1994; 2001). In opposition to Habermas' project, which—with a resemblance to Wallerstein's proposal—proposes as its central task the need to fulfill the unfinished project of modernity, Dussel's transmodernity is a project to fulfill the unfinished project of decolonization. Instead of a single modernity centered in Europe/Euro-America and imposed as a global project on the rest of the world, Dussel argues for a multiplicity of critical decolonial proposals against Eurocentric modernity and from the epistemic locations of the colonized peoples of the world. Transmodernity proposes moving beyond modernity through the resignification of the elements/signifiers

of modernity from the epistemic perspective of the "other," non-western subjects excluded, erased, rendered invisible, and/or exterminated by modernity.
A good example of transmodern, anti-capitalist decolonization is the Zapatista
struggle in Mexico. The Zapatistas are neither Eurocentric nor anti-modern
fundamentalists. They criticize and reject western liberal democracy, but without
rejecting democracy per se and without withdrawing into a form of indigenist
fundamentalism. To the contrary, the Zapatistas accept the notion of "democracy" but redefine it on the basis of local indigenous cosmologies and practice
conceptualized as "commanding obeying" or "we are equal because we are different." What looks like a paradoxical slogan is in reality a critical, decolonial,
anti-capitalist redefinition of notions of democracy and citizenship on the basis
of subaltern practices, cosmologies, and epistemologies. The Zapatistas provide
a practical decolonial example of how to transcend the monologue and deafness
established by Eurocentric modernity.

To think from the perspective of the wretched of the earth—as have
subaltern intellectuals like Frantz Fanon and Aimé Césaire—leads us to "other"
ways of thinking Utopistics. The wretched of the earth do not need a fraternity
among equals within the same hegemonic universe that relates oppressively to
those who are not the equals of the universe (for example, fascisms, fundamentalisms, Eurocentrism, liberalism, nationalisms, fraternal among themselves but
never toward "others"), but they seek instead a world which offers solidarity
between "diverse-equals" within a pluriverse (a world composed of multiple
worlds), in which people in a world can see people from other worlds as
"diverse-equals" and can be capable of solidarity and fraternity with them. To
fraternize with an other who pertains to the same world is not as radical—as the
limits of Eurocentrism, racism, and sexism demonstrate—as creating solidarity
and fraternity with an "other" from "another world" (as demonstrated in the
life-practice of Fanon and Césaire). This decolonial ethic (Maldonado-Torres
2008) cannot be understood if it sets out only from Western epistemology to
engage in Utopistics. Eurocentric Utopistics—deaf to epistemic diversity and
"ecology of knowledges"—runs the risk of reproducing imperial/colonial global
designs under the name of an alternative historical-system.

References

Dussel, Enrique. 1994. *1492: El encubrimiento del Otro: Hacia el origen del "mito de la modernidad."* La Paz, Bolivia: Plural Editores.

Dussel, Enrique. 2001. *Hacia una Filosofía Política Crítica.* Bilbao, España: Desclée de Brouwer.

Ernst, Carl W. 2003. *Following Mohammad: Rethinking Islam in the Contemporary World.* Chapel Hill and London: The University of North Carolina Press.

Eze, E. C. 1997. "The Color of Reason: The Idea of 'Race' in Kant's Anthropology." In

Postcolonial African Philosophy: A Critical Reader, edited by E. C. Eze. Cambridge, MA: Blackwell.

Gordon, Lewis. 2008. *An Introduction to Africana Philosophy.* Cambridge, MA: Cambridge University Press.

Grosfoguel, Ramón. 2003. *Colonial Subjects.* Berkeley: University of California Press.

———. 2006. "World-System Analysis in the Context of Transmodernity, Border Thinking and Global Coloniality." *Review* XXIX(2), 167–187.

Hitchens, Christopher. 2009. "Assassins of the Mind." *Vanity Fair,* No. 582 (February), 72–75.

Maldonado-Torres, Nelson. 2008. *Against War.* Durham, NC: Duke University Press.

Sousa Santos, Boaventura de. 2007. *El Milenio Huérfano.* Madrid: Trotta.

Wallerstein, Immanuel. 1974. *The Modern World System. I. Capitaliist Agriculture and the Origins of the world-Economy in the Sixteenth Century, 1450–1600.* New York: Academic Press Inc.

———. 1979. *The Capitalist World-Economy.* Cambridge and Paris: Cambridge University Press and Editions de la Maison des Sciences de l'Homme.

———. 1980. *The Modern World System. II. Mercantilism and the Consolidation of the European World-Economy, 1600–1750.* New York: Academic Press Inc.

———. 1983. *Historical Capitalism.* New York: Monthly Review Press.

———. 1984. *The Politics of the World-Economy.* Cambridge and Paris: Cambridge University Press and Editions de la Maison des Sciences de l'Homme

———. 1991a. *Unthinking Social Science.* Cambridge: Polity Press.

———. 1991b. *Geopolitics and Geoculture.* Cambridge and Paris: Cambridge University Press and Editions de la Maison des Sciences de l'Homme.

———. 1995. *After Liberalism.* New York: The New Press.

———. 1998. *Utopistics: Or, Historical Choices of the Twenty-first Century.* New York: The New Press.

———. 2003. *The Decline of American Power.* New York and London: The New Press.

10

THE QUASI-EUROPES

WORLD REGIONS IN LIGHT
OF THE IMPERIAL DIFFERENCE

Manuela Boatcă

Looking Small, Looming Large: World Regions in World-Systems Analysis

Other than as structural positions within the capitalist world-economy, world regions have tended to receive little attention in world-systems analysis and widely varied emphases when taken into account at all. One reason for the charge of Eurocentrism voiced by some of the critics of the world-systems perspective is precisely the fact that Europe itself is not dealt with as one region among several, but as the birthplace of the modern world-system, and as such unduly privileged.

Instead, the centrality of the Americas, for an understanding of both the geopolitics and the geoculture of what has increasingly come to be called "the modern/colonial world system" as a consequence, started to come into focus in world-systems work since the 1990s (Quijano and Wallerstein 1992; Mignolo 2000; Grosfoguel et al. 2005), stressing the key role that the Americas played in the very definition of modernity, and as a precondition for the concomitant emergence of coloniality. The critically important conceptual change operated by the notion of coloniality was that, while colonialism as a formal administrative status had come to an end, the coloniality inherent in the political, economic, and cultural hierarchy between Europeans and non-Europeans had not, such that crucial dimensions of the process of decolonization remained pending. At the same time, the centrality conferred the Americas in the creation of coloniality has come with a theoretical cost: by focusing on the impact of colonial power in the emergence of alternative modes of labor control, weak state structures, and subaltern epistemologies that subsequent waves of decolonization have left in place, the modernity/coloniality perspective has invited the implication that the neocolonial relation between the core and the noncore in other parts of the world besides the Americas was a later step within a postulated temporal sequence that ran from (1) colonial occupation to (2) juridical-administrative decolonization and up to (3) the postcolonial period. Although easily analyzable in terms of a structure of coloniality, and with recognizable postcolonial traits today, world regions formerly subjected to neocolonial or imperial domination fit poorly or not at all in this timeline.

By contrast, work on Eastern Europe by world-systems authors in the 1970s (Wallerstein 1974; Chirot 1976), Eastern European historians since the 1980s (Berend and Ranki 1982; Berend 2003) and a growing body of recent postcolonial and critical development studies have revealed that the economic, political, and ideological domination that different parts of Eastern Europe experienced at different times beginning in the sixteenth century followed a sequence that went from protocolonial to the neocolonial at best, but in the absence of formal colonization.

Such processes were typically linked to situations of imperial, not colonial, domination. As late as the eighteenth century, the already declining Ottoman Empire behaved more like a traditional world empire than like the expanding capitalist system, in that it exploited its colonies in order to finance luxuries and wars, and to maintain imperial structures, but not in order to industrialize the core's economy (Chirot 1976, 61). Stretching for about two hundred years, the dissolution of the Habsburg, Ottoman, and Tsarist empires often did not lead to the liberation of the previously occupied provinces in the region, but to a shift from such protocolonial systems—based on the exploitation of an unfree peasant labor force—to neocolonial ones under the jurisdiction of the Western capitalist powers, interested in an increase of agrarian production, and thus in the overexploitation and re-enserfment of rural workers. For the newly emerged states in the area, the terms of political discourse, national identity formation, and cultural change, too, were accordingly transformed by the geopolitical reshuffling that made Western Europe the new metropole.

The political, cultural, and economic legacy of empire in the region, that is, the coloniality of empire, had however left indelible marks, both on the socioeconomic organization and on the self-conceptualization of its subjects, which therefore placed them in a different relationship to the Western European core than the American colonies. While the racial, ethnic, and class hierarchies erected in the colonies marked the *colonial difference* (Mignolo 2002) from the core, the less overtly racial, more pronounced ethnic, and distinct class hierarchies accounted for the *imperial difference* among the European empires and their (former) subjects. Since the impact of the imperial difference, as I intend to show below, has not only been decisive in the nineteenth century, but continues to be so today, I argue that taking into account the imperial, not only the colonial, difference as part of the impending study of world regions represents one of the main challenges for world-systems analysis in the twenty-first century. In the following, I will restrict myself to pointing out two domains in which the imperial difference in Eastern Europe is relevant to world-systems analysis. First, in the production of epistemic frames, which will be dealt with in more detail, and second, in the conceptualisation of the alleged anomalies in the course of capitalist development, as one possible consequence of the first.

The Construction of European Others: Epistemic Parameters in the Longue Durée

Following Edward Saïd's now classical account of Orientalizing discourses as the basis for the production of otherness in the West, Latin American theorists of postcolonialism have argued that the Orientalism of the eighteenth and nineteenth centuries could not have been conceived without a previous idea of Occidentalism, whose emergence coincided with the onset of the Western European colonial expansion in the long sixteenth century. As "the expression of a constitutive relationship between Western representations of cultural difference and worldwide Western dominance" (Coronil 1996, 57), Occidentalism does not represent the counterpart of Orientalism, but its precondition, a discourse *from* and *about* the West (Mignolo 2000) that sets the stage for discourses about the West's Other(s)—that is, for Orientalism, but also for anti-Semitism and anti-Black racism, as well as for sexism. Rather than a physical location on the map, the geopolitical concept of the Occident emerging in the sixteenth century was, in this perspective, an epistemic location for the production of hegemonic mental maps, that is, of imperial maps carrying a discursive power component.

What is often neglected in this context is the fact that the Western perspective of knowledge as it emerged with the establishment of Western hegemony as a global model of power is not a mere synonym of Eurocentrism. While Eurocentrism is an essential component of Occidentalism as it is defined here, and both can be treated as interchangeable in terms of their impact on the non-European world to a certain extent, it is imperative to differentiate with respect to the distinct range of the two within Europe.

From Multiple Orientalisms to Multiple Europes

During the first modernity, when the secondary and peripheral Europe of the fifteenth century became the conquering Europe in the Atlantic and at the same time the first center of the capitalist world-system (Wallerstein 1979), both the European territorial dominance and the extent of its epistemic power were still partial. In contrast, since the second modernity beginning in the eighteenth century, hierarchies that structured Europe according to principles similar to those applied to the colonial world gradually started taking shape. If, for Anibal Quijano, the propagation of Eurocentrism in the non-European world occurred with the help of two founding myths, evolutionism and dualism (Quijano 2000), the same also served to propagate Occidentalism in Europe once the change in hegemony from the old Spanish-Portuguese core to the Northwestern one had been effectuated. On the one hand, the evolutionary notion that human civilization had proceeded in a linear and unidirectional fashion from an initial state of nature through successive stages leading up to Western civilization justified the *temporal* division of the European continent: while the East was still considered feudal, the South had marked the end of the Middle Ages, and the Northwest represented modernity. On the other hand, dualism—the idea that differences between Europeans and non-Europeans could be explained in terms of insuperable natural categories such as primitive-civilized, irrational-rational, traditional-modern (Quijano 2000, 543)—allowed both a *spatial* and an *ontological* division within Europe. By being geographically inextricable from Europe, and at the same time (predominantly) Christian and white, the European Southeast and especially the Balkans could not be constructed as "an incomplete Other" of Western Europe, as in the case of the Far East, but rather as its "incomplete Self" (Todorova 1997). Moreover, its proximity to Asia and its Ottoman cultural legacy located it halfway between East and West, thus giving it a condition of semi-Oriental, semi-civilized, semi-developed, in the process of "catching up with the West."[1] In the same vein, the European South, epitomized by the declining Spanish empire and its Moorish legacy, was gradually defined out of the Western core both for its proximity to Islamic North Africa and for its reputation as a brutal colonizer of the New World, constructed as the opposite of England's own benevolent colonialism.

Parallel to the construction of the colonial difference overseas, we thus witness the emergence of a double imperial difference in Europe (stretching onto Asia): on the one hand, an external difference between the new capitalist core and the existing traditional empires of Islamic and Eastern Christian faith—the Ottoman and the Tsarist one; on the other hand, an internal difference between the new and the old capitalist core, mainly England vs. Spain: "In this short history it is clear that the imperial external difference created the conditions for the emergence, in the eighteenth century, of Orientalism, while the imperial internal difference ended up in the imaginary and political construction of the South of Europe. Russia remained outside the sphere of Orientalism and at the opposed end, in relation to Spain as paradigmatic example of the South of Europe" (Mignolo 2006, 487).

From this moment on, we have at least two types of European subalterns to the hegemonic model of power, as well as the first imperial map of multiple Europes. In light of both the external and the internal imperial difference, we can thus distinguish between what I would like to call *decadent Europe* (which had lost both hegemony and, accordingly, the epistemic power of defining a hegemonic Self and its subaltern Others), *heroic Europe* (self-defined as the *producer* of modernity's main achievements), and *epigonal Europe* (defined via its alleged lack of these achievements and hence as a mere *re-producer* of the stages covered by the heroic Europe). While "decadent Europe" and "epigonal Europe" were both characterized by a semiperipheral position, their different trajectories in having achieved this position acted toward disuniting rather than uniting them in their interests: In Spain and Portugal, the memory of lost power and the dominion of imperial languages induced the awareness of a decline from the core, that is, an imperial nostalgia. Instead, in that part of the continent that had only emerged as "Europe" due to the growing demise of the Ottoman Empire—Eastern Europe and the Balkans—the rise to the position of semiperiphery within the world system alongside the enduring position of periphery within Europe itself made the aspiration to Europeanness—defined as Western modernity—the dominant attitude.

Thus, the subdivisions underlying the imperial map of multiple Europes served to positively sanction the hegemony of "heroic Europe," which thus became the only authority capable of imposing a universal definition of modernity and at the same time of deploying its imperial projects in the remaining Europes or through them. On one hand, the second modernity, during which hegemony was disputed among Holland, France, and England, would use the territorial gains of the first, Spanish-Lusitanian modernity in order to derive the human, economic, and cultural resources that substantiated the most characteristically modern achievements, of which the "Industrial Revolution" is a paradigmatic example. However, this will occur without integrating the contribution of either the decadent European South or of the colonized Americas in the narrative of modernity, which was conceived as being both of (North)Western and of inner-European origin.

On the other hand, and especially as of the mid-nineteenth century, the Western European core of the capitalist world-economy benefited from the end of Ottoman rule in the east of the continent by establishing neocolonies in the rural and agricultural societies of the region and thus gradually gaining control of the strategic trade routes of the Black Sea and the Danube. The subsequent modernization of the Balkans and the European Southeast through the introduction of bourgeois-liberal institutions and legislation, while pursuing the goal of making the region institutionally recognizable to the West and financially dependent on it, at the same time involved the shaping of political and cultural identities of countries in the region in relation to the Western discourse of power. Consequently, not only Austria but also Poland, Romania, and Croatia defined their contribution to European history as "bulwarks of Christianity" against the Muslim threat, while every country in Eastern Europe designated itself "frontier between civilization and barbarism" or "bridge between West and East," thus legitimizing Western superiority and fostering the same Orientalism that affected themselves as Balkan, not Christian enough, or not white enough.

From such a perspective—that of the instrumentalization of the geopolitical location of "the other Europes" for the purposes of heroic Europe in the longue durée—it becomes easier to understand that the Occidentalism directed at the subalterns never represented an obstacle to the Eurocentrism that the latter displayed on their part toward the non-European world. Quite the contrary. While Samuel Huntington accused the Orthodox and Muslim parts of Europe of marginality and passivity with respect to the achievements of modernity, situating them on the opposite side of one of the fault lines in the future clashes of civilizations, re-mapping them in the context of a hierarchical model of multiple Europes, reveals that their blindness to coloniality rather makes them accomplices of the colonial project of power underlying the emergence of modernity.

Such a classification is necessarily incomplete and meant to serve heuristic purposes, not to exhaustively or even partially explain the trajectory of any European region in the longue durée. This has been systematically done a number of times and has yielded widely differing taxonomies, depending on whether the focus of the categorization were economic or political criteria or a mixture of the two (see e.g., Therborn 1995; Rokkan 1999). On the basis of its most prototypical examples, however, the model of multiple Europes as sketched here does help illuminate the impact that the direct or indirect involvement in the

Table 10.1 Multiple Europes

Europe	Prototype	Role in the history of modernity	World-system position	Attitude	Role in coloniality
Decadent	Spain, Portugal	participant	semiperiphery	nostalgia	founding
Heroic	France, England	producer	core	hegemony	central
Epigonal	The Balkans	reproducer	semiperiphery	aspiration	accomplice

extra-European colonial endeavor has had on the definition power associated with a region's structural position within the world-system and within Europe in particular. The following section illustrates this using the case of Romania.

From the Periphery of Empire to the Periphery of the World-System

Bordering on the Habsburg, the Ottoman, and the Tsarist empires and thus strategically important for each of them for military, political, and commercial reasons, the three Romanian provinces, Transylvania, Wallachia, and Moldavia, had in time been subjected to several redrawings of borders to the territorial benefit of Austria and Russia—culminating in Transylvania's subordination to Austria in 1699—and to fiscal exploitation and political control by the Sublime Porte, respectively. It was through the geopolitical reshufflings triggered by the growing decline of the Ottoman Empire that they acquired additional relevance as part of the civilizing discourse of nineteenth-century Europe: by removing Wallachia and Moldavia from under the Russian protectorate at the end of the Crimean War and declaring them autonomous, the Great Powers—Russia, the United Kingdom, France, Austria, and Prussia—not only created a buffer state that warranted Austria and Russia the security of their frontiers against Turkey's claims, but also pushed the border demarcating the imperial difference between Christianity and Islam to include the two Orthodox provinces subsequently to be turned into "bridgeheads of Western capitalism" (Stahl 1993, 87). In sum, by exchanging the direct control of a single metropole—the Ottoman Empire—for the indirect one of "a consortium of overseers" (Chirot 1976), Romania had accomplished only "a shift of peripheral axis" (Bădescu 2004) from its condition as a periphery of the Ottoman Empire to the one of periphery of Western Europe. This trend was reversed during and after World War II, when united Romania went from being a border state (alongside Finland, Estonia, Latvia, Lithuania, Poland, Belarus, Ukraine) between the Soviet Union and the anti-Socialist West to yet another buffer state on the margins of the Soviet Empire. The most recent shift of axis at the end of the twentieth century saw Romania become once more a border state, this time exchanging the geopolitical position of Communist periphery for the one of periphery of the European Union. Thus, ever since its incorporation into the capitalist world-economy in the late nineteenth century as an agricultural periphery of Western Europe, Romania's place on the Occidentalist map has been determined by several shifts of axis in accordance with the surrounding empires' shifts in power.

The important thing this geopolitical trajectory reveals, however, is not the difference between the alternating border and buffer roles—often interchangeable, if not downright arbitrary designations—but the long-term continuity of an in-between status that the regular ascription of such military, religious-strategic, and ideological functions made apparent. This *longue durée*

Table 10.2 Romania's shifts of axis

Period	Geopolitical role	Shift of peripheral axis
after 1856 (Crimean War)	buffer state	Ottoman Empire–Western Europe
interbellum (1918–1939)	border state	–
Cold War (1947–1989)	buffer state	Western Europe–Communist Empire
after 1989	border state	Communist Empire–European Union

instrumentalization of its geopolitical coordinates was crucial in determining both Romania's location in the Occidental imaginary and its recurrent attempts at self-definition at various turning points in its history. Consequently, metaphors such as "bridge between East and West," "bulwark of Christianity," and even "border between barbarianism and civilization," although not unique to Romania, have repeatedly been mobilized within political and intellectual statements from and about Romania in order to account for what the Eurocentered hegemonic discourse constructed as the country's ambiguous identity: European but not Western; Christian but schismatic; white—but not quite.

As far as knowledge production is concerned, it has therefore been suggested that, unlike the border epistemology engendered by the clear-cut colonial difference outside of Europe, the epistemic frame that characterizes the entire ex-Second World living in or on the border between the European imperial and colonial powers is one of blurredness—of the difference from the West—as well as splitness—between being the West's partial Other and its incomplete Self (Ivakhnenko 2006, 604; Mignolo and Tlostanova 2006, 217; Todorova 1997, 18).

Or, to paraphrase Enrique Dussel: while dwelling outside the center entails not having any privileges to defend by means of theory production (Dussel 1977, 16), living on the border means partaking of those privileges at the same time as experiencing oppression. Although I agree that this in-between position implies a significant degree of blindness to full-fledged coloniality, I argue that it also entails an epistemic potential, the achievement of which is, however, contingent on the historical context. In the case of Romania, the conditions

Table 10.3 Epistemic frames

Colonial World	*Ex-Communist World*
colonial difference (qualitative)	difference within sameness (of degree)
dichotomy (the West's Other) ➔ border thinking	splitness (West's incomplete Self) ➔ blurredness

for the emergence of border thinking (Mignolo 2000) were better at the end of the nineteenth century, when the interregnum between independence from the Ottoman Empire and the incorporation into the Western European trade system and sphere of influence literally made of Romania a "no man's land" epistemologically, than today, when the near prospect of "European integration" holds out the promise of more stakes in the Western privileges. Arguably, the more privileges there are to defend, the less the transformative potential residing in the subaltern aspect of the border position is explored.

As of the middle of the nineteenth century, several Romanian theorists embarked on a search for a transformation process tailored to the country's specific needs, in an attempt to account for this shift of peripheral axis. The solutions they offered covered a wide range of options and political stances with potential for systemic change (Boatcă 2003). In the course of the intellectual debates in the decades that followed, the classical political doctrines associated with the contenders' main ideological positions experienced a substantial reinterpretation in accordance with the peripheral status for which they were meant to account. This filter presupposed Western ideological notions through the perspective of the national concerns facing Romania's geopolitical and historical context. While the extent to which each of them succeeded in transforming the underlying Eurocentric rationality into border thinking varies widely, they can therefore be reasonably designated as "border" variants of the classical doctrines.

Border Conservatism. Thus, for the conservatives, liberal policy in Romania was a form without substance[2] not simply because the country lacked the economic foundation capable of reflecting its institutional superstructure, but chiefly because the very basis of Western liberalism, a "middle class that produces something" (Eminescu 1877, 18), fulfilled the opposite function in Romanian society, where it produced nothing. Its policy therefore turned into pseudo-liberalism and ended up promoting an *underdevelopment policy.* Tackling social and economic issues therefore required an awareness of this decisive difference between Western liberalism and its Romanian counterpart. The continuity between the economic exploitation during Ottoman rule and the aggravated form in which it was practiced by the local intermediaries of the new and informal dominant powers is clearly outlined in Eminescu's conceptualization of the "shift of peripheral axis" as a shift of tribute, eventually yielding a similiarly colonial structure: "*Pro forma* independent, we pay a tribute hundreds of times higher than the old one; the freedom of our populations is similar to the freedom of dying of misery" (Eminescu 1881a, 379). Both foreign elites had formed a "xenocracy" (Eminescu 1881b, 323), but, whereas the former administrative class of the Ottoman regime represented a "xenocracy through conquest," therefore a political one, the latter was a "xenocracy through insidiousness" (ibid.), that is, one employing ideological and economic mechanisms characteristic of a neocolonial model.

Conservatives therefore perceived both the bourgeois and the socialist revolutions as a joint offensive against historicity, organicity, and tradition. From a conservative, but also historical and national, position, the peasantry was the only real producer of values in the Romanian context. Besides, there was no Romanian bourgeoisie, and the intermediate class taking its place (what Eminescu dubbed the "superimposed layer") performed no positive (or progressive) role—quite the opposite. The critical view typical of conservatism was thus transformed into a "double critique" or into what we could label peripheral or "border conservatism"—and thereby exposed both liberalism and socialism as devoid of any real basis under peripheral conditions (Eminescu 1878, 91).

As it had been elaborated in Western Europe, where the main social issue was the agrarian one, socialism was a logical response the proletarianization of formerly rural masses faced with increasing land scarcity. In agrarian countries like Romania and Russia, however, land scarcity was not an issue, and the propagation of socialist ideas in such areas acted much more in support of liberal ideology than against it (ibid.). Without a full-fledged notion of periphery or of the world-systems as a whole, the conservatives' approach to the center-periphery relationship was limited to the structure of power characterizing the transfer of economic surplus from industrial to agrarian countries, but included instead the cultural and social components of this type of domination. Cultures of scholarship such as political doctrines, Eminescu argued, could not be exported from the center to the periphery without heeding the social, economical, and cultural divide. In the case of liberalism and socialism, their uncritical exportation to Romania had turned them into "pseudo-liberalism" and "agrarian socialism," forms without substance in a society whose most momentous characteristic, peripherality, induced and maintained by the action of a parasitical superimposed layer, they could not explain.[3]

Border Liberalism. Apparently at the opposite end of the political spectrum, nineteenth century Romanian liberals pressed for specific instead of universalist solutions to development, arguing that a people's individual solutions to development—its necessary contribution to civilization—constituted the key to its national sovereignty and thereby increased its "evolutionary potential" (Xenopol 1882). The economic specialization of agrarian countries was therefore a danger to their state independence. Unlike the conservatives, the liberal historian Alexandru Xenopol nevertheless held that all progress took place from cultural forms to economic substance and that the import of liberal principles was thus inherently progressive. At the same time, he diagnosed the dependency of small, underdeveloped countries on industrial nations as a structural problem, the cause of which he identified in the unequal exchange between the Western European industrialized core and its agrarian suppliers in the periphery.

Xenopol therefore suggested that Romania should discard the free trade policy advocated by the West, which only served Western interests, and instead adopt protectionism, promote large-scale industry, and rely on state investment. Paradoxically, this was in his view the task of the liberal government, whose policy—adapted to the needs of a peripheral country—Xenopol dubbed "new liberalism": "Until now, we have been ideologues; we used to think that wealth and well-being could result from theoretical creations. We were only concerned with laws which changed the outer form of our institutions, without trying to transform the very substance of our life" (Xenopol 1882, 126).

Consequently, Xenopol saw it as his duty to "dislodge the ideologies" of sociological theories. The concrete form this took, in his case, involved the search for a strategy of *national* development, since the situation of cultural and economic backwardness that he described was important to the extent that it was a national issue.

The first step in the transition from ideology to science accordingly consisted in abandoning the claim to a universal science and to corresponding universal principles of economic development, such as those inherent in classic liberalism's doctrine of *laissez faire*. Instead of an individual party policy, "new" liberalism should become a state platform and as such take responsibility for inducing development and promoting industrialization. The issue of industrialization itself, more than just a good illustration of the periphery's general evolutionary potential, was "not only a question of gain, but one of civilization ... not one of gain, but one of nationality" (Xenopol 1882, 86), and as such stood in close connection with a liberating economic and political course: " ... crying out for liberty in a plainly agricultural country is in vain, for liberty is only possible where there are *free people*, and free people only exist in a country in which industry plays a significant role" (Xenopol 1882, 83). The "people," in this understanding, constituted the unit of progress at the national level, in which national ethnicity was articulated. Work enhancement at the level of the national economy and in international exchanges, capable of increasing the people's well-being as well as of justly distributing it, accordingly represented the right national strategy that the "new liberalism" was supposed to implement.

Border Socialism. The amount of adjustment that the socialist doctrine had to undergo before fitting a peripheral pattern of development was even greater than in the case of the liberal doctrine. In stressing that "our country is not a capitalist country like the Occidental ones, but a backward capitalist country, or a semicapitalist one, like Russia, Serbia, Bulgaria" (Gherea 1908, 160), the socialist Gherea managed to combine a teleological understanding of social development with a clear rejection of unilinearity. A Marxist in arguing that Romania had to overcome feudalism in order to attain "full" capitalism and eventually socialism, Gherea proved quite "un-Marxist" in stating that the apparent idiosyncrasies Romania displayed in its transition to capitalism were a common trait of peripheral regions, and that such cases therefore were consistent with the rule, not exceptions to it. Thus, while there was room for specific evolution from country to country, semicapitalist societies shared recognizable evolutionary patterns distinguishing them as a group from the already capitalist ones.

This shift of levels of analysis, however, meant a displacement of class struggle as a relevant factor of internal social change for individual (peripheral) societies, in which, consequently, "social transformations do not necessarily follow from class struggle, but are imposed from outside" (Gherea 1976 [1892], 435). Unlike his predecessors, notably Xenopol and Eminescu, who viewed Romania's lag vis-à-vis the West as an abnormal development contradicting the laws of organic evolution, Gherea generalized from his analysis of Romania's evolution to the evolution of all peripheral countries in capitalist transition. However greatly influenced by the "international environment," Gherea thought the process of "bourgeoisification" in Romania's case had not been *caused* but only *accelerated* by the country's political and economic ties with the capitalist core.

Gherea's belief in the lawlike character of peripheral evolution formed the basis on which, in 1910, he would ground his explanation of Romania's "peasant question." He thus argued that the mode of production instated in Romania after the land reform of 1864 represented the most prominent instance of the coexistence of capitalist superstructural elements and a feudal economic base, a mixture made possible in the wake of Romania's incorporation into the "great world division of labor" (Gherea 1910, 32). Solving the resulting "agrarian issue" therefore was primarily a matter of acknowledging its specificity to Romania as a semicapitalist country.

By binding the peasants to the land, declaring their plots inalienable, and legalizing coerced work in the form of "labor contracts," the system had thus given a contractual form to the former feudal dues that the peasant had to provide to his master, that is, it had reverted to a more radical form of serfdom. This particular regime, which had deprived the country of any possibility of development instead of providing a rational basis for it, was what Gherea termed "neoserfdom": "Thus, we possess a double economical agrarian regime, an extraordinary regime: capitalist on the one hand, serf-based on the other ... whose existence for half a century is due only to the extraordinary advantages it holds for our economically dominant class" (Gherea 1910, 95).

What Gherea described as "neoserfdom" was a form of labor control characteristic of the entire periphery of the capitalist world-economy from the sixteenth century on, one which Engels had labeled "second serfdom" in 1888. Paradoxically, Gherea agreed with both conservatives and socialists in viewing the administration as a factor contributing to the consolidation and reinforcement of neoserfdom for its own interests and for those of the large estate owners. Not only had the so-called "democratic-bourgeois" state become the biggest consumer, as Xenopol had noted, but it also deliberately employed the neoserf regime, despite the ruinous consequences it had for the national economy, as a means to the primary end of a production oriented toward consumerism and squander.

The Communist Interlude. During the period of Communist rule in the region, the logic of coloniality established in the relationship with Western Europe was overriden by the imperial reason imposed by the Soviet Union. With respect to the production of knowledge, the geopolitics of the Cold War envisaged resignifying the scholarship produced in the Communist Second World as just another object of study for the political science of the First, where an ideology-free point-zero perspective was supposed to guarantee valid intellectual production (Mignolo 2000, 313). Within the Second World itself, the forced Sovietization of culture according to the bipolar imperial logic entailed in turn reinterpreting the intellectuals' defense of religion, the national, local history, and the specific as fascist propaganda. This simultaneous epistemic silencing on the part of the Western and the Soviet Empires formed the basis on which what Immanuel Wallerstein (1991, 182) has called the "gigantic liberal-marxist consensus," and operated a double politicization of theoretical thought throughout Eastern Europe in the latter half of the twentieth century.

In Romania, the result was the enforcement of a state-controlled collective amnesia with respect to all local knowledge production, irrespective of political epistemology. Thus, while Xenopol's works were banned from publication for their liberalism, Gherea's were denounced for their unorthodox Marxism. Condemnation of Eminescu's sociological views, in turn, was undertaken along their conservative dimension, then associated with the exploitative bourgeois class and its ideological use of nationalism as a means of class struggle, yet was by far more severe than in the other cases.

Although the intellectual landscape at the end of the nineteenth century and the beginning of the twentieth was a variegated one, the extent to which each approach managed or was willing to address the imperial and/or neo-colonial difference marking the country's sociohistorical context was clear. A classification of the different political epistemologies was therefore relatively easy, as I tried to show above. This is no longer the case in the twenty-first century, when intellectual subservience to the neoliberal dictate, linked to the hope of "belonging to Europe," results in a near-uniformity of public and published opinion and when works that take issue with the imperial difference, rather than reproduce its logic, represent exceptions.

This time around, the terms of the conversation have been set by recasting the Occidentalist map of the continent in its sixteenth-century mold.

Twenty-First Century Blurredness. On the one hand, Samuel Huntington's 1993 map of the inner-European clash of civilizations argued for the renewed relevance of the 500-year-old eastern boundary of Western Christianity after the end of Communist rule in Eastern Europe, which—in his view—had entailed replacing the relatively short-lived Iron Curtain as the most significant dividing line in Europe by the more pervasive "Velvet Curtain of Culture." The latter is not only supposed to successfully predict significantly different degrees of economic advancement in Western and Eastern Europe along the lines of the cultural differences corresponding to Protestantism/Catholicism and Orthodoxy/Islam, respectively, but also to explain the regions' unequal contributions to the building of European modernity.[4]

On the other hand, the resurgence of Balkanism as part of the Western geopolitical imaginary led to the replacement of the "Communist threat" by the "danger of nationalism" in Western media and scholarly accounts of Southeastern Europe, thus reinforcing the region's essentialization as violently nationalistic, politically unstable, and undemocratic. In the case of Romania, the fact that the "Velvet Curtain of Culture" coincides with the border separating the Habsburg from the Ottoman Empires in the nineteenth century means that the new shift of axis from the periphery of the Soviet Communist Empire to that of the European Union is equivalent to a new geopolitical identity as a "border state" at the crossroads between Western democracy and "Oriental despotism." Consequently, identifying and denouncing nationalism at home became part and parcel of the strategy of political, economic, and intellectual alignment with the European norms embraced by local political elites. This anti-statist trend, fuelled on the one hand by the delegitimation of (Communist) states as agents for prosperity and by neoliberalism's promise of economic bounty on the other, acts in the form of a concerted Communist-cum-neoliberal epistemic control that old intellectual circles in need of legitimacy, as well as the newly emerged ultra-liberal intellectual and political elites of the region, exert on past and present local knowledge production. For the self-definition of social science disciplines, this amounts to a thorough delegitimation of the nineteenth century project of a "science of the nation" and to its substitution by the legitimate aim of Europeanism. Accordingly, both older and contemporary theoretical approaches are categorized as either commonsensical, desirable and responsible pro-Europeanism, or as intellectually and politically dubious, nationalist anti-Europeanism (Boatcă 2006).

In a reiteration of their nineteenth century predecessors' attempts at the decolonization of alleged universal knowledge, today's critical social theorists caution against the unilateral deconstruction of (peripheral) national identities implicit in the current project of cultural and political globalization. In their view, a "Europeanist" discourse that differentiates between the legitimate, Western (hence democratic) nationalism and the illegitimate, Balkan (hence necessarily violent) nationalism in the name of abstract universalism conceals the specificity of the local histories that it seeks to include and is itself in need of epistemological deconstruction—which would ultimately reveal it as situated, that is, as local knowledge incapable of providing the basis for a future "European" identity (Dungaciu 2004, 333). Against this background, the denouncement of nationalism in Eastern Europe and the demonization of claims to national sovereignty based on territorial integrity are regarded as proofs of a double standard that allows the unification of Germany on the basis of common ethnicity but dictates the disintegration of Eastern European states in the name of the necessary regionalization and transnationalization of Europe (David 1996, 162; Mureşan 1998, 112). Much like the nineteenth century social theorists, who perceived the forced modernization of the country as contrary to the national interest, today's critical Romanian scholars reject the European-ist anti-nationalist discourse and its political implications for the Romanian state as a universal shock therapy that Western Europe has been administering indiscriminately to the whole of Eastern Europe with a view to promoting its own geopolitical projects, to which strong nation-states in the region would be an obstacle. At the risk of being politically and professionally stigmatized as "anti-Europeanist," they therefore also reject the distinction between civic and ethnic nationalism as specific manifestations of a Western and an Eastern ethos, respectively (Bădescu 2002, 571; David 1996, 167; Dungaciu 2004, 3; Cristea 2005, 8; Georgiu 2001, 77), arguing that it operates on the basis of a methodological essentialism which reduces Eastern Europe and especially Balkan states to their violent past, while leaving any mention of racism, fascism, and genocide out of the analysis of Western Europe's nationalist manifestations. In this particular context, state sovereignty is defined as the internationally valid guarantee of current frontiers, while European integration, rather than a privi-leged access to a superior or essentially different cultural and political entity, is seen as a means of securing that guarantee in the long run (David 1996, 167).

In their criticism of globalization theories, however, many of today's Romanian intellectuals reject part of the Eurocentric epistemic frame while wholeheartedly embracing another. One the one hand, the association of Marxism with the former Communist regime, which had denied the Orthodox Church its right to existence for decades and thus had boycotted the country's constitutive spirituality, categorically excludes Marxism from the range of possible alternatives for the future. On the other hand, the recent project of a spiritualist sociology (Bădescu 2002) goes so far as to ground any potential for innovative thought in Christianity as a source of spiritual experience and corroborates this claim with the help of an expanded European genealogy of thinkers—from ancient Roman and Greek philosophers to Renaissance and Enlightenment thinkers—into which the Romanians naturally fit (2002, 585). The attempt at escaping ideology thus bridges the divide between Western and Eastern Christianity, and thus eschews one form of Occidentalism—but not Eurocentrism.

The ambitious project of the "Sociology and Geopolitics of the Frontier" (Bădescu et al. 1995a), exhibits the same oscillation between distancing itself

from the Occidentalism of Western approaches to border phenomena and embracing a European perspective with respect to the rest of the world. The basic
thesis—that the advance of imperial/colonial frontier produces critical cultures
in response (Bădescu et al. 1995a, 15ff.) is highly critical of the "liberal-Marxist
consensus" that has allowed Western thinkers to be non-Marxist without being
anti-Marxist throughout the twentieth century, thus preserving the balance of
power on the continent (Bădescu et al. 1995b, 204). Building on Turner's notion of the "frontier," the authors advance the concept of "reactionary cultures"
in order to grasp the phenomenon according to which the advance of imperial/
colonial frontiers engenders a cultural response from the dominated territories
(Bădescu et al. 1995a, 18ff.). At the same time, their contention that imperial
expansion never occurs into no man's land, although intended as a corrective
of the ethnocentric view that leaves the perspective of the colonized out of the
analysis, is in turn limited by a Christian stance that absolves the expansion of
the Christian frontier of any imperial connotations. While the current sociopolitical crisis of all East and Central European countries is traced back to a lack
of significant cultural counterprojects to the dominant model, the advance of
the US/Western frontier is seen as having produced the first major reactionary
culture, based on biblical faith and a revival of the Abrahamic family model
(Bădescu et al. 1995a, 24ff; 33ff.), but no mention is made of the impact of
this process on Native American communities.

On the whole, this explains in part why the colonial difference instituted
in former colonized world regions makes for the geopolitical assertion of Latin
America in the worldwide movement against neoliberalism today, while the
imperial difference imposed in Eastern Europe during the several imperial shifts
of power in the region much rather fosters ambivalence toward and complicity
with the hegemonic model. In other words, if the "spirit of Davos" and the
"spirit of Porto Alegre" (Wallerstein 2005) are the key actors in the current
struggle for epistemic dominance in the world-system, it is unlikely that we
will soon see the emergence of a "spirit of Prague."

By Way of a Conclusion: Anomalies Revisited

One of the most radical methodological steps undertaken by world-systems
analysis was the claim that "to be historically specific is not to fail to be analytically universal" (Wallerstein 2000, 76). For an approach explicitly conceived as
a heuristic middle ground between transhistorical generalizations and particu-
laristic accounts, therefore, the historical analysis of world regions, or, indeed,
of particular national trajectories such as undertaken above, is in no need of
legitimacy, since, in a world-systems perspective, dealing with the historically
concrete is "the only road to nomothetic propositions" (ibid.). But does the
study of world regions as such, and of the production of imperial difference

therein, hold any new promise for the world-systems analysis of the twenty-first century?

The arguments presented here intend to show that it does. Thus, while the conceptual distinction between the colonial and the imperial difference emphasized in the preceding sections is an important first step in the analytical process, it is not only the dissimilarities, but also, and especially, the study of the similarities between the geopolitical contexts generating colonial and imperial differences that enable a world-systemic perspective to arrive at analytically universal propositions. I argue that one of the main areas to which world regions with distinct geopolitical vectors can contribute insights into systemic processes concerns global inequality at its most basic, that is, conceptual level—in particular, the world working class.[5]

Ever since Marx's conceptualization of free wage labor as the defining feature of the capitalist mode of production and of the urban industrial proletariat as its expression, slaves, serfs, subsistence producers, and peasantries in and outside the core had been considered "feudal remnants," "anomalies," "historical anachronisms" typical of underdeveloped regions. From Lenin through the modernization school and classical development theory, non-wage workers were portrayed as so many variants of what Marx had called the "reserve army of capitalism," eventually to be absorbed into wage labor. At the same time, the persistence of such "lower" forms of labor despite capitalist penetration was the conventional Marxist explanation for economic underdevelopment in the periphery, Latin America in particular. World-systems analysis' crucial intervention in this debate in the 1970s had been the contention that, contrary to Marx's view, it was the *mixture* of free and unfree forms of labor control which constituted the essence of capitalism as a mode of production of the entire modern world-system, not of discrete administrative units within it. While free labor was characteristic of skilled work in core areas, coerced labor was employed for less skilled work in peripheral ones (Wallerstein 1974, 127). Thus, in the capitalist world-economy emerged with the establishment of Europe's overseas colonies in the sixteenth century, slavery, serf labor,[6] share-cropping, and tenancy were alternative capitalist modes of labor control, all of which employed labor-power as a commodity. Understood as expressions of various relations of production within a global capitalist system, they thus became "not exceptions to be explained away but patterns to be analyzed" (Wallerstein 2000, 143).

Taking the entire capitalist system as a unit of analysis amounted to a relational notion of both inequality and development, in which the bourgeoisie and the proletariat are transnational classes, while the accumulation of surplus takes place via the mechanism of unequal exchange between the core, the semi-periphery, and the periphery (Wallerstein 1979, 293). Accordingly, the world proletarian class does not only include wage workers in urban industrial areas in the core, but also petty peasant producers, sharecroppers, indentured servants, tenants, and slaves in the periphery and semiperiphery. During the next decades, this conceptualization[7] received substantial theoretical and empirical support from works on slave labor in the periphery as well as subsistence labor, including women's housework and peasant farming, in both the periphery and the core. While the former emphasized the contribution of slave labor in the colonies to the emergence and maintenance of wage-labor in the metropoles (e.g., Mintz 1986; Tomich 2004), the latter claimed that the economic role of the housewife in the core and that of slaves, serfs, and small peasants in the periphery had been the very precondition for the "rise" of the male, white wage worker and of the capital-wage labor relation to the center-stage of theories of capitalism (Mies et al. 1988). More recently, the role of the colonial peasantry as a "pedestal for metropolitan wage labor" has served as an explanation for the current inability of modern agriculture and urban industry to absorb an increasingly superfluous landless labor force and for the corresponding re-peasantization of parts of the world-system's periphery (McMichael 2006; 2008).

All of these approaches view non-wage forms of labor control as modern labor arrangements emerged as a result of capitalist development, rather than as markers of underdevelopment of the regions under discussion—typically, the Caribbean and Latin America, but also India and Africa—and they conceptualize the workers in question as members of the world working class. At the same time, whether they primarily deal with slaves, indentured servants, the peasantry, or subsistence producers, such approaches tend to concentrate on class hierarchies and forms of social organization characteristic of (post) colonial contexts and on the corresponding production of colonial differences therein. Such a focus on the specificity of world regions, however, reinforces the centrality of the Americas and of African labor for the development of the capitalist world-economy, while leaving the impact of the neocolonial relationship between Western and Eastern Europe, as well as the creation of imperial difference in the process unaddressed.

As shown above, and as dealt with in detail elsewhere (Boatcă 2003; 2005), both Western Europe's neocolonial relationship with its Eastern agrarian zones and the modes of labor control instituted as a result have been theorized in Romania as early as the nineteenth century in terms strikingly similar to those used in dependency theory a century later. The form of labor control labeled in Romania "neoserfdom" in 1910 would enter world-systems analysis as "coerced cash-crop labor," a work regime characteristic of the Americas and large parts of Eastern Europe as of the sixteenth century that accounted for a significant part of the world proletariat up to the twentieth. The centrality of the peasant question in agrarian Romania, as opposed to the proletariat question in the industrial West, was explicitly construed as proof that the peasantry was no remnant of an old mode of production, but the main social category from which the working class was recruited and on whose productivity the economic organization of predominantly agrarian zones rested (Eminescu 1878; Stere 1996). As mentioned above, these issues have been systematically dealt with in the first works on the origin and development of the capitalist world-economy (Wallerstein 1974; 1980), as well as in the ones explicitly engaging with Eastern Europe as a peripheral and later semiperipheral region of the world-system (Chirot 1976). The inner-European conceptual differentiation suggested here, which identifies the European East as bearer of a significant critical potential with respect to the hegemonic model as well as the location of apparently "anomalous" social and economic phenomena, is not meant to replace existing explanations of the region's structural position within the world-system. Instead, keeping in mind the "quasi-Europes" alongside the self-defined Europe "proper" is to act as a memento of the fact that world regions currently neglected in the discussion of systemic development and transformation come with a geopolitical trajectory and epistemic frames that substantially enrich and complete our understanding of the past and present workings of the modern world-system.

Notes

1. Maria Todorova speaks in this context of "Balkanism." Unlike Orientalism, which deals with a difference between (imputed) types, the European (Self) and the Oriental (Other), "Balkanism" as a discourse treats the differences within one type (Todorova 2004, 235), the civilized Western European and the semi-civilized, semi-Oriental Eastern European.

2. Boatcă, 2003.

3. As Romanian sociologist Ilie Bădescu has made clear using the example of Eminescu's polemics with the Romanian socialists, (Bădescu, forthcoming), the common concern of liberal, socialist, and conservative theorists with the issue of peripherality should not be mistaken for adherence to a common political doctrine. Thus, in polemicizing the socialists, Eminescu not only did not share their anti-capitalist stance but managed to overcome the limitations inherent in both socialist and liberal doctrines by pointing to the need to distinguish between the different effects capitalism produced in the core versus in the periphery.

4. According to Huntington, whereas Western Christianity was both actively involved in as well as shaped by feudalism, the Renaissance, the Enlightenment, the French Revolution, and industrialization, peoples east of the Velvet Curtain are taken to have been only "lightly touched" by them. Furthermore, these divergent trajectories are seen as accounting for the development of stable democracies in the West and their malfunction in the East.

5. How world-systems analysis can be used in the study of worldwide inequality patterns beyond the conceptual level cannot be addressed here for reasons of space, but several recent and forthcoming works are dedicated to the issue (e.g., Linden 2008). For a comprehensive world-systems approach to the empirical study of global inequality, see Korzeniewicz and Moran (2009).

6. Wallerstein's term for the modern variant of serf labor, which, for the very reason of being part of the capitalist mode of production, was essentially different from its feudal European form, was "coerced-cash crop labor" (Wallerstein 1974, 110ff.).

7. Whether or not class relations and inequality patterns more generally are a direct function of core-periphery relations has for decades been a matter of debate among world-systems theorists themselves and the object of criticism from related perspectives (for a recent overview see Linden 2008, ch. 13). While the approaches discussed in the following share some of the criticism and in part modify world-system's initial rendering of the impact of systems

of labor control on world class structure, they nevertheless adhere to the key notion of the interdependency of inequality mechanisms at the level of the world-economy, resulting in a world working class.

References

Bădescu, Ilie. 2002. Noologia. *Cunoașterea ordinii spirituale a lumii.* Sistem de sociologie noologică. Bucharest: Valahia.

———. 2004. *Sincronism european și cultură critică românească.* Cluj Napoca: Dacia.

Bădescu, Ilie, Dan Dungaciu, Sandra Cristea, Claudiu Degeratu, and Radu Baltasiu. 1995a. *Sociologia și geopolitica frontierei,* vol. 1. Bucharest: Floarea albastră.

———. 1995b. *Sociologia și geopolitica frontierei,* vol. 2. Bucharest: Floarea albastră.

Berend, Iván T., and György Ránki. 1982. *The European Periphery and Industrialization.* Cambridge: Cambridge University Press.

Berend, Iván T. 2003. *History Derailed. Central and Eastern Europe in the Long Nineteenth Century.* Berkeley: University of California Press.

Boatcă, Manuela. 2003. From Neoevolutionism to World-Systems Analysis. The Romanian Theory of 'Forms without Substance.' *Light of Modern Debates on Social Change.* Opladen.

———. 2005. Peripheral Solutions to Peripheral Development. The Case of Early 20th Century Romania. *Journal of World-Systems Research,* XI(I), 3–26.

———. 2006. Knocking on Europe's Door: Romanian Academia between Communist Censorship and Western Neglect. *South Atlantic Quarterly* 105(3:Summer), 551–579.

Chirot, Daniel. 1976. *Social Change in a Peripheral Society. The Creation of a Balkan Colony.* New York: Academic Press.

Coronil, Fernando. 1996. Beyond Occidentalism: Toward Non-Imperial Geohistorical Categories. *Cultural Anthropology* 11(1), 51–87.

Cristea, Darie. 2005. *Balcanii: Memorie și geopolitică.* Bucharest: Ed. Economică.

David, Aurel. 1996. Scenarii privind reorganizarea Europei. *Noua Revistă Română* 8–9(November-December), 159–168.

Dungaciu, Dan. 2004. *Națiunea și provocările (post)modernității.* Bucharest: Tritonic.

Dussel, Enrique. 1977. *Filosofia de la liberación.* Nueva América.

Eminescu, Mihai. 1877. Icoane vechi și icoane nouă. In Mihai Eminescu (1989), *Opere,* vol. X. Publicistică, Bucharest: R.S.R: 17–31.

———. 1878. Editorial in *Timpul.* In Mihai Eminescu (1989), *Opere,* vol. X, Publicistică, Bucharest: R.S.R: 90–91.

———. 1881a. Editorial in *Timpul.* In Mihai Eminescu (1985), *Opere,* vol. XII, Publicistică, Bucharest: R.S.R: 378–379.

———. 1881b. Editorial in *Timpul.* In Mihai Eminescu (1985), *Opere,* vol. XII, Publicistică, Bucharest: R.S.R.; 320–324.

Georgiu, Grigore. 2001. *Identitate si integrare. De la disjuncție la conjuncție.* Bucharest: Institutul de Teorie Socială.

Gherea, Constantin Dobrogeanu. 1908. Post-scriptum sau Cuvinte uitate. In Constantin Dobrogeanu-Gherea (1976): *Opere complete,* vol. 2. Bucharest: Ed. Politică; 476–504.

————. 1910. *Neoiobăgia. Studiu economico-sociologic al problemei noastre agrare.* Bucharest: Socec.

————. 1976 [1892]. Rolul Păturii Culte în Transformările sociale. In Constantin Dobrogeanu-Gherea (1976): *Opere complete,* vol. 2. Bucharest: Ed. Politică; 426–446.

Grosfoguel, Ramón. 1997. A TimeSpace Perspective on Development. Recasting Latin American Debates. *Review* XX(3/4:Summer/Fall), 465–540.

Grosfoguel, Ramón, Nelson Maldonado-Torres, and José David Saldívar, eds. 2005. *Latin@s in the World-System. Decolonization Struggles in the 21st Century U.S. Empire.* Boulder, CO: Paradigm Publishers.

Huntington, Samuel. 1993. The Clash of Civilizations? *Foreign Affairs* 72(3: Summer), 22–49.

Ivakhnenko, Eugene. 2006. A Threshold-Dominant Model of the Imperial and Colonial Discourse of Russia. *South Atlantic Quarterly* 105(3: Summer), 595–615.

Korzeniewicz, Roberto Patricio, and Timothy Patrick Moran. 2009. *Unveiling Inequality. A World-Historical Perspective.* New York: Russell Sage Foundation.

Linden, Marcel van der. 2008. *Workers of the World. Essays toward a Global Labor History.* Leiden: Brill.

McMichael, Philip. 2006. Peasant Prospects in a Neo-Liberal Age. *New Political Economy* 11(3), 407–418.

————. 2008. Peasants Make Their Own History, But Not Just as They Please. *Journal of Agrarian Change* 8(2–3), 205–228.

Mies, Maria, Veronika Bennholdt-Thomsen, and Claudia von Werlhof. 1988. *Women, the Last Colony.* London: Zed Books.

Mignolo, Walter. 2000. *Local Histories/Global Designs. Coloniality, Subaltern Knowledges, and Border Thinking.* Princeton: Princeton University Press.

————. 2002. The Geopolitics of Knowledge and the Colonial Difference. *South Atlantic Quarterly* 101(1), 57–96.

————. 2006. Introduction. *South Atlantic Quarterly* 105(3: Summer), 479–499.

Mignolo, Walter, and Madina Tlostanova. 2006. Theorizing from the Borders: Shifting to Geo- and Body-Politics of Knowledge. *European Journal of Social Theory* 9(2), 205–211.

Mintz, Sidney. 1986. *Sweetness and Power. The Place of Sugar in Modern History.* New York: Penguin.

Mureșan, Gheorghe. 1998. Utopia transnațională. *Noua Revistă Română,* 7–8(January–March), 111–113.

Quijano, Aníbal. 2000. Colonialidad del Poder y Clasificación Social. *Journal of World-Systems Research* I(2: Summer/Fall), 342–386.

Quijano, Aníbal, and Immanuel Wallerstein. 1992. Americanity as a Concept, or the Americas in the Modern World-System. *International Journal of Social Sciences* 134, 549–557.

Rokkan, Stein. 1999. A Model and Conceptual Map of Europe. *State Formation, Nation-Building, and Mass Politics in Europe,* 135–149. New York: Oxford University Press.

Stahl, Henri. 1993. Théories des processus de 'modernisation' des Principautés Danubiennes et de l'ancien Royaume de Roumanie (1850–1920). *Review,* XVI(1: Winter), 85–111.

Stere, Constantin. 1996 [1907–1908]. *Social-democratism sau poporanism?* Galaţi: Porto Franco.

Therborn, Göran. 1995. *European Modernity and Beyond. The Trajectory of European Societies, 1945–2000.* London: Sage.

Todorova, Maria. 1997. *Imagining the Balkans.* New York, Oxford: Oxford University Press.

———. 2004. Historische Vermächtnisse als Analysekategorie. Der Fall Südosteuropa. In *Europa und die Grenzen im Kopf,* edited by Karl Kaser, Dagmar Gramschammer-Hohl and Robert Pichler. Klagenfurt, 227–252.

Tomich, Dale. 2004. *Through the Prism of Slavery. Labor, Capital, and the World Economy.* Lanham: Rowman and Littlefield.

Wallerstein, Immanuel. 1974. *The Modern World System, Vol. I, Capitalist Agriculture and the Origins of the European World-Economy in the Sixteenth Century.* New York: Academic Press.

———. 1979. *The Capitalist World-Economy: Essays.* Cambridge: Cambridge University Press.

———. 1980. *The Modern World System, Vol. II, Mercantilism and the Consolidation of the European World-Economy, 1600–1750.* New York: Academic Press.

———. 1991. Marxisms as Utopias: Evolving Ideologies. *Unthinking Social Science.* Cambridge: Polity Press, 170–184.

———. 2000. *The Essential Wallerstein.* New York: The New Press.

———. 2005. Latin@s: What's in a Name? In *Latin@s in the World-System. Decolonization Struggles in the 21st Century U.S. Empire,* edited by Ramón Grosfoguel, Nelson Maldonado-Torres and José David Saldívar, 31–40.

Xenopol, Alexandru. 1882. Comertul exterior al României. In *Studii Economice* (1967). Bucharest: Ed. Academiei Republicii Socialiste România.

11

NEITHER GLOBAL NOR NATIONAL

NOVEL ASSEMBLAGES OF TERRITORY, AUTHORITY, AND RIGHTS[1]

Saskia Sassen

Introduction: Mapping an Analytic Terrain

A key yet much overlooked feature of the current period is the multiplication of a broad range of partial, often highly specialized, global assemblages of bits of territory, authority, and rights (TAR) that begin to escape the grip of national institutional frames.[2] These assemblages cut across the binary of national versus global. They continue to inhabit national institutional and territorial settings but are no longer part of the national as historically constructed. They exit the national through a process of denationalization that may or may not lead to the formation of global arrangements.

These assemblages are enormously diverse. At one end we find private, often very narrow, frameworks such as the *lex constructionis*, a private "law" developed by the major construction engineering companies in the world to establish a common mode of dealing with the strengthening of environmental standards in a growing number of countries, in most of which these firms are building.[3] At the other end of the range they include far more complex (and experimental) entities, such as the first ever-global public court, the International Criminal Court; this court is not part of the established supranational system and has universal jurisdiction among signatory countries.[4] Beyond the fact of the diversity of these assemblages, there is the increasingly weighty fact of their numbers—over 125 according to the best recent count.[5] Their proliferation does not represent the end of national states, but it does begin to disassemble the national.

Central to the argument in this chapter is that although for now these are mostly incipient formations, they are potentially profoundly unsettling of what are still the prevalent institutional arrangements (nation-states and the supranational system) for handling questions of order and justice. One of the consequences of the sharpening differentiation among domains once suffused with the national is that this can enable a proliferation of temporal and spatial framings and a proliferation of normative orders where once the dominant logic was toward producing unitary spatial, temporal, and normative framings. A synthesizing image we might use to capture these dynamics is that we see a movement from centripetal nation-state articulation to a centrifugal multiplication of specialized assemblages. This multiplication in turn can lead to a sort of simplification of normative structures: these assemblages are partial and often highly specialized formations centered in particular utilities and purposes. The valence of these particular utilities and purposes can range from the search for justice (the ICC) to narrow self-interest (*lex constructionis*).

What distinguishes these novel assemblages is that they can de-border, and even exit, what are today still ruling normative orders. Further, and equally important if not more so, they can constitute particularized "normative" orders internal to each assemblage which easily amount to what I will refer to as mere utility logics. These assemblages are not only highly specialized or particular, they are also without much internal differentiation, thereby further reducing normative orders to somewhat elementary utilities. This is still a minor process in the larger scale of our geopolity. But it may well be the beginning of a multi-sited disruption of its existing formal architecture. It is a process that lifts a variety of segments (involving dimensions of TAR) out of their nation-state normative framing, thereby reshuffling their constitutional alignments. Not even well-functioning states with their powerful *raison d'etat* can quite counteract the particularized normativities of each of these assemblages, and their easy slide into narrower utilitarian logics.

This slide into utilitarian logics is not always bad. In the case of a single-minded pursuit of human rights, we can see many positive outcomes even as it will tend to leave out important substantive matters. But a similarly single-minded pursuit of profits and disregard of state welfare functions is troubling. There are, then, both reasonable and unreasonable aspects to this process of multiplying lower-order normative framings. But whether good or bad, the de-bordering of national normative frames is a change, and it carries implications for how we are to handle the often-complex interactions of larger normative issues.

My argument is then that these developments signal the emergence of new types of orderings that can coexist with older orderings, such as the nation-state and the interstate system, but that nonetheless bring consequences that may well be critical for larger normative questions. These developments are both strategic and particular, and hence often illegible, requiring diverse modes of decoding.

Emphasizing this multiplication of partial assemblages contrasts with much of the globalization literature. That literature has tended to assume the binary of the global versus the national, and hence to focus on the powerful global institutions that have played a critical role in implementing the global corporate economy and have reduced the power of "the state." I rather emphasize that the global can also be constituted inside the national, i.e., the global city, and that particular components of the state have actually gained power because they have to do the work of implementing policies necessary for a global corporate economy. Thus my focus in the larger project (2008) and in this particular paper opens up the analysis of what is described as "globalization" to a far broader range of actors, and it repositions the powerful global regulators, such as the (reinvented) IMF or the WTO, as bridging events for an epochal transformation, rather than as the transformation itself. The actual dynamics being shaped are far deeper and more radical than such entities as the WTO or the IMF, no matter how powerful they are as foot soldiers. These institutions should rather be conceived of as powerful capabilities for the making of a new order—they are instruments, not the new order itself. The multiplication of partial assemblages examined in this paper signals a new ordering that begins to unsettle older frameworks that have held together, albeit always imperfectly, complex interdependencies between rights and obligations, power and the law, wealth and poverty, allegiance and exit.

In what follows, I first discuss the features of some of these assemblages, then examine questions of method and interpretation that shape this particular conceptualization of current transformations, and conclude with a discussion of their normative and political implications.

Specialized Assemblages as New Types of Territoriality

If you see through the eye of the national state, these assemblages look like inchoate geographies. But they are actually the bits of a new type of ordering, a reality in the making. Perhaps starting with some actual elementary spatial instances might help illuminate some of the issues for politics and normative questions to which I return in the second half of this essay. These are instances where we can detect a process of at least partial denationalizing of TAR. Here, then, follow some of these instances.

But first a brief clarification. I will use the concept of territoriality, usually used to designate the particular articulation of TAR marking the modern state, in a slightly different way so as to capture a far broader range of such articulations. The national state functions as the standard against which I identify the following four types of territoriality assembled out of "national" and "global" elements, with each individual or aggregate instance evincing distinct spatio-temporal features. (In the larger project, I examine yet other emergent assemblages.) These four types of instances unsettle national state territoriality; that is to say, the institutional framing of territory that gives the national state exclusive authority in a very broad range of domains that go well beyond territory itself. The territory of the national is a critical dimension in play in all four instances: diverse actors can exit the national institutionalization of territory yet act within national territory, and do so in ways that go well beyond existing extra-territorial arrangements. What gives weight to these four types of instances is not simply a question of novelty but their depth, spread, and proliferation. At some point all of this leads to a qualitatively different condition. We can conceive of it as emergent institutionalizations of territory that unsettle the national encasement of territory.

A first type of territoriality is being constituted through the development of new jurisdictional geographies. Legal frameworks for rights and guarantees, and more generally the rule of law, were largely developed in the context of the formation of national states. But now some of these instruments are strengthening a non-national organizing logic. As they become part of new types of transnational systems, they alter the valence of older national state capabilities. Further, in so doing, they are often pushing these national states to go against the interests of national capital. A second type of instance is the formation of triangular cross-border jurisdictions for political action, which once would have been confined to the national. Electronic activists often use global campaigns and international organizations to secure rights and guarantees from their national states. Furthermore, a variety of national legal actions involving multiple geographic sites across the globe can today be launched from national courts, producing a transnational geography for national lawsuits.

The critical articulation is between the national (as in national court, national law) and a global geography outside the terms of traditional international law or treaty law. A good example is the lawsuit launched by the Washington-based Center for Constitutional Rights in a national court against nine multinational corporations, both American and foreign, for abuses of workers' rights in their offshore industrial operations, using as the national legal instrument the Alien Torts Claims Act. In other words, this is a global three-sited jurisdiction, with several locations in at least two of those sites: the locations of the headquarters (both the United States and other countries), the locations of the offshore factories (several countries), and the court in Washington. Even if these lawsuits do not quite achieve their full goal, they signal that it is possible to use the national judiciary for suing US and foreign firms for questionable practices in their operations outside their home countries. Thus, besides the much-noted new courts and instruments (e.g., the new International Criminal Court, the European Court of Human Rights), what this example shows is that components of the national rule of law that once served to build the strength of the national state, are today contributing to the formation of transnational jurisdictions. Another instance is the US practice of "exporting" prisoners to third countries (rendition), *de facto* to facilitate their torture. This is yet another instance of a territoriality that is both national and transnational. Finally, diverse jurisdictional geographies can also be used to manipulate temporal dimensions. Reinserting a conflict in the national legal system may ensure a slower progression than in the private jurisdiction of international commercial arbitration.[6]

A second type of specialized assemblage that is contributing to a novel type of territoriality is the work of national states across the globe to construct a standardized global space for the operations of firms and markets. What this means is that components of legal frameworks for rights and guarantees, and more generally the rule of law, largely developed in the process of national state formation, can now strengthen non-national organizing logics. As these components become part of new types of transnational systems, they alter the valence of (rather than destroy, as is often argued) older national state capabilities. Where the rule of law once built the strength of the national state and national corporations, key components of that rule of law are now contributing to the partial, often highly specialized, denationalizing of particular national state orders. For instance, corporate actors operating globally have pushed hard for the development of new types of formal instruments, notably intellectual property rights and standardized accounting principles. But they need not only the support but also the actual work of each individual state where they operate to develop and implement such instruments in the specific context of each country. In their aggregate, this and other emergent orderings contribute to produce an operational space that is partly embedded in particular components of national legal systems which have been subjected to specialized denationalizations;[7] thereby these orderings become capabilities of an organizing logic that is not quite part of the national state even as that logic installs itself in that state. Further, in so doing, they often go against the interests of national capital. This is a very different way of representing economic globalization than the common notion of the withdrawal of the state at the hands of the global system. Indeed, to a large extent it is the executive branch of government that is aligning with global corporate capital and ensuring this work gets done.

A third type of specialized assemblage can be detected in the formation of a global network of financial centers. We can conceive of financial centers that are part of global financial markets as constituting a distinct kind of territoriality, simultaneously pulled in by the larger electronic networks and functioning as localized micro-infrastructures for those networks. These financial centers inhabit national territories, but they cannot be seen as simply national in the historical sense of the term, nor can they be reduced to the administrative unit encompassing the actual terrain (e.g., a city), one that is part of a nation-state. In their aggregate they house significant components of the global, partly electronic, market for capital. As localities they are denationalized in specific and partial ways. In this sense they can be seen as constituting the elements of a novel type of multi-sited territoriality, one that diverges sharply from the territoriality of the historic nation-state.

A fourth type of assemblage can be found in the global networks of local activists and, more generally, in the concrete and often place-specific social infrastructure of "global civil society."[8] Global civil society is facilitated by global digital networks and the associated imaginaries. But this does not preclude that localized actors, organizations, and causes are key building blocks of global civil society as it is shaping up today. The localized involvements of activists are critical no matter how universal and planetary the aims of the various struggles—in their aggregate these localized involvements are constitutive. Global electronic networks actually push the possibility of this local global dynamic further. Elsewhere I have examined the possibility for even resource-poor and immobile individuals or organizations to become part of a type of horizontal globality centered on diverse localities.[9] When supplied with the key capabilities of the new technologies (decentralized access, interconnectivity, and simultaneity of transactions), localized, immobilized individuals and organizations can be part of a global public space, one that is partly a subjective condition, but only partly because it is rooted in the concrete struggles of localities.

In principle, we can posit that those who are immobile might be more likely to experience their globality through this (abstract) space than individuals and organizations that have the resources and the options to travel across the globe. These globalities can assume complex forms, as is the case with first-nation people demanding direct representation in international fora, bypassing national state authority, a longstanding cause that has been significantly enabled by global electronic networking. They can also be more indirect, as is the case with the Forest Watch network, which uses indigenous residents in rain forests around the world as they can detect forest abuse long before it becomes visible to the average observer. They then pass on this information to what are often long chains of activists, eventually ending in the central office; the early links in the chain, where the deep knowledge resides, are typically not via digital media nor are they in English.

We can see here at work a particular type of interaction between placeless digital networks and deeply localized actors/users. One common pattern is the formation of triangular cross-border jurisdictions for political action, which once would have been confined to the national. Local activists often use global campaigns and international organizations to secure rights and guarantees from their national states; they now have the option to incorporate a non-national or global site in their national struggles. These instances point to the emergence of a particular type of territoriality in the context of the imbrications of digital and non-digital conditions. This territoriality partly inhabits specific subnational spaces and partly gets constituted as a variety of somewhat specialized or partial global publics.

While the third and fourth types of territoriality might seem similar, they actually are not. The subnational spaces of these localized actors have not been denationalized as have the financial centers discussed earlier. The global publics that get constituted are barely institutionalized and mostly informal, unlike the global capital market, which is a highly institutionalized space both through national and international law and through private governance systems. In their informality, however, these global publics can be seen as spaces for empowerment of the resource-poor or of not very powerful actors. In this sense the subjectivities that are emerging through these global publics constitute capabilities for new organizing logics.

Although these four types of emergent territorialities are diverse, each containing multiple, often highly specialized and partial instances, all four evince specific features. First, they are not exclusively national or global but are assemblages of elements of each. Second, in this assembling they bring together what are often different spatio-temporal orders, that is, different velocities and different scopes. Third, this can produce an eventful engagement, including contestations and the frontier zone effect, a space that makes possible kinds of engagements for which there are no clear rules. The resolution of these encounters can become the occasion for playing out conflicts that cannot easily be engaged in other spaces. Fourth, novel types of actors can emerge in this assembling, often with the option to access domains once exclusive to older established actors, notably national states. Finally, in the juxtaposition of the different temporal orders that come together in these novel territorialities, existing capabilities can get redeployed to domains with novel organizing logics.

These emergent assemblages begin to unbundle the traditional territoriality of the national historically constructed overwhelmingly as a national unitary spatio-temporal domain.

Avoiding Old Binaries

A major methodological, theoretical, and political implication of the type of analysis I am proposing is that it is insufficient to focus on the nation-state and the global system as two mutually exclusive and distinct entities. There are global formations that are indeed distinct and mutually exclusive with the nation-state, and I have studied these as well. But the transformations that concern me here crisscross this binary and enter the national and even the state apparatus itself. They may be a global condition that gets endogenized into the nation-state, or they may be endogenous to the nation-state but become denationalized in this process of change.

To historicize both the national and the global as constructed conditions, I have taken three transhistorical components present in almost all societies and examined how they became assembled into different historical formations. (This is fully developed in the larger project on which this paper is based.) These three components are territory, authority, and rights (TAR). Each can assume specific contents, shapes, and interdependencies across diverse historical formations. The choice of these three rests partly on their foundational character and partly on the contingency of my fields of knowledge. One could choose additional components or replace one or another of these.

TAR are complex institutionalizations arising from specific processes, struggles, and competing interests. They are not simply attributes. They are interdependent, even as they maintain their specificity. Each can, thus, be identified. Specificity is partly conditioned by levels of formalization and institutionalization. Across time and space, TAR have been assembled into distinct formations, within which they have had variable levels of performance. Further, the types of instruments and capabilities through which each gets constituted vary, as do the sites where each is in turn embedded (private or public, law or custom, metropolitan or colonial, national or supranational, and so on).

Using these three foundational components as analytic pathways into the two distinct formations that concern me in the larger project—the national and the global—helps avoid the endogeneity trap that so affects the globalization literature. Scholars have generally looked at these two complex formations *in toto* and compared them to establish their differences. This is not where I start. Rather than comparing what are posited as two wholes—the national and the global—I disaggregate each into these three foundational components (TAR). They are my starting point. I dislodge them from their particular historically constructed encasements (in this case, the national and the global) and examine their constitution and institutional location in these different historical formations, and their possible shifting valence as the global grows. An example is the shift of what were once components of public authority into a growing array of forms of private authority. One thesis that arises out of this type of analysis is that particular national capabilities can be dislodged from their national institutional encasement and become constitutive of globalization, rather than being destroyed or sidelined by it.[10]

This type of approach produces an analytic that can be used by others to examine various phenomena, be it countries in the context of today's globalization, or be it different types of assemblages across time and space.[11] In the modern state, TAR evolve into what we now can recognize as a centripetal scaling, where one scale, the national, aggregates most of what there is to be had in terms of TAR. Although never absolutely, each of the three components is constituted overwhelmingly as a national domain and, further, exclusively so. Whereas in the past most territories were subject to multiple systems of rule, the modern state gains exclusive authority over a given territory and at the same time this territory is constructed as coterminous with that authority, in principle ensuring a similar dynamic in other nation-states. This in turn gives the sovereign the possibility of functioning as the exclusive grantor of rights. Territory is perhaps the most critical capability for the formation of the nation-state. But it is not for today's global regulators, for whom authority is more critical than territory. Nor is it for the human rights regime, for whom rights are more critical than territory.

Globalization can be seen as destabilizing the particular scalar assemblage represented by the nation-state. What scholars have noticed is the fact that the nation-state has lost some of its exclusive territorial authority to new global institutions.[12] What they have mostly failed to examine in-depth are the specific, often specialized, rearrangements inside the highly formalized and institutionalized national state apparatus aimed at instituting the authority of global institutions. This shift is not simply a question of policy-making—it is about making a novel type of institutional space inside the state. In overlooking such rearrangements, or interpreting them as simply national changes, it is also easy to overlook the extent to which critical components of the global are structured inside the national, producing what I refer to as a partial, and often highly specialized, denationalizing of what historically was constructed as national.

Thus today particular elements of TAR are becoming reassembled into novel global configurations. Therewith, their mutual interactions and interdependencies are altered, as are their institutional encasements. These shifts take place both within the nation-state—for example, shifts from public to private—and through shifts to the inter- and supra-national and global levels. What was bundled and experienced as a unitary condition (the national assemblage of TAR) now increasingly reveals itself to be a set of distinct elements, with variable capacities for becoming denationalized. For instance, we might say that particular components of authority and of rights are evincing a greater capacity to partial denationalization than territory; geographic boundaries have changed far less (except in cases such as the disintegration of the Soviet Union) than authority (i.e., the greater power of global regulators over national economies) and rights (the further institutionalizing of the international human rights regime). It points to possibly sharp divergence between the organizing logics of the earlier international and current global phases; these two phases are often seen as analogous to the current global phase, but I argue this understanding may be based on a confusion of analytical levels. In earlier periods, that international logic was geared toward building national states, typically through imperial geographies. In today's phase, it is geared toward setting up global systems *inside* national states and national economies, and in that sense, at least partly denationalizing what had historically been constructed as national. This denationalizing can take multiple concrete forms. Two critical ones are global cities and specific policies and institutions within the state itself, including such different regimes as instituting human rights and instituting the rights of foreign firms. The Bretton Woods agreement, often seen as the beginning of the current global era is, in my interpretation, not part of the current phase: it sought to protect national states from excessive fluctuations in the international economy.

The scholarship on the state and globalization contains three basic positions: one finds the state is victimized by globalization and loses significance; a second one finds that nothing much has changed and states basically keep on doing what they have always done; and a third, a variant on the second, finds that the state adapts and may even be transformed, thereby ensuring that it does not decline and remains the critical actor. There is research to support critical aspects of each one of these three positions, partly because much of their difference hinges on interpretation. For some, states remain as the key actors no matter how the context has changed, and hence not much has changed about states and the interstate system.[13] For others, even if states remain important there are today other key actors, and globalization has changed some important features of states and the interstate system.[14] But notwithstanding their diversity, these scholarships tend to share the assumption that the national and the global are mutually exclusive.

A second line of argumentation concerns what has changed. Thus for Mann, the present era is merely a continuation of a long history of changes that have not altered the fundamental fact of state primacy.[15] Both the "strong" and the "weak" version of neo-Weberian state theory share certain dimensions of this conceptualization of the state.[16] While acknowledging that the primacy of the state may vary given different structural conditions between state and society, these authors tend to understand state power as basically denoting the same conditions throughout history: the ability to successfully implement explicitly formulated policies. A second type of literature interprets deregulation and privatization as the incorporation by the state of its own shrinking role.[17] In its most formalized version, this position emphasizes the state's constitutionalization of its own diminished role. In this literature, economic globalization is not confined to capital crossing geographic borders as is captured in measures of international investment and trade, but is in fact conceptualized as a politico-economic system. A third, growing literature emphasizes the relocation of national public governance functions to private actors both within national and global domains.[18] Key institutions of the supranational system, such as the World Trade Organization, are emblematic of this shift. Cutting across these types of literatures are the issues raised earlier as to whether states are declining, are remaining as strong as they have ever been, or, have changed but as part of an adaptation to the new conditions rather than a loss of power.

Given my effort to expand the analytic terrain within which to map the question of the global and the national, the larger research and theorization agenda needs to address aspects of globalization and the state, which are lost in these dualized accounts about their relationship. In these accounts, the spheres of influence of, respectively, the national and the global are seen as mutually exclusive. While there are indeed many components of each the national and the global that are mutually exclusive, there is a growing, often specific set of components that does not fit in this dual structure.

Factoring in these types of conditions amounts to a fourth position alongside the three referred to above. While this fourth type of approach does not necessarily preclude all propositions in the other three, it is nonetheless markedly different in its foundational assumptions. For instance, in my own research I find that far from being mutually exclusive, the state is one of the strategic institutional domains where critical work for developing globalization takes place. This does not necessarily produce the decline of the state, but neither does it keep the state going as usual or produce merely adaptations to the new conditions. The state becomes the site for foundational transformations in the relation between the private and the public domains, in the state's internal balance of power, and in the larger field of both national and global forces within which the state now has to function.[19] One feature of the larger field of forces is the multiplication of specialized assemblages described earlier. I now turn to this in greater detail with a particular focus on the political and normative implications of this development.

Normative and Political Implications

The centrifugal multiplication of specialized and/or particular assemblages of TAR is a partial rather than all-encompassing development. Yet its character is strategic in that it unsettles existing normative arrangements and produces a new type of segmentation. One way of formulating the consequences is in terms of novel types of systemic inequality and novel locations for the normative.

We can begin with the novel types of systemic inequality that are being produced. These are kinds of inequality that can cut across every scale, nation-state, major city, and state apparatus. It is not the kind of intra-systemic inequality that emerges from inside a unitary, albeit highly differentiated system, such as a nation-state. Nor is it the kind of inequality that exists between developed and less developed regions of the world. These are two types of recognized and named inequalities, and we have developed massive institutional and discursive domains to address them; although all this effort has only partly reduced those inequalities, they are a recognized target for existing efforts and resources.

In contrast, the proliferation of specialized assemblages that exit the grip of existing normative frames and cut across countries produces a kind of inequality we might conceive of as multiplying particular types of intersystemic segmentations, where the systems are these particularized assemblages. It is, then, also a kind of inequality that can coexist with older and recognized forms of differentiation inside countries and among countries. But it is to be distinguished from these.

Secondly, on the locations for the normative, these assemblages tend to have rules for governance wired into the structures of their system in a way reminiscent of how free markets function. That is to say, these are not explicated rules and norms. The new forms of unaccountable power within the executive branch of government and in global markets illustrate this; but so does the world of NGOs, perhaps especially when they function internationally. This wiring of rules and norms in the structure itself of the system can be distinguished from formalized systems for governance where rules and norms are meant to be explicated and are located both inside and outside the system itself, in that they are accountable to external authorities.[20]

We can see here a disaggregating of the glue that for a long time held possibly different normative orders together under the somewhat unitary dynamics of nation-states. The multiplication of partial systems, each with a small set of sharply distinctive constitutive rules produces a proliferation of simple systems. This also brings with it a reshuffling of constitutive rules. Not all of these new specialized assemblages contain such constitutive rules, but it is evident in a number of those that constitute themselves precisely as disembedded from state authority and normativity and as systems of justice and authority (for instance, the ICC), including private systems of justice (for instance, international commercial arbitration).[21]

Perhaps it is tempting to see in these trends arrangements akin to European feudalism, a period marked by the absence of centralized national states. Some of the globalization literature positing the weakening, and even "disappearance" of the nation-state has made this type of argument. I see this as a mistake (2006: Part One). In identifying a multiplication of partial orders, I find a foundational difference with the medieval European period, one when there were strong broadly encompassing normative orders (the church, the empire) and the disaggregations (the feuds, the cities) each contained within them a fairly complete structure involving many, if not most, aspects of life (different classes, norms, systems of justice, and so forth). Today these assemblages are highly specialized, partial, and without much internal differentiation. In contrast, the localized and limited world of the manor or the fief of the medieval lord was a complex world encompassing constitutive rules that addressed the full range of spheres of social life.

The multiplication of partial, specialized, and applied normative orders is unsettling and produces distinct normative challenges in the context of a still prevalent world of nation-states. Just to mention one instance, we can deduce from these trends that normative orders such as religion reassume great importance where they had been confined to distinct specialized spheres by the secular normative orders of states. Thus I posit the rise of religion in the last two decades especially as part of a new modernity rather than a fallback on older cultures, no matter how "traditional" its contents. It is a systemic outcome of cutting-edge developments. In brief, this can then be shown to be not pre-modern but a new type of modernity, arising out of the partial unbundling of what had been dominant and centripetal (secular) normative orders into multiple particularized segmentations.[22]

This incipient formation of specialized or particularized orders extends even inside the state apparatus. I argue that we can no longer speak of "the" state, and hence of "the" national state versus "the" global order. There is a novel type of segmentation inside the state apparatus, with a growing and increasingly privatized executive branch of government aligned with specific global actors, notwithstanding nationalist speeches, and a hollowing out of the legislature whose effectiveness is at risk of becoming confined to fewer and more domestic matters.[23] A weak and domesticated legislature weakens the political capacity of citizens to demand accountability from an increasingly powerful and private executive, since the legislature gives citizens stronger standing in these matters than the executive. Further, the privatizing of the executive has partly brought with it an eroding of the privacy rights of citizens—a historic shift of the private-public division at the heart of the liberal state, even if always an imperfect division.[24]

A second critical divergence is between the increasing alignment of the executive with global logics and the confinement of the legislature to domestic matters.[25] This results from three major trends. One is the growing importance of particular components of the administration, such as ministries of finance and central banks (respectively, Treasury and Federal Reserve in the United States), for the implementing of a global corporate economy; these components actually gain power because of globalization. Secondly, the global regulators (IMF, WTO, and others) only deal with the executive branch; they do not deal with the legislature. This can strengthen the adoption of global logics by the executive. A third becomes evident in such cases as the Bush-Cheney Administration's support for the Dubai Ports proposed management of several major port operations in the United States. In contrast to these trends, the legislature has long been a domestic part of the state, something which begins to weaken its effectiveness as globalization expands. This then also weakens the political capacity of citizens in an increasingly globalized world.

This participation of the state in the implementation of a corporate global economy engenders a particular type of international authority for the state *vis-à-vis* global firms and it engenders a kind of internationalism in state practice. But for now the deployment of this authority and new internationalism has largely been confined to supporting private corporate interests. Such a conceptualization introduces a twist in the analysis of the state and corporate economic globalization because it seeks to detect the actual presence of private agendas inside the state, rather than the more common focus in the globalization literature on the shift of state functions to the private sector and the growth of private authority.[26] Further, it differs from an older scholarly tradition on the captured state, which focused on cooptation of states by private actors.[27] In my own research I emphasize the privatization of norm-making capacities and the enactment inside the state of corporate private logics dressed as public norms.[28]

An important question is whether these new properties of state practice could be reoriented to questions concerning the global common good. For this to become an aim, a number of issues need to be addressed. What type of state authority is this mix of public and private components, and, most importantly, could it accommodate other interests besides private corporate ones? Does the weight of private, often foreign, interests in this specific work of the state become constitutive of that authority and indeed produce a hybrid that is neither fully private nor fully public? My argument is that we are seeing the incipient formation of a type of authority and state practice that entails a partial denationalizing of what had been constructed historically as national. This denationalizing consists of several specific processes, including importantly, the re-orienting of national agendas towards global ones, and the circulation inside the state of private agendas dressed as public policy. But this denationalizing also can open up space for non-corporate international agendas.

For the purposes of this essay it matters whether this participation by the state in global processes, and the consequent partial denationalization, can also take place in domains other than that of economic globalization. Among these are recent developments in the human rights regime, which make it possible to sue foreign firms and foreign dictators in national (rather than international) courts. Can denationalization be extended to aims other than those of global corporate actors including an attempt to develop a global economy with broader social justice aims, and aims other than economic ones?[29] Elsewhere I have argued that yes, like globalization, denationalization can be multivalent: it can include the endogenizing into the national of the global agendas of diverse actors, not only corporate firms and financial markets, but also human rights and environmental agendas.[30] The existence of a dynamic and growing transnational sphere[31] becomes critical at this juncture as it can sustain this entry by national actors into global struggles using national instruments.[32] Sometimes these processes of denationalization allow, enable, or push the construction of new types of global scalings; other times they continue to inhabit the realm of what is still largely national.

An issue in all of this is the considerable illegibility, ultimately, of this shift from a centripetal to a centrifugal logic. We cannot quite see that this centrifugal logic has replaced important segments of the centripetal logic of the nation-state. This is partly because the national state continues to be the dominant ordering institution and because war and militarized border controls mark the geopolitical landscape and have mostly been sharpened rather than diluted in much of the world. It leads many observers to overlook the fact that wars and borders can coexist with centrifugal logics. Even more difficult to apprehend is the fact that, through processes of denationalization, some of the components of the nation-state and the state apparatus are themselves part of the new centrifugality. Elsewhere I have shown how this trend holds even for particular segments of the executive branch of government,[33] in spite of varied nationalisms. The ongoing prevalence of strong state politics and policies may well increasingly be a matter more of raw power than the more complex category that is authority. The new types of wars, whether "civil" or international, suggest this rise of raw power over authority. Even as the raw power of national states in many cases has increased, this may not necessarily mean that sovereign territorial authority has become more significant. This distinction is critical to the analysis in the larger project on which this essay is based.[34]

Important to my argument is that some of the most complex meanings of the global are being constituted inside the national, whether national territories and institutions or national states. A good part of globalization consists of an enormous variety of subnational micro-processes that begin to denationalize what had been constructed as national—whether policies, laws, capital, political subjectivities, urban spaces, temporal frames, or any other of a variety of dynamics and domains.[35] This argument can perhaps be developed most persuasively at this time through an examination of the critical role of national states in setting up the basic conditions, including governance structures, for the implementation of a global economy.[36] Ministries of finance, central banks, legislatures, and many other government sectors have done the state work necessary to secure a global capital market, a global trading system, the needed competition policies, and so on.

Conclusion

Both self-evidently global and denationalizing dynamics destabilize existing meanings and systems. As the unitary character of the nation-state becomes disaggregated, even if only partially, sovereign authority is itself subject to partial disaggregations. The weakening of the centripetal dynamic of the nation-state also can generate exit options for the disadvantaged. Denationalization is the category through which I attempt to capture these transformations because they are not necessarily global in the narrow sense of that term. This is a historicizing categorization with the double intent of de-essentializing the national by confining it to a historically specific configuration and of making it a reference point by positing that its enormous complexity and large capture of society and the geopolity make it a strategic site for the transformation—the latter cannot simply come from the outside. What this categorization does not entail is the notion that the nation-state as a major form will disappear. Rather, in addition to being the site for key transformations, it will itself be a profoundly changed entity.

Except for the most superficial and self-evident instances (e.g., globalized consumer markets), this constituting and shaping of global dynamics inside the national generally gets coded, represented, formulated, or experienced through the vocabularies and institutional instruments of the national as historically constructed. This is to be expected insofar as nation-states, and national states are enormously complex organizations, with often very long histories of developing the needed capabilities. In contrast, the current phase of global institutions and processes is young and an as yet thin reality. Part of the research task is then decoding, and, more generally, discovering and detecting the global inside the national.

These and other denationalizing dynamics (e.g., the insertion of human rights in national judiciary decisions) have additional consequences. They begin to disassemble bits and pieces of the nation-state and the state apparatus itself as containers. This disassembling is one dynamic feeding the multiplication of partial, often highly specialized, cross-border assemblages of bits of TAR once lodged inside the national. Many of these are beginning to function as formal or informal entities for both operational and governance tasks in a growing range of global processes stretching across nation-states. The clearest normative implication is a proliferation of particularized normative orders, including their downgrading to utility logics. Whether this is the beginning of a phase that might still see the formation of larger and more encompassing normative orders, remains, in my reading, an open question.

All of this points to at least three distinct subjects for further research and theorization. One concerns the degree of specificity of these emergent assemblages that result from the partial disassembling of unitary nation-state framings. That is to say, what is the extent of their normative and analytic legibility? The second concerns the level of complexity and power these assemblages can assume, given their as yet elementary character compared to the internal diversity, organizational complexity, and social thickness of the national. A third subject concerns the move away from unitary normative and spatio-temporal alignments inside nation-states resulting from this proliferation of multiple assemblages. In brief, what are the normative and political implications of these moves toward centrifugal dynamics, and away from the centripetal dynamics that have marked the development of nation-states?

Notes

1. This is based on a larger project published as *Territory, authority, rights: From medieval to global assemblages* (Princeton, NJ: Princeton University Press, 2008), henceforth referred to as *Territory*. There readers can find full bibliographic elaboration of the issues raised here.

2. This is clearly an analysis that emerges from European history, with all the limitations that entails. Critical here is Gayatri Spivak's thinking about the diverse positions that can structure an "author's" stance. Donna Landry and Gerald MacLean (eds.) 1996. *The Spivak reader.* New York and London: Routledge.

3. See generally Teubner, Gunther (ed.) (1997) *Global law without a State.* Aldershot, UK: Dartmouth Publishing.

4. See Sadat, Leila Nadya, and Richard Carden, S. (2000) The new international criminal court, *Georgetown Law Journal* 88(3), 381–474.

5. See http://www.pict.org.

6. *Territory,* Chapter 5.

7. *Territory,* Chapters 4 and 5.

8. This term remains underspecified in the view of many. But there is now a vast scholarship that has documented various features, measures, and interpretations. See for instance, the *Annual Global Civil Society* volumes published by Oxford University Press.

9. *Territory,* Chapter 7.

10. In the larger project (*Territory,* Chapters 1, 8, and 9) there are lengthy discussions of questions of method and interpretation. I propose a distinction between capabilities (for example, the rule of law) and the organizing logics (the national, the global) within which they are located. Thus capabilities are multivalent: as they switch organizing logics, their valence can change. But they may look the same, and detecting their change may well require decoding.

11. I use the concept assemblage in its most descriptive sense. However, several scholars have developed theoretical constructs around this term. Most significant for the purposes of the book on which this chapter is based, is the work of Deleuze and Guattari, for whom "assemblage" is a contingent ensemble of practices and things that can be differentiated (that is, they are not collections of similar practices and things) and that can be aligned along the axes of territoriality and deterritorialization. More specifically, they posit that particular mixes of technical and administrative practices "extract and give intelligibility to new spaces by decoding and encoding milieu." Deleuze, Gilles and Félix Guattari. 1987. *A thousand plateaus: capitalism and schizophrenia.* Minneapolis: University of Minnesota Press, 504–505. There are many more elaborations around the concept assemblage, including not surprisingly, among architects and urbanists (vide the journal *Assemblages*). While I find many of these elaborations extremely important and illuminating, and while some of the assemblages I identify may evince some of these features, my usage is profoundly untheoretical compared to that of the above-cited authors. I simply want the dictionary term. I locate my theorization elsewhere, not on this term.

12. For a number of critical scholars, even if states remain important there are today other key actors, and globalization has changed some important features of states and the interstate system. Phillip G. Cerny. 2000. "Structuring the political arena: public goods, states and governance in a globalizing world." In *Global political economy: contemporary theories,* edited by Ronen Palan. London, Routledge, 21–35. Phillip G. Cerny. 1990. *The changing architecture of politics.* London and Newbury, CA: Sage. Ferguson, Y.H. and Barry Jones, R.J. (eds.). 2002. *Political space: Frontiers of change and governance in a globalizing world.* Albany, NY: SUNY Press. Susan Strange. 1996. *The retreat of the state.* Cambridge: Cambridge University Press. Cutler, A. Claire, Virginia Haufler, and Tony Porter. 1999. "Private authority and international affairs." In *Private authority and international affairs,* edited by Claire A. Cutler, Virginia Haufler and Tony Porter. Albany, NY: SUNY Press. For others more centered in canonical propositions, states remain as the key actors no matter how the context has changed, and hence not much has changed about states and the interstate system. Stephen Krasner. 2003. "Globalization and the state." In: *Contemporary debates in international relations,* edited by Edwards and Sisson. Miami, OH: Ohio University Press. Eric Helleiner. 1999. "Sovereignty, territoriality and the globalization of finance." In *States and sovereignty in the global economy,* edited by D. Smith, D. Solinger, and S. Topic. London: Routledge. Pauly. 2002. "Who governs the bankers." In *The emergence of private authority in*

global governance, edited by Rodney Bruce Hall and Thomas J. Biersteker. Cambridge: Cambridge University Press.

13. Krasner, "Globalization and the state"; Pauly, "Who governs the bankers"; Helleiner, "Sovereignty, territoriality and the globalization of finance."

14. For example, Cerny, "Structuring the political arena"; Cerny, The changing architecture; Strange 1996; Cutler et al. 1999; Ferguson and Jones, Political Space; Koskenniemi, Martii. 2009. "The Politics of International Law-20 Years Later." *European Journal of International Law* (20)1: 7–19.

15. Michael Mann. 1997. "Has globalization ended the rise and rise of the nation state?" *Review of International Political Economy* 4(3), 472–496.

16. Skocpol, Theda. 1985. "Bringing the state back in: strategies of analysis in current research." In *Bringing the state back in*, edited by Peter Evans, Dietrich Rueschemeyer and Theda Skocpol. Cambridge and New York: Cambridge University Press. Evans, Peter. 1997. "The eclipse of the state? Reflections on stateness in an era of globalization," *World Politics* 50(1), 62–87.

17. Panitch, Leo. 1996. "Rethinking the role of the state." In *Globalization: critical reflections*, edited by James Mittelman. Boulder, CO: Lynne Rienner Publishers, 83–113. Gill, S. 1996. "Globalization, democratization, and the politics of indifference." In *Globalization: critical perspectives*, edited by James Mittelman. 205–228. Mittelman, James H. 2000. *The globalization syndrome: transformation and resistance*. Princeton, NJ: Princeton University Press.

18. For example, Hall and Biersteker (2002) and Cutler et al. (1999); Cutler, A Claire. 2009. "Constituting Capitalism: Corporations, Law, and Private Transnational Governance." Saint Anthony's International Review (5)1: 99–115; Kingsbury, Benedict, and L Casini. 2009. "Global Administrative Law Dimensions of International Organizations Law." *International Organization Law Review* (63)2.

19. *Territory*, Chapters 4 and 5.

20. I intend this to capture a considerable diversity of formations. For instance, Hezbollah in Lebanon can be seen as having shaped a very specific assemblage of TAR that cannot be easily reduced to any of the familiar containers nation-state, internal minority-controlled region, such as the Kurdish region in Iraq, or a separatist area such as the Basque region in Spain. It intensifies the difference with the "home country" and in fact extends beyond the latter through specific translocal networks and more difuse subjectivities. This type of development strengthens types of territorial and authority fractures that the project of building a nation-state sought to eliminate or dilute.

21. I develop these issues at length in *Territory*, Chapters 5, 6, and 8.

22. We also see these incipient novel mixes of TAR in far less visible or noticed settings. For instance, when Mexico's (former) President Fox met with undocumented Mexican immigrants during his visit to the United States in May 2006, his actions amounted to the making of a new informal jurisdiction. His actions did not fit into existing legal forms that give sovereign states specific types of extraterritorial authority. Nonetheless, his actions were not seen as particularly objectionable; indeed, they were hardly noticed. Yet these were, after all, unauthorized immigrants subject to deportation if detected, in a country that is now spending almost two billion dollars a year to secure border control. No INS or other police came to arrest the undocumented thus exposed, and the media barely reacted, even though it was taking place at a time when Congress was debating whether to criminalize illegal immigrants. Or when Chavez, seen as an "enemy" of sorts by the US government, is somehow enabled (through the state-owned oil enterprise) to bring oil to the poor in a few major cities in the United States. All of these are minor acts, but they were not somehow acceptable or customary even a short time ago. I see these practices as producing novel types of mostly informal jurisdictions, and these are, in the last analysis, assemblages of TAR.

23. *Territory*, Chapter 4. In fact, nationality itself is a legal format undergoing change (see, for instance, Karen Knop [2002] *Diversity and Self-Determination in International Law*. Cambridge:

Cambridge University Press; Kim Rubenstein and Daniel Adler [2000] "International Citizen-ship: The Future of Nationality in a Globalized World," *Indiana Journal of Global Legal Studies* 7(2): 519–48). Nationality can no longer be easily deployed as a singular condition. Some of the main dynamics at work today are destabilizing its singular meaning; for example, the granting of dual nationality (see Peter J. Spiro [2007] *Citizenship Beyond Borders*) and the incorporation of international human rights norms in national law (Harold Hongju Koh [1997] "How is International Human Rights Law Enforced?," *Indiana Law Journal* 74(4): 1397–1417). In this regard nationality may well evolve into an instance of Benhabib's "constitutive tensions in liberal democracies." For a more detailed discussion of these issues,see the special issue on Benhabib's work and my response in the *European Journal of Political Theory,* 6 (4: 2007), 431–444.

24. This is a complicated issue that I do not address here, but see *Territory*, Chapter 6. One question is whether there is a necessary relationship between an increasingly privatized executive branch and the erosion of citizens' privacy rights.

25. An issue here is the relationship between this executive branch alignment with global logics, on the one hand, and, on the other, the proliferation of various nationalisms. I address this in *Territory*, Chapters 6 and 9. Helpful here is Calhoun's (1997) proposition that nationalism is a process articulated with modernity; this makes room for the coexistence of globalization and nationalization. Craig Calhoun. 1997. *Nationalism*. University of Minnesota Press.

26. For example, Cutler, C. (2000) "Globalization, law, and transnational corporations: a deepending of market discipline," in: T.H. Cohn, S. McBride and Wiseman, J. (eds) *Power in the global era: grounding globalization*, 53–66. London, Macmillan.

27. Panitch, "Rethinking the Role of the State." op.cit. Cox.

28. *Territory*, Chapters 4 and 5; Sassen (1996) *Losing control? Sovereignty in an age of global-ization*. New York, Columbia University Press, Chapter 2.

29. For example, Lourdes Beneria (2003). *Global tensions: challenges and opportunities in the world economy*. New York: Routledge; Max Kirsch (ed.). 2006. *Inclusion and exclusion in the global arena*. New York: Routledge; Kate E. Tunstall (ed.). 2006 *Displacement, asylum, migration: the 2004 amnesty lectures*. Oxford: Oxford University Press; Linda Lucas (ed.). 2005. *Unpacking globalisation: markets, gender and work*. Kampala, Uganda: Makerere University Press; Natalia Ribas-Mateos. 2005. *The Mediterranean in the age of globalization: migration, welfare, and borders*. Somerset, NJ: Transaction; Rami Nashashibi. 2007 "Ghetto cosmopolitanism: making theory at the margins." In *Deciphering the global*, edited by Saskia Sassen. 241–262.

30. *Territory*, Chapters 8 and 9.

31. For example, Khagram, S., Riker, J.V. and Sikkink, K. (eds). (2002) *Restructuring World politics: transnational social movements, networks, and norms*. Minneapolis, MN: University of Min-nesota Press; Valentine M. Moghadam. 2005. *Globalizing women: transnational feminist networks*. Baltimore: Johns Hopkins University Press; Nancy A. Naples and Manisha Desai. 2002. *Women's activism and globalization: linking local struggles and transnational politics*. New York: Routledge.

32. *Territory*, Chapter 6.

33. *Territory*, Chapter 4.

34. *Territory*, Chapter 4.

35. A focus on such subnationally based processes and dynamics of globalization requires methodologies and theorizations that engage not only global scalings but also subnational scal-ings as components of global processes, thereby destabilizing older hierarchies of scale and nested scalings. Studying global processes and conditions that get constituted subnationally has some advantages over studies of globally scaled dynamics, but it also poses specific challenges. It does make possible the use of long-standing research techniques, from quantitative to qualitative, in the study of globalization. It also gives us a bridge for using the wealth of national and subnational data sets as well as specialized scholarships such as area studies. Both types of studies, however, need to be situated in conceptual architectures that are not quite those held by the researchers who generated these research techniques and data sets, as their efforts mostly had little to do with

globalization. I develop this in Saskia Sassen 2007. *A sociology of globalization.* New York: W. W. Norton.

36. For example, Alfred C. Aman 1998. "The globalizing state: a future-oriented perspective on the public/private distinction, federalism, and democracy." *Vanderbilt Journal of Transnational Law* 31, 769–870; Giselle Datz. 2007. "Global national interactions and sovereign debt-restructuring outcomes." In *Deciphering the global: Its spaces, scales and subjects*, edited by Saskia Sassen. New York and London: Routledge, 321–350.; Rachel Harvey. 2007. "The subnational constitution of global markets." In *Deciphering the global: Its spaces, scales and subjects*, edited by Saskia Sassen. New York and London Routledge, 199–216.; *Territory*, Chapters 1 and 2; Balakrishnan Rajagopal. 2003. *International law from below.* Cambridge: Cambridge University Press.

12

THE GLOBAL STREET
COMES TO WALL STREET

Saskia Sassen

Street struggles and demonstrations are part of our global modernity.[1] The uprisings in the Arab world, the daily neighborhood protests in China's major cities, Latin America's *piqueteros* and poor people demonstrating with pots and pans—all are vehicles for making social and political claims. We can add to these the very familiar antigentrification struggles and demonstrations against police brutality in US cities during the 1980s and in cities worldwide in the 1990s and continuing today. Then there is the recent huge march of over one hundred thousand people in Tel Aviv, a first for that city, whose aim was not to bring down the government but to petition for access to housing and jobs; part of the demonstration is Tel Aviv's tent city, which houses mostly impoverished middle-class citizens. Spain's *Indignados,* who have been demonstrating peacefully in Madrid and Barcelona for jobs and social services, have now become a national movement, with people from throughout the country gathering for a very long march to EU headquarters in Brussels. These are also the claims of the six hundred thousand who went to the street in late August in several cities in Chile. And in September 2011, the United States saw its *indignados* call for a literal and symbolic occupation of the street at the center of global finance, Wall Street. These are among the diverse instances that together make me think of a concept that goes beyond the empirics of each case—the Global Street.

In each of these cases, I would argue that the street, the urban street, as public space is to be differentiated from the classic European notion of more ritualized spaces for public activity, with the piazza and the boulevard the emblematic European instances. I think of the space of "the street," which of course includes squares and any available open space, as a rawer and less ritualized space. The Street is a space where new forms of the social and the political can be *made*, rather than a space for enacting ritualized routines. With some conceptual stretching, we might say that politically "street and square" are marked differently from "boulevard and piazza": the first signals action, and the second, ritual.

Seen this way, there is an epochal quality to the current wave of street protests, no matter their enormous differences, from the extraordinary courage and determination of protesters in Syria, to the flash crowds convoked via social media to invade commercial blocks in Chile, the United Kingdom, and the United States, to the unarmed Occupiers being tear-gassed, beaten, and arrested by militarized police forces across America.

In this short essay, I first examine some aspects of the uprisings in the Middle East and North Africa. The effort is to situate these specifics in a larger conceptual frame: the focus is on dimensions of these diverse politics that have at least one strategic moment in the space that is the Street—the urban street, not the rural or suburban street. The city is the larger space that enables some of this and also the lens that allows us to capture the history-making qualities of these protests, whose larger background includes a sharp slide into inequalities, expulsions from places and livelihoods, corrupt political classes, unfettered greed, and in the most significant of these struggles, extreme oppression.[2] I then explore the role communication technologies have to play. Finally, I look at how Occupy Wall Street shows us the limits of superior armed force but also the antidemocratic character of the neoliberal state. The Occupy movement also brings to the fore the return of territory as one crucial stepping ground in social struggles, from antigentrification protests to Tahrir Square.

When Powerlessness Becomes Complex

The city is a space where the powerless can make history. That is not to say it is the only space, but it is certainly a critical one. Becoming present, visible, to each other can alter the character of powerlessness. I make a distinction between different types of powerlessness. Powerlessness is not simply an absolute condition that can be flattened into the absence of power. Under certain conditions, powerlessness can become complex, by which I mean that it contains the possibility of making the political, or making the civic, or making history—there is a difference between powerlessness and invisibility/impotence. Many of the protest movements we have seen in the Middle East and North Africa (MENA) are a case in point: these protesters may not have gained power; they are still powerless, but they are making a history and a politics. This then leads me to a second distinction, which contains a critique of the common notion that if something good happens to the powerless, it signals empowerment. The concept that powerlessness can become complex can be used to characterize a condition that is not quite empowerment. Powerlessness can be thereby consequential.

What is being engendered in the uprisings in the cities of the MENA region is quite different from what it might have been in the medieval city of Max Weber. Weber identifies a set of practices that allowed the burghers to set up systems for owning property and protecting it against more powerful actors, such as the king and the church, and to implement various immunities against despots of all sorts. Today's political practices, I would argue, have to do with the production of "presence" by those without power, a politics that claims rights to the city and to the state rather than protection of property. What the two situations share is the notion that new forms of the political (for Weber, citizenship) are being constituted, with the city as a key site for this type of political work. The city is, in turn, partly constituted through these dynamics. Far more so than a peaceful and homogenous suburb, the contested city is where the civic is made.

We see this potential for the making of the civic across the centuries. Historically, the overcoming of urban conflicts has often been the source for an expanded civicness.[3] The cases that have become iconic in western historiography are Augsburg and Moorish Spain. In both, a genuinely enlightened leadership and citizenry worked at constituting a shared civicness. But there are many other both old and new cases. Old Jerusalem's bazaar was a space of commercial and religious coexistence for long periods of time. Modern Baghdad under the brutal leadership of Saddam Hussein was a city where religious minorities (though not necessarily the majority, always a threat), such as Christians and Jews, lived in more relative peace than they do today. Outsiders in Europe's cities, notably immigrants, have experienced persecution for centuries; yet in many a case, their successful claims for inclusion have had the effect of expanding and strengthening the rights of citizens as well.

We see some of this capacity to override old hatreds, in its own specific forms, in Cairo's Tahrir Square. But also in Yemen's Saana, where once-conflicting tribes have found a way to coalesce with one another and with the protesters against the existing regime. Tahrir Square has become the iconic case, partly because key features of the process became visible as they stretched over time: the discipline of the protesters; the mechanisms for communicating; the vast diversity of ages, politics, religions, and cultures; and the struggle's extraordinary trajectory. But in fact, we now know that these features are also at work in other sites. Yemen's protest movements have been intent on being peaceful and unarmed, and indeed many members expressed distress when one tribe—a long-standing enemy of the regime for political and economic reasons—launched an armed attack. In a matter of weeks, the ethics of the protest movements and the complexity of the situation created conditions that allowed enemy tribes to find a system of trust in the city for sharing the struggle against the regime. This was not a minor achievement.

The conditions and the mechanisms of protest are specific to each of the several uprisings we have come to refer to as the Arab Spring. Yet in every case, the overcoming of conflicts has become the source for an expanded civicness. This is not urban per se, but both the conflicts and the civicness assume particularly strong and legible forms in major cities. Further, we see an enabling of the powerless: urban space makes their powerlessness complex, and in that complexity lies the possibility of making the political, making the civic.

The Limits of Even Powerful Communication Technologies

Beyond complex questions of norms, the city also makes visible the limits and the unrealized potential of communication technologies, such as Facebook and Twitter. Much has been written and debated about their role in Egyptian mobilizing and protest organizing. In the United States, there has been a great deal of discussion of the notion of a "Facebook revolution," signaling that the protest movement was at the limit a function of communication technologies, notably social media. It seems to me that this conflates a technology's capacities with a massive on-the-ground process that uses the technology. In my research, I have found that this type of conflation results from a confusion between the logics of the technology as designed by the engineer and the logics of the users—the two are not one and the same. The technical properties of electronic interactive domains deliver their utility through complex ecologies that include: (a) non-technological variables—the social, the subjective, the political, material topographies; and (b) the particular cultures of use of a technology by different actors.

Thus, Facebook can be a factor in very diverse collective events—a flash mob, a birthday party, the uprising in Tahrir Square. But that is not the same as saying they all are achieved through Facebook. As we now know, if anything, Al Jazeera was a more significant medium for the revolution in Egypt, and mosques served as the foundational communication network in the case of the Tahrir Square Friday mobilizations.

One synthetic image we can use is that these ecologies are partly shaped by the particular logics embedded in diverse domains. Thus, a Facebook group doing financial investment aims at something quite different from Cairo protestors using Facebook to organize their next demonstration. This difference is there even when the same technical capabilities are used by both, notably rapid communication to mobilize around one aim—making money or going to Tahrir Square.

When we look at electronic interactive domains as part of these larger ecologies, rather than as a purely technical condition, we make conceptual and empirical room for the broad range of social logics driving users and the diverse cultures of use through which these technologies are employed. Each of these logics and cultures of use activates an ecology (the "typical" Facebook subscriber letting "friends" know she will be at a new restaurant) or is activated by it (the Egyptian protesters' struggle, which included as one element using Facebook to signal an upcoming action). The effect of taking this perspective is to position Facebook in a much larger world than the thing itself.

In this way, we capture a sort of minimalist version of Facebook as well as the *larger ecology* within which a Facebook action is situated. This contrasts with the more common perspective on the "internal world" of Facebook, with its vast population of subscribers, approaching one billion and growing fast. The protest movement in Tahrir Square had the power to bring a new ecology to the repertory of ecologies within which Facebook is used; this showed both the limits of the existing Facebook format and the capacity of urban collective action to inscribe a technology.

Facebook space itself is today mostly described by experts as part of social life for a large majority of its subscribers. But the network capability involved clearly cannot be confined to this function. The shifts that become visible when we take into account the types of ecologies mobilized point to a far larger range of uses and practices. The Tahrir Square protest movement embodies these shifts and relations: in Tahrir Square, Facebook space is not "social life"; it is more akin to a tool. Social thickness can come about as well when the space is used for other purposes, but it is likely that in many cases it will not. *Toolness* rules. And what stands out, what gives us the dramatic entry of Facebook as "actant," is the larger ecology that shapes the use of Facebook space in these cases.

The potential of digital media to enable immobile or place-centered activists concerned with local, not global, issues points to the making of larger ecologies that will be different from the ecologies of globally oriented users. For instance, the fact that specific types of local issues (jobs, oppression) recur in localities across the world and engage local, immobile activists in each place means that a kind of globality can be engendered that does not depend on them *communicating* with each other.

This is also a feature of the ongoing Arab Spring—a recurrence of protests in very diverse places in the region that do not depend on direct communication across these different sites and yet all together make for a larger and more complex formation than each individual struggle. This points to a kind of imaginary where the actual communications are a third point in a triangle—they are part of the enabling ecology of conditions, but that ecology is not simply about communication among participants. This does invite us to ask: How can the new social media add to functions that go beyond mere communication and thereby contribute to more complex and powerful capabilities for such movements? The rapid spread of Occupy initiatives across the United States and most recently extending to over eighty countries is one instance of such a multisited global formation that does not require direct communication, even when social media is a critical tool.

The 99% Take to the Street, and the State Protects the 1%

The militarized police actions in New York City against Occupy Wall Street protestors and supporters, and nationwide against the growing Occupy movement, test the limits and the potential of street actions and social media as the powerless employ these tools to take on the powerful. Unlike Spain, Germany, and other European countries with social uprisings, the United States has deployed antiterrorism units from local police departments and the federal Department of Homeland Security to "keep order." These are civic protests—not attempts to destroy or take over the government. With these antiterrorist measures, the US government re-marks the civic as a threat to national security.

Such re-markings can lead to deep distortions in how a government responds to protesters and civil unrest, signaling how the epochal quality of these social uprisings can bring out and make visible some of the more sinister elements of the neoliberal state right there at home, not only in remote war zones. Elsewhere, I have examined this strengthening of antidemocratic forces deep inside the neoliberal state with the rise of global corporate capitalism.[4] I would argue that the deployment of antiterrorism units to contest a peaceful social movement on native soil is yet another material step in this process.

And yet, the "social physics" of the city set limits to the direct abuse that superior power can exercise in a concrete urban situation.[5] It is worth remembering last year's student occupation on the campus of the University of Puerto Rico. It lasted for months, and the protestors were surrounded, literally, by the military. But they were not attacked, given the high visibility of the urban campus. And they had enough space to themselves to develop the elements of an alternative politics and way of life: they did urban agriculture and collective cooking, used environmentally sustainable practices, and made art and music. In brief, they strived to build a different society even while encircled by the state.[6] And they eventually won several of their demands from the university administration.

Social media magnifies this urban visualness, further circumscribing power. Police action against the Occupy movement is instantly documented by countless cameras, with photographs tweeted and video streamed live to cries of "the whole world is watching." In downtown Manhattan, the invisible crimes being committed in the towers of finance are made visible by the people marching in the street below, claiming their city as they call and respond to one another, for all to hear, "Whose street? Our street!" By calling on the 99% to share the struggle, the Occupiers seek to override the partisan liberal/conservative conflict that divides (and conquers) the US electorate and coalesce the powerless against the powerful, using social media to circumvent a monolithic mainstream media and drive a perceptibly leaderless movement, rendering twenty-first-century powerlessness all the more complex. Even the powerlessness of individual police officers within the forces deployed by the 1% is exposed: "You are the 99%!" By taking their voices to the Street, the protestors make the civic, and by employing technology that increasingly allows all to see, they make the political.

Conclusion

This essay explored a few of the vectors at work in the worldwide uprisings of the past year, with the aim of opening up a larger conceptual field to understand the complex interactions between power and powerlessness. This exploration makes it possible to examine the heuristic potential of these events, in that they tell a larger story.

We can aggregate the factors and conditions that these uprisings make visible into two sets. The first has to do with the dynamic interaction between power and powerlessness, between armed forces and peaceful demonstrators, that is possible in urban space. On the one hand, these uprisings tell us something about how the "social physics" of the city can obstruct, though not destroy, superior armed power in situations as diverse as Tahrir Square and OWS. On the other hand, they also make visible the increasingly powerful antidemocratic forces present not only in recognized dictatorships but also in the neoliberal state.

The second set of factors made visible contests some widespread beliefs about communication technologies that are in need of serious qualifying, one concerning the new social media and the other the role of territory in an increasingly digitized world. On the first count, these urban uprisings show us both the limits and the potential of these technologies, especially social media. In Cairo, the mosques and Al Jazeera proved more important than Facebook and Twitter. In the United States, social media is driving a new form of largely leaderless protest. These new interactive tools deliver their utilities though larger ecologies that include nontechnical factors, notably the larger social, political, and cultural processes of a place, of a user, of a network.

As for the second count, both Tahrir Square and OWS bring to the fore the question of occupying territory. Tahrir Square was a highly dramatic instance that made legible the importance for the powerless of claiming physical space. We see elements of this in the Occupy movement, notably the extent to which making an encampment in the heart of New York's financial district anchored the movement and encouraged and enabled others to form their own encampments around the country. This highlights both the complexity of the territorial moment in diverse processes and the limits of the digital option, no matter its vast technological powers. It illustrates, again, the fact of a larger ecology through which these technologies deliver their utilities: the existence of the encampments in Tahrir Square or in Zuccotti Park adds to the powers of the new social media.

Some of the key features of a broad range of struggles happening in the MENA region but also, with their own specific features, in places as diverse as cities in China, Israel, Chile, Greece, Spain, the United Kingdom, and the United States lead me to argue that the question of public space is central to giving the powerless rhetorical and operational openings. But this public space needs to be distinguished from the concept of public space in the European tradition. This brings me to the concept of the Global Street, a contrast to the piazza and the boulevard of the European tradition. And it calls attention to territory, a category flattened into one meaning—national territory—over the last century, which is now coming to life through occupations such as those of Tahrir Square and OWS.

(Reprinted with permission from Possible Futures, A Project of the Social Science Research Council, http://www.possible-futures.org/2011/11/22/the-global-street-comes-to-wall-street.)

Notes

1. This essay is based on "The Global Street: Making the Political," *Globalizations* 8(5: October 2011), 565–71; and the conceptual tools developed in *Territory, Authority, Rights: From Medieval to Global Assemblages* (Princeton, NJ: Princeton University Press, 2008).
2. See "Globalization and Crisis," special issue, *Globalizations* 7(1–2: February/April 2010).
3. Saskia Sassen, *Guests and Aliens* (New York: The New Press, 1999).
4. Sassen, *Territory, Authority, Rights,* chaps. 4 and 5.
5. Saskia Sassen, "When the City Itself Becomes a Technology of War," *Theory, Culture, & Society* 27(6: November 2010), 33–50, http://www.columbia.edu/~sjs2/PDFs/city_technology _of_war.pdf.
6. Saskia Sassen, "Beyond Protests: Students Making the Pieces of a Different Society," *Huffington Post,* May 22, 2010, http://www.huffingtonpost.com/saskia-sassen/beyond-protests -students_b_586138.html.

ABOUT THE AUTHORS

Manuela Boatcă, Professor of the Sociology of Global Inequalities at the Freie Universität Berlin, Germany; co-editor (with Encarnación Gutiérrez Rodríguez and Sérgio Costa) of *Decolonizing European Sociology: Transdisciplinary Approaches,* Aldershot: Ashgate 2010.

Christopher Chase-Dunn, Sociology, Director of the Institute for Research on World-Systems, University of California, Riverside; editor, *Global Social Change* (with Salvatore Babones), Johns Hopkins University Press, 2007.

Brett Clark, Department of Sociology and Anthropology, North Carolina State University; Author of *The Science and Humanism of Stephen Jay Gould* (with Richard Clark), Monthly Review Press, 2010.

Bahar Davary, Theology and Religious Studies, University of San Diego; author of *Women and the Qur'an: A Study in Islamic Hermeneutics,* Edwin Mellen Press, 2009.

Walter Goldfrank, Professor Emeritus, Sociology, University of California Santa Cruz; editor of *Ecology and the World-System* (with David Goodman and Andrew Szasz), Praeger, 1999.

Ramon Grosfoguel, Ethnic Studies, University of California Berkeley; Author of *Colonial Subjects: Puerto Ricans in a Global Perspective,* University of California Press, 1993.

Michelle M. Jacob, Ethnic Studies, University of San Diego.

Andrew K. Jorgenson, Sociology, University of Utah; editor of *Globalization and the Environment* (with Edward Kick), Haymarket Books, 2009.

Bruce Lerro, Sociology, University of California, Riverside.

Alberto López Pulido, Chair, Department of Ethnic Studies, University of San Diego, author of *Moving Beyond Borders: Julian Samora and the Establishment of Latino Studies* (with Barbara Driscoll de Alvarado and Carmen Samora), University of Illinois Press, 2009.

Tom Reifer, Sociology, Affiliated Faculty, Ethnic Studies, University of San Diego; Associate Fellow, Transnational Institute, editor of *Globalization, Hegemony and Power: Antisystemic Movements and the Global System,* Paradigm Publishers, 2004.

Saskia Sassen, Sociology, Columbia University. Author of *Territory, Authority, Rights,* Princeton University Press, 2007.

Gershon Shafir, Department of Sociology and Institute for International, Comparative, and Area Studies (IICAS), University of California, San Diego. Author of *Being Israeli: The Dynamics of Multiple Citizenship* (with Yoav Peled), Cambridge University Press, 2002.

Immanuel Wallerstein, Senior Research Scholar, Yale University. Author of *European Universalism: The Rhetoric of Power,* New Press, 2006.

POLITICAL ECONOMY
OF THE WORLD-SYSTEM
ANNUALS SERIES

Immanuel Wallerstein, Series Editor

I.   Kaplan, Barbara Hockey, ed., *Social Change in the Capitalist World Economy.* Political Economy of the World-System Annuals, 01. Beverly Hills/London: Sage Publications, 1978.

II.   Goldfrank, Walter L., ed., *The World-System of Capitalism: Past and Present.* Political Economy of the World-System Annuals, 02. Beverly Hills/London: Sage Publications, 1979.

III.   Hopkins, Terence K., & Immanuel Wallerstein, eds., *Processes of the World-System.* Political Economy of the World-System Annuals, 03. Beverly Hills/London: Sage Publications, 1980.

IV.   Rubinson, Richard, ed., *Dynamics of World Development.* Political Economy of the World-System Annuals, 04. Beverly Hills/London: Sage Publications, 1981.

V.   Friedman, Edward, ed., *Ascent and Decline in the World-System.* Political Economy of the World-System Annuals, 05. Beverly Hills/London/New Delhi: Sage Publications, 1982.

VI.   Bergesen, Albert, ed., *Crises in the World-System.* Political Economy of the World-System Annuals, 06. Beverly Hills/London/New Delhi: Sage Publications, 1983.

VII.   Bergquist, Charles, ed., *Labor in the Capitalist World-Economy.* Political Economy of the World-System Annuals, 07. Beverly Hills/London/New Delhi: Sage Publications, 1984.

VIII.   Evans, Peter, Dietrich Rueschemeyer, & Evelyne Huber Stephens, eds., *States versus Markets in the World-System.* Political Economy of the World-System Annuals, 08. Beverly Hills/London/New Delhi: Sage Publications, 1985.

IX.   Tardanico, Richard, ed., *Crises in the Caribbean Basin*. Political Economy of the World-System Annuals, 09. Newbury Park/Beverly Hills/London/New Delhi: Sage Publications, 1987.

X.   Ramirez, Francisco O., ed., *Rethinking the Nineteenth Century: Contradictions and Movements*. Studies in the Political Economy of the World-System, 10. New York/ Westport, CT/London: Greenwood Press, 1988.

XI.   Smith, Joan, Jane Collins, Terence K. Hopkins, & Akbar Muhammad, eds., *Racism, Sexism, and the World-System*. Studies in the Political Economy of the World-System, 11. New York/Westport, CT/London: Greenwood Press, 1988.

XII.   (a) Boswell, Terry, ed., *Revolution in the World-System*. Studies in the Political Economy of the World-System, 12a. New York/Westport, CT/London: Greenwood Press, 1989.

XII.   (b) Schaeffer, Robert K., ed., *War in the World-System*. Studies in the Political Economy of the World-System, 12b. New York/Westport, CT/London: Greenwood Press, 1989.

XIII.   Martin, William G., ed., *Semiperipheral States in the World-Economy*. Studies in the Political Economy of the World-System, 13. New York/Westport, CT/London: Greenwood Press, 1990.

XIV.   Kasaba, Resat, ed., *Cities in the World-System*. Studies in the Political Economy of the World-System, 14. New York/Westport, CT/London: Greenwood Press, 1991.

XV.   Palat, Ravi Arvind, ed., *Pacific-Asia and the Future of the World-System*. Studies in the Political Economy of the World-System, 15. Westport, CT/London: Greenwood Press, 1993.

XVI.   Gereffi, Gary, & Miguel Korzeniewicz, eds., *Commodity Chains and Global Capitalism*. Studies in the Political Economy of the World-System, 16. Westport, CT: Greenwood Press, 1994.

XVII.   McMichael, Philip, ed., *Food and Agrarian Orders in the World-Economy*. Studies in the Political Economy of the World-System, 17. Westport, CT: Greenwood Press, 1995.

XVIII.   Smith, David A., & József Böröcz, eds., *A New World Order? Global Transformations in the Late Twentieth Century*. Studies in the Political Economy of the World-System, 18. Westport, CT: Greenwood Press, 1995.

XIX.   Korzeniewicz, Roberto Patricio, & William C. Smith, eds., *Latin America in the World-Economy*. Studies in the Political Economy of the World-System, 19. Westport, CT: Greenwood Press, 1996.

XX.   Ciccantell, Paul S., & Stephen G. Bunker, eds., *Space and Transport in the World-System*. Studies in the Political Economy of the World-System, 20. Westport, CT: Greenwood Press, 1998.

XXI.   Goldfrank, Walter L., David Goodman, & Andrew Szasz, eds., *Ecology and the World-System*. Studies in the Political Economy of the World-System, 21. Westport, CT: Greenwood Press, 1999.

XXII.   Derluguian, Georgi, & Scott L. Greer, eds., *Questioning Geopolitics*. Studies in the Political Economy of the World-System, 22. Westport, CT: Greenwood Press, 2000.

XXIV.   Grosfoguel, Ramón, & Ana Margarita Cervantes-Rodriguez, eds., *The Modern/ Colonial/Capitalist World-System in the Twentieth Century: Global Processes,*

Antisystemic Movements, and the Geopolitics of Knowledge. Studies in the Political Economy of the World-System, 24. Westport, CT: Greenwood Press, 2002.

XXV.   (a) Dunaway, Wilma A., ed., *Emerging Issues in the 21st Century World-System, Volume I: Crises and Resistance in the 21st Century World-System*. Studies in the Political Economy of the World-System, 25a. Westport, CT: Greenwood Press, 2003.

XXV.   (b) Dunaway, Wilma A., ed., *Emerging Issues in the 21st Century World-System, Volume II: New Theoretical Directions for the 21st Century World-System*. Studies in the Political Economy of the World-System, 25b. Westport, CT: Greenwood Press, 2003.

XXVI.   (a) Reifer, Thomas Ehrlich, ed., *Globalization, Hegemony & Power*. Political Economy of the World-System Annuals, 26a. Boulder, CO: Paradigm Publishers, 2004.

XXVI.   (b) Friedman, Jonathan, & Christopher Chase-Dunn, eds., *Hegemonic Decline: Present and Past*. Political Economy of the World-System Annuals, 26b. Boulder, CO: Paradigm Publishers, 2005.

XXVII. Tabak, Faruk, ed., *Allies as Rivals: The U.S., Europe and Japan in a Changing World-System*. Political Economy of the World-System Annuals, 27. Boulder, CO: Paradigm Publishers, 2005.

XXVIII. Grosfoguel, Ramón, Nelson Meldonado-Torres, and José David Saldívar, eds., *Latin@s in the World-System: Toward the Decolonization of the Twenty-first Century U.S. Empire*. Political Economy of the World-System Annuals, 28. Boulder, CO: Paradigm Publishers, 2005.

XXIX.   Samman, Khaldoun, and Mazhor Al-Zo'by. eds., *Islam and the Orientalist World-System*. Political Economy of the World-System Annuals, 29. Boulder, CO: Paradigm Publishers, 2008.

XXX.   Trichur, Ganesh K., ed., *The Rise of Asia and the Transformation of the World-System*. Political Economy of the World-System Annuals, 30. Boulder, CO: Paradigm Publishers, 2009.

XXXI.   Jones, Terry-Ann, & Eric Mielants, eds., *Mass Migration in the World-System: Past, Present, and Future*. Political Economy of the World-System Annuals, 31. Boulder, CO: Paradigm Publishers, 2010.

XXXII. Reifer, Tom, ed., *Global Crises and the Challenges of the 21st Century: Antisystemic Movements and the Transformation of the World-System*. Political Economy of the World-System Annuals, 32. Boulder, CO: Paradigm Publishers, 2012.

www.ingramcontent.com/pod-product-compliance
Ingram Content Group UK Ltd.
Pitfield, Milton Keynes, MK11 3LW, UK
UKHW020430010325
455677UK00029B/1092